CLYDE WELLS

C L Y D E
WELLS

A POLITICAL BIOGRAPHY

CLAIRE HOY

First published in 1992 by
Stoddart Publishing Co. Limited
34 Lesmill Road
Toronto, Canada
M3B 2T6

Canadian Cataloguing in Publication Data

Hoy, Claire
Clyde Wells: a political biography

Includes bibliographical references.
ISBN 0-7737-2652-7

1. Wells, Clyde K., 1937-   . 2. Newfoundland —
Politics and government — 1972-   . 3. Canada —
Politics and government — 1984-   .4. Prime
ministers — Newfoundland — Biography. I. Title.

FC2176.1.W45II7 1992   971.8′04′092   C92-094967-3
F1123.W45II7 1992

Typesetting: Tony Gordon Limited

Printed and bound in Canada

Stoddart Publishing gratefully acknowledges the support of
the Canada Council, Ontario Arts Council and Ontario
Publishing Centre in the development of writing and
publishing in Canada.

To lydia
my own island of sanity

Contents

Preface

LIKE MOST CANADIANS, certainly those living outside of Newfoundland, the first time I saw Clyde Wells — I mean, really saw him — was in November 1989 when he confronted Brian Mulroney at the first ministers' conference in Ottawa over the Meech Lake accord.

I liked him then. Or, at least, respected him. Here, finally, was a guy who couldn't be bullied by Mulroney; a politician who not only had a view, but wasn't afraid to express it without first checking the latest printouts from public opinion polls.

I was reminded of a scene in the movie *Butch Cassidy and the Sundance Kid*. Having been tracked literally to the ends of the earth, facing the unhappy choice of surrendering to the pursuing posse or jumping off the cliff into the treacherous water hundreds of feet below, the two lovable outlaws look back at their tracker and, exuding a combination of admiration and disgust, ask, "Who are those guys, anyway?"

That's exactly what Mulroney, Robert Bourassa, David Peterson, the national media, and millions of Canadians watching this dramatic showdown and the subsequent constitutional events over the next seven months must have been asking themselves.

Who is that guy, anyway?

This book will answer that question. Not only who, but what, and, I hope, why.

He is not the selfless saint many of his most ardent worshippers see him as. Nor is he the dogmatic sinner his enemies portray. But he is different. A far cry from your standard issue, Central Casting politician. He is a man the fishermen's union president Richard Cashin has dubbed "the Anglican Bishop": unbending, austere, dogmatic to a fault. And yes, there is something slightly unnerving about his messianic fervor and his absolute conviction that what he says and thinks and does is not only right, but proper. Yet most of his critics at least concede he has a sense of honesty and integrity rarely seen in today's politics.

Clyde Wells is still wildly popular in much of Canada — apart from Quebec, of course. And for that matter, more and more popular outside his own province than inside it. As the speaker of choice for Liberal riding associations across the country, nobody comes close to him, something that has put several federal Liberal noses out of joint over the past two years.

Regardless of the merits or demerits of his actions and his style, he is a fascinating political study. His sudden rise from obscurity to the status of a household name is a rare phenomenon in this country. Ask anybody in Canada if they've heard of Clyde Wells and chances are they have. Ask what they know about him, and chances are that, beyond his Meech performance, they don't know much.

He is a man of little humor, an odd quality in a person from an island where the raw brand of folksy humor has helped its people endure the physical rigors of hacking out lives on the Rock. Nor does he have an accent. To hear him speak, you could be listening to a Bay Street baron instead of a guy from Stephenville Crossing. He touched the collective hearts and souls of so many Canadians during Meech, yet on a human level, he seems aloof and uncomfortable even with the everyday concerns of his people. He's a man who can move an audience of rural Newfoundlanders with a technical speech about constitutional philosophy, yet a man who appears to be either unable or unwilling to reach out on a human level to them. He came from poverty, and by his own enterprise rose out of it, yet he doesn't relate to the poor. He is fixated by creature comforts, by financial security, and is clearly haunted by the shortcomings of his early educational experiences.

For several months, Wells flatly refused to be interviewed for this book, even though he had earlier indicated he would be co-operative. In two letters turning down requests for interviews, Wells said he was concerned the book would accord blame for the failure of Meech instead of focusing on trying to find a solution to the present difficulties, and he did not want to be part of that. But finally, in April 1992, after appeals from his own staff and several federal Liberals, Wells changed his mind and granted a lengthy interview. I thank him for that.

As with any book, of course, many more people are involved. First there's the publisher, Nelson Doucet of Stoddart, who accepted the idea. Then there's the invaluable help provided by Erik Spicer and his staff in the Parliamentary library. For a political journalist, librarians are among the few people in the whole political process whose job it is to *find* information for you rather than hide it. And they do it well.

Another challenge in writing a book about a subject who doesn't live in the same neighborhood is to find a way to collect local information without having to move there for several months. In that regard, St. John's freelancer Carol Crocker not only dug up tons of exhaustive background on Wells, but also conducted many interviews herself in St. John's, Corner Brook, and Stephenville Crossing and opened some doors for me when I did go to Newfoundland. I thank her, too, for her fine work.

In total, more than 200 people were interviewed for this book and, as the bibliography shows, considerable reading was also involved in an effort to discover the essence of this unique political figure. I'm grateful to all those who agreed to interviews, even those who wished to remain anonymous.

The only real certainty in politics is uncertainty, they say. But in Wells, there's more certainty than you'll find in any other politician. One constant theme during the interviews, from friend and foe alike, is that, with Wells, what you see is exactly what you get.

Globe and Mail columnist Jeffrey Simpson told me that one thing that struck him in his many interviews for a lengthy feature he did on Wells is that no matter whom he interviewed — old schoolmates, former legal colleagues, political friends and enemies, personal friends — the story about the man's character was essentially the same. It's a character not everyone admires — although many do — but it's certainly consistent.

What's more, Clyde Wells yearns to be prime minister. The fact he refuses to rule it out alone tells us that, not to mention his ongoing French lessons. But at this stage, his chances seem remote. Then again, what were the chances of a poor kid from Stephenville Crossing, stuck in an ill-equipped, one-room school, growing up to become first a successful lawyer, and then one of the best-known political figures in all of Canada?

Wells succeeded because of his single-minded devotion to a cause — his cause — and he may well do it again. People have underestimated him before and lived to regret it. Just ask the man who currently holds the job Wells covets.

CLAIRE HOY
Ottawa
June 1992

CLYDE WELLS

Prologue

EVERYBODY WAS WAITING for the Newfoundland premier. The three other Atlantic premiers were already there. A gaggle of reporters and cameramen were swapping stories, sipping coffee, and periodically peering out into the March snow looking for him. Political aides bustled about the lobby of Corner Brook's Glynmill Inn looking extremely busy in the way aides do even when they're not.

Finally he arrived.

Wearing a heavy formal coat, a scarf, but no hat to ward off the winter's worst storm, Clyde Wells stomped the snow off his shoes, took a few deliberate steps into the lobby, then stopped, grudgingly it seemed, when a scrum of journalists instantly formed around him.

Without a word, he reached out to a microphone held by Halifax radio reporter Chris Dover and pulled it down.

He was in control and wanted everybody to know it.

The troubled Commons-Senate Beaudoin-Dobbie report on national unity had been released in Ottawa two days before, but Wells, his blue eyes blazing, snapped, "I can't possibly comment on it without reading it. That would be irrational on my part and I try to avoid being irrational."

He certainly does.

No spontaneity here. No Rowdyman. Nothing but the

straight, cold logic of a remarkably self-assured man who not only knows what his own views are, but believes they are right.

Wells had spent much of that weekend, before the Atlantic premiers' meeting, skiing at nearby Marble Mountain ski resort with Nova Scotia's Donald Cameron and New Brunswick's Frank McKenna and their families. He hadn't invited Prince Edward Island Premier Joe Ghiz. He was still angry that Ghiz — who swore at him during the private Meech Lake sessions — just three months earlier in December 1991, had shown up at a $500-a-plate testimonial dinner at the Radisson Plaza Hotel in St. John's along with Brian and Mila Mulroney to honor John Crosbie's twenty-five years in elected politics. Worse, Ghiz, likely the only Liberal in the room, had delivered a tough constitutional speech, indirectly knocking Wells right on his own turf for his stubborn refusal to bend during the Meech Lake negotiations. Wells, of course, did not attend the dinner.

While the national news had been dominated during the week leading up the premiers' meeting by the partisan bickering of the Beaudoin-Dobbie committee, in Newfoundland, escalating outrage over foreign overfishing had held the spotlight.

Wells had had something to say about the Constitution, but nothing about fishing. He was biding his time. At the end of the one-day premiers' meeting, flanked by his three colleagues, Wells went on the attack, demanding that Ottawa order Spanish and Portuguese fishing trawlers out of the international waters off the Grand Banks or, if they refused, send in the navy to clear them out.

Cameron agreed. McKenna waffled. Ghiz had no comment.

Wells, who a couple years earlier had dismissed the same suggestion by two local Liberal MPs as irresponsible, was perhaps having second thoughts himself, so he ordered his press secretary, Judy Foote, to phone Canadian Press reporter Beth Gorham, who was covering the meeting, hoping to have his plea for military intervention toned down. It didn't work.

He'd said it, and Gorham, an experienced professional, reported it. So did everybody else. Yet a week later, after Mulroney had dismissed "gunboat diplomacy" as counterproductive, Wells lamely claimed the media had misconstrued his remarks.

Which is it? Does Wells really feel so strongly about protecting cod stocks he'd be willing to risk an act of war? Or was he simply pandering to local sentiment, as politicians often do, to push his own partisan agenda and grab a few easy headlines?

Wells's comments on the federal constitutional proposals were another sideshow. Several days passed before he formally commented on them — he wasn't impressed — yet the night of the premiers' meeting, in the same hotel, the man who complained bitterly about the secretive aspects of the Meech constitutional process had plenty to say about it in private to a gathering of Liberals at a party fund raiser.

One who attended said Wells blasted the report, but "the interesting thing is that the audience was not very enthusiastic about his remarks. And these are the same people, remember, who cheered him wildly when he was dumping on Meech."

In much of Canada, people are still cheering. But many remain angry.

Wells is a man who is both easy to love and easy to loathe; a genuine, made-in-Canada enigma; a leader who can be admired for the courage of his convictions, yet condemned for his dogmatic adherence to what he defines as unalterable principle whether anybody else does or not.

Apart from Brian Mulroney, who upsets most Canadians, none of our leaders evokes the passionate responses Wells does, positive or negative. Joe Clark has called him an egomaniac. Others have called him worse. Yet for every critic, there are dozens of fans. In person, Wells is civil, amiable, a true gentleman. In public, he appears cold and aloof. He's also maddeningly finicky about details, and almost completely humorless. Asked why he lacks a sense of humor, Wells ac-

knowledges people say that about him, but insists it isn't true.
To support his contention, he launches into a serious discussion on humor, concluding with the argument that people
think he is humorless only because he doesn't make jokes
about "serious subjects." Unfortunately, everything is a serious
subject for Wells, ranging from the precise legal wording of a
technical constitutional clause to whether to spread jam or
marmalade on his morning toast.

Deborah Coyne, Wells's former constitutional adviser, in her
book *Roll of the Dice*, tells the story of a January 1990 column
by what she described as hostile Montreal *Gazette* editor
Norman Webster, the day after the two men met face-to-face,
which began with the plea: "Save us from principled politicians!" To Coyne, "principled politicians are precisely what
the Canadian people want and what they are entitled to."

She may be right. And on that score, Wells has a substantial
edge over the current crop of political leaders in the country.

But people want more than principles. They want leaders
with compassion, men or women they can warm up to and who
can warm up to them. They don't want a cold fish, a mechan-
ical being who will protect their tax dollars but never take a
moment to smell the roses.

Wells, in fact, is warmer than he seems. Yet, while he has
brilliantly marketed his ideas, his principles, his sense of
propriety, he has failed to convey to people that, while he may
not be the Wizard of Oz, able to solve all our problems, he is
also not the Tin Man, in danger of seizing up at the next spray
of salt water from the sea-tossed island on which he was reared.

1

The Crossing

THE TWO-ROOM CLAPBOARD All Saints Anglican schoolhouse in Stephenville Crossing is boarded up now. The tiny Anglican church nearby sits unused on this snowy, blowy, February 1992 day, the bell, rung only by members of the Wells family for twenty-five years, silent now except for the odd Sunday when a circuit priest drops by to serve the town's faithful. Next to the church is a faded yellow, squat, two-storey house. It is the old Wells homestead, which Ralph Wells built himself, log by log, with a little help from Clyde and two of his brothers.

There are few people out in the hamlet's main street and laneways. Those who are have their faces covered by woollen scarfs, their bodies packed into snowmobile suits, and are trudging back and forth between their modest homes and a small groceteria, bracing themselves against the bitter wind. At the far edge of town, where Station and Main streets collide, two orange cabooses and three boarded-up Pullman cars sit rotting on a short railway spur, a mute reminder of the town's former glory. The station where Ralph Wells once worked as an express agent is gone, replaced by a funeral home.

The Crossing, as locals call it, is where Clyde Wells lived with his family from the age of seven until he entered university. He rarely mentions the place now although, in the 1990 update of Joey Smallwood's autobiography, *Call Me Joey*, Wells confesses it was here, as an eleven-year-old boy, that he initially saw Newfoundland's first premier. It was 1948 during the bitter Confederation debates, and Smallwood was campaigning "in the back of a truck on a dusty road behind the railway station in Stephenville Crossing."

Still, it is almost as if he has deliberately closed this part of his life. Unlike other Newfoundlanders, even those who have been well educated and spent many years off the Rock, Wells has no accent. To hear him speak, he could be mistaken for a lawyer from Toronto. And while Brian Mulroney boasts of rising above his alleged poor beginnings, Wells religiously avoids discussing his background, the family of nine children, where he slept four to a bed with his brothers and a cousin, and had to work part-time to help the family survive. It's been a long, tough journey to the premier's office, the big house on the hill, the sleek thirty-eight-foot sailboat *Piper*, and the expensive monogrammed shirts.

The second-oldest of the nine — he has four brothers and four sisters — Clyde was born November 9, 1937, in Buchans, a mining town located literally in the heart of the island of Newfoundland and established in 1920 to exploit the rich deposits of copper, lead, and zinc. A year later, brother Alan was born, and the family moved down the road to Millertown Junction, his mother Maude's (née Kirby) hometown, another hamlet on the railway line. Named after Lewis Miller, a lumber entrepreneur, it was the western repair depot of the Newfie Bullet, the narrow-gauge railway train once used to ship ore from Buchans north to the port of Botwood on the Bay of Exploits.

The Kirby family was originally from King's Cove, another Newfoundland port on the rugged coastline of the Bonavista Peninsula, famous for its spectacular springtime views of gigantic icebergs. Maude's great-grandfather was one of the first Anglican priests on the island, and as with most Newfoundland families, their lives revolved around the church. Clyde's father, Ralph, was born in Twillingate, a small island community north of Gander in Notre Dame Bay, which was once a prosperous fishing centre, with its own newspaper, the *Twillingate Sun*, and a championship cricket team.

Just after the start of World War II, the Wells family moved again, Ralph's railway duties taking him up the line to Bishop's Falls in the heart of Exploits Valley, a maintenance depot for the Newfie Bullet and a major forest-product centre since the early 1800s. Clyde's older brother, Harold, began school in Bishop's Falls, and a year later, Clyde joined him in the one-room Anglican school.

The Americans had established a military base near Bishop's Falls, and the trains carried equipment and building materials there on their way to the airbases at Gander, Botwood, Argentia, and Stephenville. The Newfoundland Regiment was stationed in nearby Grand Falls and practised mock battles in backyards. Harold, who has taken early retirement from his job as administrator at Sir Thomas Roddick Hospital in Stephenville, recalls how as kids he and Clyde got a thrill out of riding on the backs of the huge army trucks, watching the mock battles, and practising blackouts in case of air raids.

In November 1944, ten days after Clyde's seventh birthday, the family moved again, this time to Stephenville Crossing, where Ralph was an express agent, one of six at the station. Not long after the move, says Clyde's sister Gladys, recalling a story her mother told many times, Clyde was sitting at the kitchen table staring outside. It was one of those cold winter afternoons with darkness lumbering in. Suddenly he noticed that the moon had appeared, even though it was still daylight.

"Don't hang out the moon, God b'y," he said. "The sun hasn't gone down yet."

"I often thought about that little quote during the Meech Lake thing," she says. "That's vintage Clyde. 'Wait now. Don't do it just yet until we get everything straightened out.' It seems to always be his way. He even wanted God to get it right."

Unlike other teenage boys in the village who studiously ignored their kid sisters, Clyde was always considerate of Gladys, allowing her to tag along with him to social events. "He was the one who would wait for me, or come back and take my hand," she says fondly.

She recalls that Clyde was never given to compromise. "When he deems it important not to, then he will not. He will listen to alternatives or consider it. But when compromise means something less than he'd consider, he won't do it. It's the result of a particular type of upbringing."

Part of that upbringing was to keep to your own group, which in practice meant keeping away from the Roman Catholics who made up about seventy per cent of the town's population. "We were raised in a very strict family with strong moral views," Gladys explains. "Part of the stricture was we were required to stay within our own bounds. Our parents were never critical of the R.C. faith, and we weren't allowed to criticize it either. But we knew our parents would prefer us to stick to our own, so we did pretty much. There were tensions between the two groups. They had what we thought was a much better school. It was certainly bigger. They had subject teachers for goodness' sake, whereas we had one teacher for all subjects from kindergarten to grade five and another teacher from grade six to eleven."

While brothers Harold and Alan, and to a lesser extent Cliff, had their share of scrapes with the Catholics, Clyde rarely got involved.

He was eleven before he became a Canadian, old enough to have witnessed the divisive battles leading up to Newfoundland's joining Confederation. He couldn't help but be affected by the passions unleashed during that time. His parents, being such staunch Anglicans, would have joined the rest of the Protestants on the island in the widespread outrage at the efforts of Roman Catholic Archbishop Edward Patrick Roche, who turned *The Monitor*, a small parish newspaper, into a political war cry against Confederation. Beginning in the summer of 1947, it was sent to every Catholic family on the island. Religious differences exploded after the first referendum ended inconclusively on June 3, 1948, with the Catholic-supported independent Responsible Government option garnering forty-four and a half per cent of the vote compared to forty-one per cent for Confederation with Canada. (A majority was needed, and the third option, the old British-run Commission of Government, took away fourteen per cent of the vote.)

Richard Gwyn, in his book *Smallwood: The Unlikely Revolutionary*, describes how, during the second referendum campaign — between June 3 and July 22, 1948, when Smallwood's Confederation option squeaked through — "repression and jealousy flared into an ugly and consuming religious war. Catholic was pitted against Protestant, and Irish puritanism and Orange fanaticism. . . . The roots of sectarianism are deep in Newfoundland's history, and owe more to race and politics than to religion. In contrast to both the American melting pot and the Canadian mosaic, Newfoundlanders spring from two scarcely adulterated racial stocks: West Country English and Southern Irish. Since until 1782 the colony's official religion was Anglican, conflict between the two groups was inevitable. In the early years, Catholic priests were forbidden to come to the island, and Catholic marriages and funerals were banned."

This emphasis on religion led to the inefficient and second-rate denominational school system. Rather than the island's limited resources being pooled, schools were split along religious lines, and until most of the Protestant denominations were consolidated many years later, there were six separate denominational schools — Anglican, United, Roman Catholic, Salvation Army, Pentecostal, and Seventh Day Adventist. Each had its own autonomous school board and received a proportionate share of the meagre education budget. Many small communities, barely big enough to offer decent education in one school, ended up supporting two or three one-room schools.

A case in point was Stephenville Crossing, where neither the Anglican school nor the Roman Catholic school were large enough to merit qualified teachers, let alone reasonable facilities. The man who taught Wells, for example, had as his academic qualifications just grade eleven plus two terms at summer school.

Even so, Wells seemed to prosper. Both of his parents had graduated from high school, a rare feat in those days in rural Newfoundland and achieved by only two of their nine children. Still, his older brother Harold recalls that their parents always stressed the importance of education. "They said it gave us a choice." As children, they weren't permitted to have comic books. "Our parents would say if we have time to read we should read our lessons. We were allowed to read *Reader's Digest* though."

His sister Gladys says that Clyde "was always good in school. He skipped grade seven or eight. He never had a problem with schoolwork. He wasn't particularly rebellious. There were occasions when he had to stand his ground, even with the teacher, and he certainly did that. It was never a case of insubordination with a superior, but he always stood up for what he considered important at the time." Clyde graduated from high school — grade eleven was the final year at that time — in 1952, when he was fifteen.

His brother Alan recalls that Clyde was the only one who would debate their father's commands. He would never disobey. But if his father said he couldn't do a certain thing, "the rest of us would just grumble and accept it, but Clyde would insist on an explanation. And if he didn't like the explanation, he'd argue the point. Of course, he always lost the argument, but it didn't stop him from making his points."

Alan says Clyde avoided much of the rough-house stuff other boys did for fun. "He never had any meanness in him. I wouldn't say he didn't have a sense of humor exactly, but he was just more serious than the rest of us were."

Clyde shared a room in the crowded house with brothers Alan and Cliff, along with a cousin who often stayed with them. For meals, everyone sat around a big wooden table in the spacious kitchen. Ralph was a very strict father. "If you had something to say," says Alan, "you directed it to mom or dad."

The family spent many hours in the parlor gathered around the large wood-encased radio listening to the popular shows of the day — "Amos 'n Andy," "Dragnet," and "The Shadow." But during the Confederation debates, Alan recalls, Clyde was glued to that radio. "Even at a young age he was very, very interested in what was going on. The rest of us were interested in normal things kids like, but Clyde was always into the more serious stuff. During the Confederation debates my mother thought Joey Smallwood was God. As far as politics was concerned, she was a little more vocal than dad."

Because the Wells family lived so close to the church and the school — the churchyard actually served as their back-yard, with the school just across the road — they had the task of not only ringing the bell but also lugging in the firewood in the winter and lighting the fire before the other students or parishioners arrived. During class in the school that Clyde describes as consisting of "four walls and a potbellied stove," the boys would take turns carrying the coal bucket down to the basement, loading it up, and carrying it back up to the old stove in the middle of the tiny room. The girls got to scrub the floors, dust, and look after the younger children.

At home they all had their regular chores as well, and Clyde, who still likes to cook, was no stranger to the kitchen. "When you have nine kids living together in a small house with none of the modern amenities — just one bathroom and originally a wood and coal stove, later an oil stove — there was no shortage of chores. And obviously, with that many children, there were times when mother was obviously incapacitated, so everybody had to fill in. There was no argument about that," says Gladys.

The Crossing was too small for organized sports, but they did fish and play some baseball in the summer, and skated and played hockey in the winter. "Clyde had a pair of skates I remember that belonged to my mother when she was a young girl," says Gladys. "They were ladies' skates, but they were black. I remember him selling those later on to get a second-hand pair of boys' hockey skates. He used to be embarrassed about wearing ladies' skates. But that's the way it was in those days. If you had only one elbow pad, you used it. If you didn't have any, you went without."

Harold recalls that Clyde began smoking Camels and Lucky Strikes — the influence of the nearby American Harmon base — when he was only eight. This didn't stop him as a teenager from laying down the law about not smoking with his younger sister Margaret. Years later, she told *Toronto Star* columnist Thomas Walkom that when their father died suddenly of a heart attack at the age of forty-nine in 1959, Clyde returned from university to help with the small grocery store Ralph Wells had been running. "I was close to my dad," she says, "and when he died I was angry and resentful at him for going. I started smoking. My brother caught me and tried to get me to admit it. I guess I was as stubborn as he was. I didn't, so he spanked me and I was grounded for a week. . . . It was the only time in my life I've been spanked. . . . He probably spanked me not for smoking but for lying. I know that doesn't sit well with him."

Clyde came by this Cromwellian sense of moral absoluteness honestly, from his strict training both at home and at church.

Alan tells the story of when he and Clyde were caught smoking by their father. Clyde was twelve, Alan, ten. "Dad sat us down and started giving us Camel cigarettes, one after the other, to smoke. I got sick, but Clyde didn't. My dad was determined he was going to get Clyde sick, but he got a call from the railway that a train was coming in, so he had to leave the house. There's a tradition in Newfoundland of having a snack before bedtime, and that night Clyde was determined he was going to have a cigarette after his snack. I remember him taking some cigarette paper and rolling another cigarette. Mom got very upset. But Clyde was trying to prove a point."

"We were all taught to respect our elders," says Harold. "Mother taught us to put a hand to our cap and nod to elders and ministers when passing them on the street."

The Reverend Isaac Butler, now retired in Halifax, was the priest at All Saints in The Crossing from 1947 to 1955, nearly all of the years Clyde lived there. "He was always a great help to me in the church," says Butler. "He looked after the fire and the altar. Of course, he came from a very fine Christian family. But he was, really, just what you would expect from a boy brought up in a Christian environment. Nothing outstanding, except even then he had this moral integrity. The whole family attended church regularly."

When Clyde decided he wanted to be a lawyer, it was Butler who wrote a letter to Memorial University in St. John's to obtain the necessary application forms and to learn the requirements and procedures for entering university.

That story, like many others, has evolved over the years into a tale about how Butler actually convinced Wells to become a lawyer. Wells has lent credence to that version himself. On the other hand, in an April 1990 *Chatelaine* interview with journalist Michael Harris, when asked why he decided to go into law, Wells said, "I don't know where the idea came from, and

I didn't have the faintest idea of how to become a lawyer, but that's what I always wanted to be."

Still, Butler says, Wells is never one to forget a favor. In late 1991, Butler went to hear Wells speak in Halifax. "As soon as he saw me, he told people how I had helped him. He was always like that, very conscientious, a man of integrity. I said to him that it's remarkable he didn't lose his integrity, even though he is mixed up in politics. And I said, 'I think you're a hero on the mainland.' He replied, 'So they tell me.'"

Besides going to the town's only movie theatre, McFatridge's, where Clyde and his friends spent many a Friday night and Saturday afternoon watching Hollywood westerns, one of the major summer attractions were wiener roast beach parties about twice a week at Black Bank on Barachois Brook just a couple of miles outside of town. Gladys describes the parties as "innocent affairs . . . like one of those scenes you see in the fifties' beach movies," where they'd roast marshmallows and jive and waltz in the sand.

It was at these parties that Clyde became friendly with his future wife, Eleanor Bishop, who taught Sunday school at the church, but they didn't start dating until after he'd left for university. By local standards, the Bishop family was at the top of the social heap in The Crossing. They lived in a large, comfortable white house; Eleanor's father was an accountant, and her maternal grandfather, Charles McFatridge, owned shops, hotels, and apartments, as well as the theatre. Her mother, Daisy, still spends Christmas with Clyde and Eleanor, and whenever they're in the area they bring her peppermint candy.

Clyde also visits Eleanor's grandmother, the feisty ninety-eight-year-old Mable McFatridge, who taught Eleanor quilting. He brings her fresh flowers, usually pansies. "I always liked Clyde," she says. "Can't help liking him. I'll take his part always. He told Archbishop [Stewart] Payne in Corner Brook if he was in The Crossing to visit me. He did."

While The Crossing remained dirt poor by mainland standards during Clyde's formative years, one thing that elevated it slightly above most Newfoundland towns was its proximity to the U.S. Air Force base at nearby Stephenville, which pumped up the local economy and generated hundreds of jobs.

It must be remembered that in 1934, virtually bankrupt, Newfoundland voluntarily surrendered its dominion status, gave up its Responsible Government, and put itself in the hands of a specially created Commission of Government, appointed by Britain, chaired by the island's British governor and composed of three commissioners chosen from the U.K. and three from Newfoundland.

By the time Clyde was born in 1937, the economic situation, bad everywhere, had deteriorated to catastrophic conditions in Newfoundland, with almost a third of the population of 290,000 trying to live on relief, at the rate of six cents a day. During the next two years, things did not improve, and because Britain declared war against Germany in 1939, which meant Newfoundland was at war too, the U.K. commissioner of finance announced even further cuts in grants-in-aid to Newfoundland. In 1940, Britain followed with even more cuts and higher taxes.

Help, however, was close at hand. Despite objections from the Newfoundland members of the Commission of Government, in September 1940 the British negotiated an agreement with the United States, which was, of course, still officially neutral in the war effort, that allowed it to set up military bases on three large chunks of the island. In exchange for these strategic locations — in the days when aircraft couldn't make it across the ocean without a fuel stopover — Britain received fifty old destroyers to assist in its war against Hitler. The properties were under American law and tax free.

Political scientist Sid Noel, who studied with Clyde Wells at Memorial University, wrote in his 1971 book *Politics in Newfoundland*: "For Newfoundland the economic impact of the exchange was immense and almost immediate. On 29 January 1941 the troop ship *Edmund B. Alexander* became the largest vessel ever to squeeze through the narrows of St. John's harbour, bringing the first of many thousands of American servicemen and the beginning of an economic boom which has been compared to 'frontier days on the American continent.' Full employment, rising prices, and increased imports quickly pushed the revenue of the government to an all-time high of $23 million by 1942, producing a budget surplus of nearly $7,250,000. (In 1934 the total revenue of the government had been only $8,718,979.)" As a result of this sudden influx of Yankee dollars, the government upgraded public health and education facilities, although a large portion of the surplus funds went back to Britain.

One of the four bases built between April and June 1941 was the U.S. Air Force Ernest Harmon Field at nearby Stephenville, with an American military presence of 6000. At the time, Stephenville had a population of just 250. The district had no all-weather roads and no industries other than the fishery. But the base, just outside of Stephenville (it has since been annexed by the town) created an immediate demand for hundreds of unskilled and semi-skilled laborers for jobs that paid far more than most of the area's residents were making at the time.

One of those influenced directly by the American presence was Clyde Wells. While he and his brothers and sisters were growing up in The Crossing, their father never allowed them to go to the Stephenville base or associate with the Americans (although Clyde, his brothers, and some friends did sneak off periodically to the Dhoon Lodge, where many Americans hung out).

But at fifteen, finished high school and too young for university, Clyde got a job with his brother Harold as a records-keeper in the maintenance shop of a construction company at the Harmon base. They worked forty-eight hours a week at $1 an hour and then made $1.50 an hour for a further twelve hours at the tire grease shop. Harold says when they first told their father they'd been hired, he laughed about it, but was later upset, because he'd been working for the railway for twenty-five years and wasn't making as much money as they were.

Of their gross of $66 a week, they cleared $56, paid $3 a week for bus fare, gave their mother $40, and each kept $13 for themselves. That was an enormous amount of money for them at the time, and Clyde, unable to resist the lure of the automobile, bought his first car. The money not only helped their father finish the house and put an addition on the back, but helped finance the little grocery store he opened on Main Street in The Crossing in 1955.

In October 1953, Emerson Rudderham, an RCMP officer who lived next door to the Wells family, decided to get out of the force and go into plumbing full-time. He hired Clyde as a plumber's helper for $54 a week, $45 of which Clyde turned over to his father for his education.

"Clyde was a good worker," Rudderham says. "Everybody liked him. But I was aware of his ambitions to become a lawyer and he wasn't making enough money with me. But I couldn't pay him any more because he wasn't far enough advanced. He was quick to learn, and was doing just basic plumbing, new installations and repair work, that sort of thing. So, after discussing it with Ralph, I laid him off. I took him to Corner Brook to apply for UI. We had to make the thing official. And I told his dad if he didn't get a job in two weeks, I'd take him back with me."

Clyde has joked, "It was great money in those days. If I hadn't been laid off, I probably would have been a plumber."

Rudderham says Clyde's parents "were both people of strong principles. They lived well together, but they were two different characters. They both had their own minds. Clyde gets his character from both of them. I don't think he's bullheaded, really. I honestly believe he reasons everything out. By the same token, when they [other politicians during Meech Lake] started pushing him, the last thing you did was bully Clyde Wells.

"His father was just like that, too. He wouldn't back down from anybody. He had his principles. He had nine kids and didn't make much money, but nobody pushed him. I see a lot of that in Clyde. They worked hard and had a good, wholesome, clean life."

Emerson's former wife, Margaret, says the Wells family "often went without in those days. But Clyde was a quiet boy, not very outgoing. I remember him being at my house, and my niece thought Clyde, who was sixteen at the time, was so cute and she had such a crush on him. But he was paying no attention to her. He was too shy. But we always figured he was going places. He just had that extra something which makes people stand out above the crowd."

Wells certainly has his detractors, such as Myrle Vokey, a well-known Newfoundland humorist and teachers federation official, who played hockey with Wells when they were both students at Memorial University during the 1950s. He recalls a favorite saying of MUN professor Harry Pullen: "'You have strengths, you have weaknesses. And unless you're careful, your greatest strength can be your greatest weakness.' If you want to apply that to Clyde, you can see his greatest strengths are his rigidity, his task-oriented approach, his determination, steadfastness, straight and narrow, the right and proper way, all these phrases. Yet that certainly is his biggest criticism, as well. . . . All these things, if taken to the extreme, can be a big weakness." A former classmate at Dalhousie Law School in Halifax has a colorful way of putting Wells's failure to live up to his election-campaign promise of more jobs: "It reminds me of that old English song: 'The working man can kiss my ass, I've got the foreman's job at last.'"

But people like Margaret Rudderham aren't among them. She was in St. John's for a wedding in 1991 and telephoned

Wells at his office the day he signed the Hibernia deal with Ottawa. Told the premier likely wouldn't have time to see her, she received a telephone call from him shortly afterward, and he invited her to his office.

"I felt like a real celebrity going in there," she says. "He was so down to earth. He hadn't changed a bit. He wasn't putting on any airs at all. So I said to him, 'The next time I see you it might be in Ottawa,' and he said, 'Oh God, Marg, don't think that.' So I said, 'Well, the last time I saw you before this, I didn't expect you'd be premier of Newfoundland at our next visit.'

"He replied, 'Well, I guess if you look at it that way . . .'"

2

Memorial

IN 1497, GIOVANNI CABOTO, better known as John Cabot, officially "discovered" the island of Newfoundland while sailing under the English flag. Of course, the earliest-known evidence of human life on the island predated this "discovery" by about 4500 years, when the Vikings set up shop near the tip of the island's Great Northern Peninsula.

But it wasn't until the Society for the Propagation of the Gospel in Foreign Parts (SPGFP) organized a school in Bonavista in 1722, and then one in St. John's in 1744, that the island's children had any organized schooling at all.

Since the beginning then, God, or the way the various denominations saw him, was the educational system's most important product.

For more than 150 years, after the British parliament outlawed settlements on the island except those that were necessary to maintain the cod fishery for the mother country, growth in settlements was stunted though not stopped, and by 1832 Britain gave in to local demands for a popularly elected assembly. Twenty-three years later, Newfoundland was granted full responsible government after a vicious dispute between the Irish Catholics, who favored the fishermen and service class, and the newly arrived Protestant middle class, centred largely in St. John's, a split that exists to this day.

The formal educational system was set up between 1874 and 1876, giving the churches power to own and operate their own schools, as well as select and train their own teachers, and receive per-capita grants from the legislature. Remarkably, even today, about ninety-five per cent of Newfoundland's population is of British origin, mainly English and Irish. The major denominations then, as now, were Roman Catholic, Anglican, and Methodist (now United). At the time, the Anglicans and Roman Catholics each represented about one-third of the island's population, while about one-quarter of Newfoundlanders were Methodists.

One of the major arguments used by those opposed to Newfoundland's joining Canada in 1949 (only fifty-two percent voted in favor) was that it would lead to the end of church authority over the schools. Indeed, this was one of the major concerns Newfoundland expressed in fighting Pierre Trudeau's constitutional package in 1981, and the federal Liberals hired Clyde Wells, among others, to argue this would not be the case.

But Term 17 of the 1949 Terms of Union specifically gave the churches the right to retain their traditional power over the school system. Thus the province had "exclusive authority to make laws in relation to education, but the Legislature [did] not have authority to make laws prejudicially affecting any right or privilege with respect to denominational schools, common [amalgamated] schools, or denominational colleges, that any class or classes of persons have by law in Newfoundland at the date of Union, and out of public funds of the Province of Newfoundland provided for education."

During the 1950s and early 1960s, the churches themselves introduced a program of consolidation among the more than three hundred various school boards in the province. In 1962, for example, the Roman Catholic Church had eighty school boards. In less than two years they'd chopped the number to twelve. Even so, the emphasis in the schools was decidedly religious, and this church-based system resulted in myriad tiny, ill-equipped schools, especially outside St. John's, and a resulting high failure rate.

In his 1985 book *The Smallwood Era*, former Liberal cabinet minister Dr. Frederick Rowe writes that of the 1187 schools in Newfoundland in 1949, 778 had only one room, and of the 778 teachers in these schools, more than 700 hadn't spent a single year in university. Indeed, of the 2375 Newfoundland teachers at the time, only fifty-seven were university graduates. Only one in 700 pupils in these tiny outport schools ever received their grade eleven, qualifying them to go to Memorial or any other post-secondary institution.

Rowe writes that "there was little to distinguish the average Newfoundland school from its predecessor of fifty or sixty years earlier. There was no electricity and therefore no lighting except in the very rare instance when kerosene lamps were used. The schools were almost invariably constructed of wood, and were heated by wood or coal stoves. There was no water supply either for drinking or sanitation. Proper ventilation was non-existent, as were school libraries, gymnasiums, and laboratory facilities. The only concession to sanitation was the decrepit and obnoxious outhouse."

Out of this system then, came Clyde Wells.

In his maiden speech in the Newfoundland House of Assembly on December 4, 1966, Wells, then Minister of Labor in Joey Smallwood's cabinet, betrayed the bitterness he harbored about the school system. Endorsing Smallwood's plan to abolish school fees in the province, he said, "I went to such a school. I went to a one-room school where the teacher taught every subject in every grade until I was in grade seven, then a two-room school, and the teacher taught every subject in every grade from grade five to grade eleven. I know just how bad and unsatisfactory those schools are."

Throughout his initial term as a Smallwood cabinet minister and then as an independent Liberal, between 1966 and 1970, Wells attacked the province's education system many times and called for one completely integrated non-parochial system. In 1992, he endorsed a royal commission on education that recommends exactly that.

On April 15, 1969, a year after he and John Crosbie had walked out of Smallwood's cabinet over a dispute about financing the Come By Chance oil refinery, in an extraordinary public display by such a private man, Wells literally bared his soul during debate on a Smallwood bill to consolidate the major Protestant school boards.

"There was also present . . . the proverbial wooden stick, not all the teachers used it, not a yardstick, but it had those dimensions, and he used to use it on the edge, hold your wrist and slap down. . . . There is only one spot where it hurt, maybe it hurt everywhere else, but it hurt so bad in the one spot . . . that thumb joint, and when the edge of that stick hit your thumb joint, that was bad. . . .

"I count myself one of the fortunate ones, very fortunate ones. I was lucky I got through it. . . . I was able to go to university . . . and I was told at the university that I was there on condition, I was there by grace, I was permitted to remain in the university provided during my first year . . . I passed grade nine, ten, and eleven Latin, altogether in one course."

He went on to point out that hundreds of others in the province have had to face the same situation — all because the teachers in their schools knew no foreign languages and taught only the traditional subjects. "Every parent and every teacher and every clergyman and every priest and every bishop, all of us in this province have for too long been perpetrating a sin against the majority . . . and what is worse, we have been doing it all [the denominational system] in the name of God. . . . I do not accept that anymore because I have seen . . . some of the practical results of the maintenance of our system."

Wells said a secular system works in most other countries and provinces, so why not in Newfoundland? Primarily, he argued that the province cannot afford the multiple systems, but the people who suffer the most from the attempt "are the children who go through it. The people who flunk out in grade eight, the people who cannot get into university . . ."

Smallwood, a staunch defender of denominational schools, said it would be unconstitutional to abolish them and unfair to remove religious rights. Wells vehemently disagreed. "I do not want to be the one to tell this to the boy from Port au Choix or the girl from White Bay South . . . ten years from now that we protected your religious rights, but unfortunately you are condemned forever to washing dishes in a restaurant because that is all you are qualified to do."

And so, for most Newfoundlanders in the 1950s, university was, if not completely out of reach, certainly a place that catered to the rich. Particularly in rural Newfoundland, the gap between the tiny ruling elite — primarily the St. John's merchant class — and the rest of the people was more pronounced than anywhere else in the country, making the chances of university education for a fisherman's son or daughter, or for that matter, a railway express agent's son, remote. Indeed, until a few years earlier, Newfoundlanders didn't even have a university to go to. The elite were sent to Ontario, the Maritimes, or abroad, usually to Oxford or somewhere else in England, for their university training.

While rural Newfoundlanders had to put up with appalling conditions in their ill-equipped one- and two-room schools, the children of the St. John's merchant class could usually be found attending one of the three main church-based "colleges" in the capital city — well-equipped high schools modelled after the British system — either Prince of Wales College (United), Bishop Feild College (Anglican), or St. Bonaventure's College (Roman Catholic).

"Nowhere else in North America," wrote Sid Noel, "had colonial society evolved in quite the same way as in Newfoundland, and nowhere were social classes more sharply polarized. With the decline of the English West Country influence, virtually the entire export and import trade of the country had fallen into the hands of a small group of St. John's merchants, who, with the government officials, churchmen, and others they supported, formed the dominant social class. They were invariably English and Protestant. And not only were they wealthy, they were also immensely powerful, for the financial structure of the fishery had become totally dependent upon their capital."

For outsiders, moving into the world of the St. John's merchant class was no easy task.

Veteran Newfoundland Liberal MP Roger Simmons, fresh from a small Salvation Army school in Lewisporte, a timber town and seaport near the Bay of Exploits northwest of Gander, remembers his feelings upon arriving at the Memorial campus in 1957:

"If you went to Memorial University in those days, the first thing that hit you like a ton of bricks was 'I don't belong here.' Your pedigree was extremely important. Being from outside St. John's, you would notice this strong St. John's clique, the 'Townies,' who didn't have much time for the outporter crowd, or 'Baymen,' as we were called.

"So you did one of [three] things: either you packed up and went home in two weeks, or you kept completely to yourself by burying yourself in your books, or you said, 'I'm not going to let this beat me,' and you got involved in all sorts of activities. That's what Wells did, hoping to break into the St. John's clique. Everybody had their own way of doing it. Clyde joined all kinds of organizations and played sports. I did it by working at the university newspaper."

Wells was certainly not a Townie, but strictly speaking not a Baymen either, since he didn't come from a remote seaside outport. Still, like most students from outside the major urban area, he was the first in his family to attend university. Indeed, when he walked onto the old Parade Street–Merrymeeting Road campus in 1955, he was the first person ever from

Stephenville Crossing to attend university. He was eighteen and had a burning desire not only to be a lawyer, but to be accepted as an equal in what he saw as the glittering world of St. John's.

With a population of about 60,000 at the time, the capital seemed like an enormous metropolis to the eager hard-working kid from The Crossing.

"I'd never been outside Newfoundland. I'd never seen anything larger than Corner Brook," says Wells. "I thought Corner Brook was big. Then I arrived in St. John's. It was big. I was quite surprised. Remember, there wasn't any television at home. I'd never seen anything that indicated what St. John's might be like. Oh, you'd see a picture sometimes of the basilica or the cathedral. I'd seen pictures of St. John's in history books, that kind of thing. That's really all I knew about St. John's. Although it was a smaller city then than it is now, it was still big by Stephenville Crossing standards, I can tell you that."

Simmons says that for most people in rural Newfoundland, whose fathers inevitably were fishermen, loggers, or other semi-skilled workers, the only ticket out was university, and usually the only option most could afford was the education faculty, because there were provincial government grants as incentives. They couldn't get enough teachers in those days, especially in the outports and smaller communities elsewhere. So if you wanted to be a teacher, you could get help," he says. "But if you wanted to become a doctor or a lawyer, you were on your own."

Emerson Rudderham, the neighbor in The Crossing who had employed Clyde as a plumber's helper, recalls the young man coming home from Memorial his first Christmas "and he was really troubled. He figured he wasn't going to make it, and he couldn't afford to hire a tutor at the time. So I suggested he approach a professor and explain the situation and he could get extra help. And that's what he did."

It was Mose Morgan to the rescue.

Political science professor Mose Morgan scouted for potentially good students, whom he recruited as cadets for the Canadian Officer Training Corps (COTC). The Corps' appeal was that it paid cadets $15 for a weekly drill parade — extra if you took range practice on weekends — and a regular army salary for training during the summer months.

But Morgan would become much more than just Wells's COTC recruiter. He also became his faculty adviser, his mentor, a father figure, and to this day, a trusted friend and political adviser.

J. Douglas Eaton, now retired Director of Student Affairs and a MUN vice-president, recalls, "No one in this world has had more influence on Clyde Wells than Mose Morgan. Clyde has an abiding love and respect for Mose. If we ever had a Mafia at Memorial, Mose was our boss. There were six of us who ran Memorial in those days, and Mose was the top. He had a tremendous influence on Clyde. I shouldn't be surprised if Clyde consults him weekly."

Wells is greatly enamored of Morgan who, as dean of arts at the time, clearly made the difference between his receiving his undergraduate degree or flunking out, but not all MUN graduates see Morgan as the selfless hero.

Current MUN professor Patrick O'Flaherty, a Roman Catholic, well-known Newfoundland writer, and honors student who attended MUN during the same years as Wells, says somewhat sardonically, "If you fell under Morgan's protective influence as a student, all doors would be opened. But it sure helped if you were an Anglican."

Another current MUN professor, Everard King, who was a graduate student when Wells arrived, says he doesn't remember Wells at university, but if he wanted a eulogy, he'd talk to Mose Morgan. "I went to the alumni banquet two years ago when Clyde was declared Alumnus of the Year, and it was a glorification of Mose Morgan night, especially Clyde's speech.

It's almost as if Mose had found a disciple and sent him out into the wilderness, or God knows where, perhaps Ottawa eventually."

Morgan himself concedes he had his favorites, Clyde among them.

"He was a serious-minded student. I took to him, quite apart from the fact that I was his faculty adviser. I didn't take to all the students I had, I can assure you of that. He seemed to know what he wanted to do. He was straightforward, honest and hard-working."

Morgan taught Wells the theories of federalism of his own great hero, Australian K.C. Wheare, who had taught them to Morgan at Oxford. Wheare's theory of federalism is a balance between two levels of government with a tilt toward a strong central government. The model, as applied to Canada, means Ottawa should hold most of the power, with no special jurisdictional arrangements for any constituent parts of the federation. It was precisely this view that made Clyde Wells oppose the Meech Lake accord in 1990 — and made him a household name in this country.

Reading through Wheare's influential book *Federal Government*, one can hear the echoes of Wells's objections to the Meech lake accord in 1990, and his dogged insistence on and faith in the ability of strong central governments to solve the problems of the regions. The book is essentially a comparative study of the government systems in Canada, the United States, Australia, and Switzerland, and these are the examples regularly cited by Wells in his constitutional arguments.

Wheare touches on what has also become a consistent Wells theme — that all provinces must be equal, hence his devotion to the Triple-E Senate. A federal government, wrote Wheare, "based on the principle that government by a bare majority of the people is not the only way in which to govern well and in some cases is equivalent to bad government. Majorities of regions have a significance which majorities of people have

not; two-thirds and three-quarters majorities have a significance which bare majorities have not."

In addition to Wheare, Wells's political-science reading included the work of R. McGregor Dawson and J.A. Corry, both
of which promoted the view of federalism that would later be
championed by Wells — but not before Pierre Trudeau had
turned this particular vision of Canada into his own lifelong
crusade.

There is no doubt, though, that Wells's faith in strong central
government was cast in stone during those years under
Morgan's influence. In a 1990 interview with the *Toronto Star's*
Tom Walkom, Wells said, "I don't think there's been much
change in my basic thinking on the principles from the days
when I studied political science at Memorial."

Morgan was also the one who convinced Wells to study Latin,
not French, for his prerequisite foreign language training. "He
always kids that he didn't take French because I advised him
to take Latin," says Morgan. "I advised him to take Latin
because at that time Latin was a prerequisite to get into law
school." Wells has since attempted to learn French, but with
little success. He ultimately graduated with a BA and a B
average, without earning in those years a single academic
award or scholarship.

Like so many outport students, Wells had jumped at the
chance to join the COTC. Morgan had strongly advised it.
"These service units were a great means of enabling students
to get the income to finish their university education, and that
was one of the reasons I suggested it to Clyde. And also because
they trained in the summertime on the mainland and got to
meet other students. It was quite an experience for them. . . .
He had no way of getting through university without that."

In addition to the COTC, Canada's military also sponsored
the University Navy Training Division (UNTD), the University
Reserve Training Plan (URTP, air force), and the Regular
Officer Training Plan (ROTP, full-time army personnel who

were paid to attend university). Wells later took advantage of this program to get one year's paid schooling at Dalhousie University. Under the plan, the students were promoted to a commissioned rank in the regular army and were supposed to spend three years in the service. Wells spent two, buying his way out of the third. The program was discontinued in 1966, but not before helping thousands of Canadians get a university education, which otherwise would have been impossible.

At the time, Memorial had a varsity hockey team that, because the university couldn't afford to send it to the mainland to play other university teams, played exhibition games against area senior teams such as Bell Island, a real hockey powerhouse at the time, the St. John's Caps, and Harbor Grace Seabees. Clyde Wells was goalie for one year and played in weekend tournaments at Gander and Clarenville, travelling with the team on the old Newfie Bullet.

J. Douglas Eaton, who was not only a faculty adviser with the COTC but head of physical education and the university team coach, says, "I wouldn't put Clyde down as one of the better goalies Memorial ever had, but he loved playing in goal. I could never understand why. He didn't have a goalie's personality. He wasn't physically aggressive. He was more, well, contemplative, you know."

Years later, commenting on Well's performance as premier, someone said that goaltenders have a natural tendency to block everything sent their way.

Besides the Varsity teams, each of the faculties at Memorial also had their own teams. Fellow student Myrle Vokey, who played both varsity hockey and intramural for the education faculty, said competition was "pretty keen" between the faculties. Wells played goal for the arts faculty, and Vokey remembers him well: "He wanted to win. But not wanting to win at all costs. I remember discussions sometimes between periods that you have in the dressing room and we'd be talking about taking out so and so, and his attitude always was, well, he wouldn't condone any kind of violence or hurtful approach. By all means take him out, but take him out fairly. And I think that's to his credit, and I think that's the way he operates today pretty much."

He also describes Wells as a friendly person. He said he and his wife were waiting for an airplane recently at the Empress Club at the Halifax airport when Wells, on his way back from Prince Edward Island, came in.

"He saw Marilyn and me and he came right over to shake my hand and embrace Marilyn and to show care and concern. Even though I did something terrible a few years ago and ran for the PCs — I lost by twenty-seven votes in my home of Bell Island — he is still very sociable whenever he sees me. He always has a kind word, which somehow doesn't fit in with the reputation he has of being an autocratic, independent type of leader, not a team person. I think he finds it difficult to compromise. . . . I find myself struggling. There are times I admire him and like what he's doing. Admire his courage, sympathize with his position. And there are times I get quite upset with what I perceive to be his autocratic and insensitive way of dealing with things."

Memorial math professor Ben Gardner was one of four people, including Wells, who founded the Memorial Liberal Club in 1958. Arthur Knight, now a University of Saskatoon professor, was the prime mover behind the club, arguing that because the upcoming federal Liberal convention (won by Lester Pearson) would have openings for university delegates, they could become delegates if they had a formal club. Gardner, Knight, Wells, and Dave Warren formed the club, but it turned out they could only send three delegates to the convention. "We figured Art should go since he organized the club," says Gardner, "and we drew lots for the other two spots. We just put our three names in a hat and drew two of them out, and the one guy who didn't go was Clyde Wells, the only guy of the four of us who actually went into politics. I don't think we ever had any other members. Just the four of us. Art was president, and Clyde, vice-president."

Wells also served a term as advertising director of the university yearbook *The Cap and Gown*, and took one turn as a member of the student union. The latter gave him a relished opportunity to serve on the university discipline committee and students' court, where students were punished for breaches of discipline within the university, usually by such things as removal of privileges to attend functions, sports activities, dances, or other social events, a system Wells once said "worked well."

Wells was named to the John Lewis Paton Honor Society, the highest non-academic honor Memorial's student union can confer, a recognition of good academic standing and "outstanding contribution to the university and its students."

Another Paton society colleague was Memorial education professor Noel Veitch. "I like the guy," he says. "I differ with him fundamentally on many political issues, but that's beside the point. He was an active student. We weren't close friends or anything, but we knew each other. "I remember Clyde being active in model parliament, and he was as personable then as he is now. But he didn't have some of the, well, I'll use the word 'dictatorial' qualities he seems to display now. I'll say this for him. He was willing to stand up against Joey [Smallwood], along with Crosbie, and he took the slings and arrows of politics that went along with that. But he didn't show the aspects of being such a strong leader that he'd run roughshod over other people back then. He didn't show that side of his character," Veitch insists. "Some veteran Liberal people here, and I'm not one, tell me their biggest disappointment in him is he runs a one-man show. He doesn't tolerate different views. There's no sense of value in other people's views from him."

The Reverend Carl Major, a priest at St. Thomas (Anglican) Church in St. John's, also went to Memorial with Clyde and grew up next door to The Crossing in Stephenville. "He was a fine young straightforward fellow," says Major. "One of the things you might want to change is his present style of leadership. He operates pretty much with his fingers and hands on everything. He wants to run everything. At university he wasn't like that. He didn't try to dominate, although you couldn't really when you came from outside St. John's like we did. They wouldn't allow you to dominate.

"I think Clyde was somewhat affected by the American culture which flowed from the base in Stephenville. So we didn't really grow up in an outport in the same way that, say, somebody from Arnold's Cove would have. There was quite a different background and culture in those outports. In Stephenville and Stephenville Crossing, we saw a lot more. Lots of airplanes, military people, a fair amount of money around, a more dynamic environment. They had black people there, for example, and I don't want this misunderstood, but you would not see that anywhere else other than St. John's.

"At that time, we had just come into Confederation, and for a student to be able to come from Stephenville Crossing and go to university was a very big thing. Not many were able to do that. Most of the people who went to Memorial at that time have ended up in leadership positions. Clyde had his goals to pursue, and he pursued them."

The main goal, of course, was graduating, so he could go off to Dalhousie and pursue his dream of being a lawyer. With no law school in Newfoundland, he had no other choice but to pack his bags and head for the mainland, in late summer 1959.

3

Law
Times

WHILE BRIAN MULRONEY was boozing, womanizing, partying — and flunking — his first and only year at Dalhousie Law School in 1959, his less flamboyant classmate Clyde Wells was, true to form, grinding his way through. The two men, who would clash in such dramatic fashion thirty years later over the failed Meech Lake accord, were as different then as they are now.

While Mulroney spent his free evenings trolling Halifax's black slum, Africville — where he eventually contracted a social disease that put him in hospital — Wells spent his spare time with his girlfriend, Eleanor Bishop, who was studying nursing at the Royal Victoria Hospital in Halifax. While Mulroney organized political events on campus, boasting to his peers of his regular telephone chats with John Diefenbaker, Wells stayed away from such secular pursuits, preferring to seek comfort in the Canterbury Club, the Anglican campus organization at Dalhousie.

In 1988 just after Wells became Newfoundland's premier and threatened to rescind his predecessor's approval of the accord,

Mulroney, while on a flight to an economic summit in Europe, was asked by some journalists what he thought of Wells. "I don't know the man," Mulroney said. "I've never met him. I'm looking forward to getting to know him."

This is not surprising. First, Mulroney spent only one year at Dalhousie, and he and Wells clearly travelled in different circles, although they would have shared several classes. Second, for many years Mulroney did not mention his Dalhousie experience at all, preferring a different version of his academic career.

Dalhousie is one of Canada's oldest institutions. Founded as Dalhousie College in 1818 by George Ramsay, the ninth earl of Dalhousie and then lieutenant-governor of Nova Scotia, it was elevated to a university in 1863. The law school was opened twenty years later, making it the first in the British Commonwealth to teach common law.

In the 1950s, getting into Dalhousie wasn't too difficult, but graduating was another matter. There were no admission tests and certainly no lineups for spots as there are in universities today. But the law school did form a reputation for academic toughness and for weeding out about one-third of the first-year students.

Wells wasn't weeded out, but he didn't ace it, either. Unlike another contemporary politician, Prince Edward Island Premier Joe Ghiz, who a few years later won the top academic achievement award for constitutional law at Dalhousie, Wells never rose above the B student he was at Memorial. And again, there is no record of his having won any academic honors at Dalhousie.

While he had participated in numerous extracurricular activities at Memorial, apart from the Canterbury Club, he didn't belong to anything at Dalhousie. There were two reasons: one, academic — he was having a tough enough time passing as it was, without robbing study time for social reasons; and two, the pressures he felt as a Bayman to gain favor among the St.

John's Townies at Memorial meant nothing at Dalhousie. As Newfoundland Liberal MP Roger Simmons explains, "When you go to Dalhousie, it's not the number of social graces you have, old man. It's the number of A's you had academically."

The university's traditional stuffiness would likely have appealed to Wells. He didn't have to wear a gown, which was mandatory at Memorial, but Dalhousie law students were forced to wear suits or sports jackets, with shirts and ties, leading the *Dalhousie Gazette* to label them "Blue-Suited Boobs." Wells would have also approved of the daily attendance-taking, especially since by all accounts, he rarely missed a day during his three-year stint there.

Among the fifty freshmen, a record high, who showed up in 1959 in the historic stone law school building was well-known Halifax lawyer Brian Flemming, who represented Dalhousie's debating team along with Mulroney, and in the 1970s ran Pierre Trudeau's office. He recalls Wells as "a plugger, a middle-of-the-road, middle-of-the-class kind of guy. He wasn't particularly flashy. A guy who did his work, who didn't goof around, a serious student. He certainly wasn't what you'd call one of the boys. You couldn't find him at the Lord Nelson Hotel on Friday nights lifting a few brews like the rest of us did."

Flemming says Wells may have been involved marginally in model parliament in his third year. "I was the Liberal leader at the time, and he certainly wasn't a front-bencher, if he was involved at all.

"He was nothing like Mulroney. A guy who was never fucking around, never took shortcuts, who did his work, and probably never padded his legal bills. In contrast to Mulroney, Wells is the kind of guy you'd trust sleeping naked in the bed with your wife when you were away, the kind of person you can rely on to do the right thing, the kind of person you could appoint as your executor. Clyde is as principled as Brian is unprincipled. That's a big spectrum there. He's probably never patted a bum like John Turner did. In fact, he probably never thought of it."

Clyde Wells, in Flemming's opinion, was as solid a lawyer as he was a student. "He was a good appeal-court lawyer. To say that is to say somebody is marginally boring, if not totally boring. A flamboyance that you need for trial lawyers, you don't see at appeal. You need to be more grey, more cerebral, more patient, more plodding, and I think Clyde is all those things and always has been."

In his 1991 book, *Mulroney: The Politics of Ambition*, John Sawatsky paints a picture of Mulroney as a student who, during tutorials, "needed no prodding and fired off his analysis with speed and assurance, his voice booming with confidence from the back of the room." As for Wells, Sawatsky quotes an unidentified classmate as saying Wells was the only other first-year student as blatant at sucking up to the professors as Mulroney, only Mulroney did it with more finesse. "Brian was more sophisticated than just going up and kissing ass. Brian knew how to kiss ass in an artistic way. Clyde was simple and direct, just like he is today."

But this is not the picture of either man painted by most other Dalhousie classmates.

For example, Toronto lawyer Lawrence Hebb, a gold-medal student and one whom Mulroney turned to for help in passing his first-year exams, says, "Mulroney was one of those guys who, when he was in class, which wasn't all that often, sat at the back and tried to keep his head down so the professor wouldn't see him. That was a tremendous contrast with Wells, who was an incredibly serious guy. He still is. I saw him at a conference a couple of years ago, and life is still a very serious thing for him. But he always knew, or thought he knew, he was right. That was my impression of Clyde, as one of the stronger students in the class."

Dalhousie law professors generally used what is called the Harvard case law study method, where students are assigned a number of cases to read and the professor comes into class, announces they are discussing *Jones vs. Smith,* and calls a student by name to discuss the key aspects of the case. This leads to considerable analysis and debate, prodded by the professor, on particular points of law.

Halifax lawyer Larry Hayes, another Dalhousie classmate, says, "Clyde was always quick to volunteer his views. I remember that about him. He was very keen to join the discussions. And he was always prepared. He wasn't always right, but none of us were, but he was quick off the mark, not one of those guys who would hang back and see which way the debate was going."

Niagara Falls lawyer John L. den Ouden says Wells is "about the only honest politician in the country. He calls a spade a spade. That's what I appreciate. He was like that at law school, too. He wasn't a gregarious type of person, that's true. But by the time you got into graduate school, a lot of the guys were already married. [Only] about one-third were single, so there wasn't that rat-pack mentality anyway.

"At Dalhousie, he was a very analytical chap, almost like a machine, a no-nonsense kind of approach. But there was no real indication, at least none that I saw, that he had any real political aspirations at the time. With Mulroney, it was different. He spent more time politicking than he did studying law."

Late in 1987, Ottawa lawyer Roger Barrette was having lunch in the Elephant and Castle, an English-style pub in the downtown Rideau Centre, within sight of Parliament Hill. "This guy walks up to me and says, 'Hello, Roger Barrette,' and I looked up at him and couldn't remember who he was. He said 'I'm Clyde Wells. I was in your class.' He had just become Liberal leader at the time. He wasn't premier. But I didn't remember him at all."

Still, after having time to think about Wells, especially seeing him so much in the news, Barrette recalled that his Newfoundland classmate had a pit bull mentality even back then. "He was a bit of a loner, but he's not a two-faced type of individual. He's got his convictions and he articulates them. You have to wonder how long he can survive as a politician with those convictions, but he seems to be hanging in there, although he may bring the country down the drain with his convictions.

"It's funny, I remember Mulroney more, even though he was absent most of the time. We had a lot of characters. Rick Cashin and Gerry Doucette were around during those years, too. But Clyde wasn't that communicative. He tended to keep more to himself than the rest of us did."

Helenanne Carey, one of just two women in the entire law school at the time, remembers Wells as a pleasant, friendly person. "He was always very nice to me. It was purely a student kind of relationship, but you know, some of the guys didn't want to be seen talking to the women, particularly me since I was married. Some of them had that macho attitude, what were we [women] doing there, we should be home doing something else," Carey says. "But Clyde was not like that. He was a warm, friendly guy."

No family in Prince Edward Island has stronger political ties than that of Melville Campbell, a Summerside lawyer, whose brother Alex was a long-time premier and his father, Thane, was both premier and chief justice of the PEI Supreme Court. Ironically, Melville's one plunge into elected office was as a Liberal candidate in the 1968 federal election. While Trudeaumania swept the rest of the nation, it didn't happen on the island, as the Tories won all four seats and Melville Campbell stuck with practising law.

As a student at Dalhousie, Campbell was in the navy, while Wells was in the army's ROTC program. He has a picture in his office of himself, Wells, and two others being sworn in to the Nova Scotia bar in 1963. Of Wells, he says, "He was very steady, much the same as you see today. There's not an awful lot of emotionalism in him, but there is no bullshit. He was always a straight shooter and highly respected."

Donald A. Thompson, a Cambridge, Ontario lawyer, considered Clyde a very close friend. They roomed next to each other at King's College at the time and shared that residence with divinity students. Clyde, he says, used to love to debate the issues with them, and Thompson has fond memories of him. Yes, he, too, found him serious, but also possessed of a good sense of humor.

Thompson offers a view of Wells that's different from all his other classmates. "He liked to drink and carouse and go crazy the odd time like the rest of us. He placed great value in his friends. He loved to debate and he loved the bull sessions at night.

"Remember when the Meech week wound up on the Friday night how drained he was and how glad he was to get home to escape the pressure he'd been under? Well, I had telephoned him a few days earlier, and he found the time to call me back on the Sunday night. I was quite touched by that. I can't say enough good things about Clyde. He's a very important man in our country. This country really needs him."

Wells's best friend at Dalhousie was Middleton, Nova Scotia lawyer Clare Durland. The two roommates had more than their friendship in common. At the time, Durland's girlfriend, Joan Webber, now his wife, and Clyde's girlfriend, Eleanor Bishop, also roomed together in the nurses' residence at the Royal Victoria Hospital, and the couples regularly double-dated.

"With Clyde," he says, "what you see is what you get. There is nothing pretentious or ostentatious about him. He certainly was a stubborn scoundrel. When he formulated a view, he'd hold it until the cows came home. But his fundamental values were built on his affection and allegiance to his home province. I wouldn't say he had an interest in politics, per se, in those days. Certainly he was a student of political history and always a good debater."

The two students spent their first summer together travelling around Nova Scotia and New Brunswick as Maritime distributors of a machine that sprayed a graphite grease on the bottoms of cars to keep them from rusting, earning enough to pay most of their expenses for their second year.

"Clyde's dad had died, and we both shared a need to be pretty prudent with our limited resources. Clyde always had an old car. We drove around to the various garages with a demonstration model of this undercoating machine in the back seat. We'd drag it out, put on a demonstration, and hope they'd buy it."

Their social life was pretty limited during their freshmen year. Wells and Durland shared a room at the King's College residence, moving the next year to the basement of an old fraternity house. "Our fun at night was to watch the mice run around. We were both as poor as church mice anyway, so we qualified.

"We went to the odd movie as a foursome, and we had other friends we'd visit sometimes in the city. The student nurses had to be in residence most of the time by ten or eleven, so you couldn't do much. Occasionally they'd have days off, too, and then we'd usually go out to my wife's parents' place in Mahone Bay. The school sometimes had dances, but we weren't very much into that."

Neither had much interest in fraternity life. "Clyde may have actually pledged to the Zeta Xi frat house, but I don't think he ever became a brother. We only stayed there because it was so cheap."

The irony is that, of all the fraternities, Zeta Xi — known locally as Zetes — was described in Sawatsky's book as "one of the shabbiest and raunchiest: it was the fraternity most notorious for drinking. Zetes had a six-foot beer bottle in the basement as a symbol of its true interest; patrons, so the joke went, had to wear hard hats for protection from falling beer bottles."

According to Durland, another close friend at the time was Russell Hatton, who later became principal of Huron College in Ontario, but at the time was a fledgling Anglican priest and chaplain at the Canterbury Club. On most Sunday nights, between fifty and sixty people would show up at the Canterbury Club meetings. "It was basically a discussion club," says Durland, "but also an opportunity to meet some other kids. Our [future] wives went to the meetings, too.

"Religion has always been important to Newfoundland. It's important to Clyde, too. He's very honest. He's got a tremendous sense of integrity. He's stubborn as hell. People say he's hard to work for. He has to be the boss. That's probably true. He does have strong ideas about everything."

Durland fondly recalls Clyde's helping him to work up the courage to pop the question to Joan. Clyde and Eleanor were already engaged. "I was hesitating and Clyde said, 'Let's go.' So he took me to Birks in Halifax. We saw this ring that I liked, but I was still fidgeting, and Clyde said, 'Pay him. Pay him. It's perfect.' So I bought it, and then we went by and picked up Eleanor and Joan, and Clyde drove us to the Dingle [a local park] and we got out for a walk, while Clyde and Eleanor waited in the car. It was a beautiful summer day, and Joan and I walked around the Dingle, where I got up the nerve to propose. Then Joan came roaring back to the car, all excited, and said, 'Look. Look! I got my ring!' I've always been grateful to Clyde for that. And I think about it whenever I see people saying that Clyde doesn't have any romance in his soul. He does. He just doesn't flaunt it."

Like most students who were part of the COTC during their undergraduate years, Wells hadn't had anything more to do with the army since he'd left. The only obligation was to be on what was called the supplementary reserve list, which essentially meant that in the event of war, you'd be the first called, because you at least had some level of military training.

"During my second year at Dalhousie, jobs were a bit scarce and I didn't know what I was going to do for the summer," says Wells. "But I was talking to somebody and they said, 'You were in the COTC, weren't you? How about a summer call-out?' They frequently had what they called call-outs, or job opportunities in those years, where the military needed somebody who was trained as an officer to do summer work, because of vacations and so on. So I went down and spoke to Colonel Hutchinson of the Judge Advocate General's office in Halifax and told him that I'd been in the COTC and would like an opportunity to work for the JAG and, I thought, work in his office in Halifax. That's what I had hoped for, partly, or course, because Eleanor was there at the Victoria General in training, and I would have preferred to say in Halifax."

Hutchinson told Wells there was an opportunity, all right, not in Halifax, but in Ottawa. "I needed a job," Wells explains, "so off I went. It was interesting. I enjoyed it. I was then going into my final year of law school and I didn't know any lawyers really. There weren't many in western Newfoundland. I didn't see any prospect of setting up a private practice in Stephenville at the time, so I didn't know where I'd be going when I got out of law school."

But during that summer, he was offered a permanent job upon graduation and promised financial help from the army if he accepted. "With no means of income, and already in debt, that was a great inducement."

In his final year at Dalhousie then, Wells was enrolled in the regular army, and his fees and living expenses were picked up by the service. After graduation, he articled in Halifax, because he had to be admitted to a provincial bar in order to work for the JAG. "The condition was that I work for three years. I had no quarrel with that."

So he and Eleanor got married — on August 20, 1962, in The Crossing — and moved to Ottawa. The Judge Advocate General's office there had four major sections — court martial, property, claims, and international — and Wells and the other officers were rotated regularly among all four. In those days, the military was substantially larger than it is now. The army had close to 80,000 people alone. So did the air force, while the navy had about 35,000. The JAG was the legal branch of the service and handled such matters as property acquisitions, licences, courts martial, leasing arrangements, civil and criminal court cases, and accident claims.

It was while handling an accident claim in Corner Brook that Wells ran into Kevin Barry, who was desperately looking for help for his law firm because his partner, Bill Smith, had gone into politics. Wells was sent down to handle the legal side of the case in which Barry, as one of the few lawyers in town, was involved. Barry tried to convince Wells to leave the service and move to Corner Brook.

"I said I just can't think about it at this stage," Wells recalls. "I've got to finish my time. . . . I said, 'Well, gee, I've got a lot to think about. I've got a good position now. It is paying $672 a month. I can't just throw that to one side and come back to Corner Brook and practise law.'"

Wells had already decided he would stay his promised three years with the legal branch of the service, but no more. "I had come to realize that I wouldn't want to make it a permanent legal career, because while I learned a lot, from what I could see, the lieutenant drafted the letter, and the captain vetted it, then it went to the major, who vetted it again, and if it got by him it went up to the lieutenant-colonel, and finally the colonel saw it, and it might have a chance of going out without the brigadier having a go at it. So I didn't see this as a great legal career. I saw it as too confining and too military-structured to be a good, challenging professional career."

When Wells returned to Ottawa, Barry called him a couple of times, still trying to talk him into joining the firm. Finally Wells approached his superiors at JAG about the offer. "The colonel told me, 'We'd rather you stayed, but if you want to go you can get out if you pay back what you owe.' I thought because I'd been there for two of the three years I would have to pay an appropriate amount. But they insisted on me paying the whole amount, $8000. I'll tell you, for somebody earning a whole $672 a month . . . that was an awful lot of money. I'll never forget the advice I got from one fellow that I talked to.

He said, 'Look, in the first year you'll be paying that much in income tax. So don't worry about it.'"

And so, in June 1964, Clyde, Eleanor, and their five-month-old baby, Mark, returned home to Newfoundland. Clyde didn't know, couldn't have known, that in two years, at only twenty-eight, he'd become the youngest cabinet minister in Newfoundland's history, setting off a chain of events that twenty years later would make him the obvious choice of Newfoundland Liberals to end sixteen years of continuous Tory rule, and the "great white hope" of millions of English Canadians to stop the Meech Lake constitutional accord.

4

Joey's Man

THE NEWFOUNDLAND CLYDE WELLS returned to in 1964 was still firmly in the grip of Canada's most enduring demagogue, Joey Smallwood. While ruthless in dispatching his political enemies, the Liberal premier was still genuinely loved by most Newfoundlanders for delivering on his promise that joining Confederation would put cash in their pockets — by way of the baby bonus and other social programs the island had not been able to afford on its own.

Until Wells and John Crosbie openly defied Smallwood in the House of Assembly in 1968, there was no real political opposition and no Newfoundland Liberal party. There was only Joey, the Sun King. He chose the candidates. He decided who would, and who wouldn't, be hired by the provincial government, everybody from local road paver to deputy minister. Constituencies that voted for him had paved roads. Tory constituencies did not.

Wells had got his own first-hand look at Smallwood in action in 1959 when he and his friends from the Memorial University Liberal Club watched the House of Assembly, in the old Colonial Building, crush the International Woodworkers of America (IWA) after a bloody strike against the feudal lords of Bowater Newfoundland Ltd. at Corner Brook and the Anglo-Newfoundland Development Company at Grand Falls. Smallwood unilaterally decertified the union, but not before accusing them of being gangsters, goons, and murderers.

In October 1964, when Wells joined Kevin Barry's and Gerald Doucette's Corner Brook law practice, he decided to pick up on his university Liberal activity. He attended the founding convention of the Newfoundland Young Liberals Association in Grand Falls, where he succeeded in snatching the presidency from Smallwood's hand-picked candidate.

Smallwood, who hated to lose and rarely did, was furious for a time, but also impressed by the clean-cut appearance and superior speaking style of this brash young newcomer. Two years later, with Smallwood at the height of his remarkable popularity and a provincial election in the offing, Smallwood summoned Wells to Corner Brook's elegant Glynmill Inn to recruit him as a candidate. But twenty-eight-year-old Wells was just beginning to enjoy the good life as a pillar of local society, and with two small children — Mark, two and Heidi, one — he was not anxious to sacrifice his lifestyle, even for somebody he admired as much as Smallwood. The premier responded by not only proposing to appoint Wells to cabinet, and the higher stipend that comes with that, but said he would raise the sessional pay for all members from the current $6500 to $8500. And, to help Wells defeat Humber East Tory incumbent Dr. Noel Murphy, who was leader of the six-member Opposition, Smallwood agreed to run in the adjoining riding of Humber West, a tremendous boon for any candidate in those years.

To make room for Wells in his cabinet, Smallwood summarily announced that veteran Labor Minister Charlie Ballam, who'd held the post since Confederation seventeen years earlier, had decided to "retire." Ballam said later that, if he'd been asked, he probably *would* have agreed to retire, but

Smallwood hadn't bothered to ask him. None of this, apparently, troubled either Smallwood or Wells, and may even have served as an early model for Wells's own autocratic style when he became premier.

A joke going around Liberal circles at the time was that cabinet ministers were afraid to go to sleep at night for fear they would wake up in the morning to learn they'd retired overnight. Smallwood had gone around the province "retiring" several veterans and bringing in a new team of Young Turks. Two of them — John Crosbie, Municipal Affairs, and Alex Hickman, Justice — he named to cabinet, as he'd done with Wells, before they were even elected. Smallwood also recruited such political stalwarts as Bill Rowe, whose father was a veteran senior minister, and Ed Roberts, who later became Liberal leader and in 1992 was brought back into cabinet by Wells and appointed justice minister, also without benefit of holding a legislative seat at the time. The appeal for all these young hotshot Liberals was that Smallwood made it quite clear the 1966 campaign would be his last, and they would all have the opportunity to become premier themselves.

Long-time Liberal MHA (member of House of Assembly) Steve Neary, one of many who took turns leading the party during the Tory rule in the 1970s and 80s, admits to being angry when Smallwood picked Wells as labor minister. For Neary, a past president of the Newfoundland Federation of Labor (NFL), had impressive labor credentials. But, he says, "Joey explained to me that in the interest of the party I had to be a good team man. I accepted that, of course, because I had a lot of respect for Joey. But I'd heard Wells was not a team player and didn't like St. John's, and he proved that afterwards when he quit. He more or less referred to the people of St. John's as parasites at one point. The minute he arrived, he was very unhappy and saying he was losing money. He more or less tried to crash the St. John's elite, rather than associating with what Joey used to call 'the ragged-arsed artillery.' He hob-nobbed with Crosbie and Alex Hickman and that crowd."

Nevertheless, on August 16, 1966, a private plane owned by the influential Lundrigan clan of Corner Brook picked up Clyde and Eleanor Wells at the Deer Lake airport and flew them to St. John's for Clyde's swearing-in ceremony as labor minister. Afterwards, Wells and Smallwood flew back to Corner Brook where, with the deposed Ballam sitting dutifully at the table, Smallwood introduced his newest minister. Smallwood said Wells should "be able to bring a young man's, a new man's way of looking at things in Humber East."

But while Ballam had a legitimate history as a staunch union man — an electrician by trade and one-time president of the Newfoundland Federation of Labor — Wells had no such track record. This prompted the NFL, at its convention a week later, to pass a resolution asking Smallwood to appoint somebody else, saying, "The premier has appointed a person to this most important portfolio unknown to the workers of this province."

That would soon change. And the unions wouldn't like what they got to know.

Smallwood formally ended all the election speculation on August 18, when he invited reporters into his cabinet room in the Confederation Building and told them that Newfoundland's sixth election since Confederation would be held September 8. In addition to confirming that Wells would run in Humber East and himself in Humber West, he also announced that local newspaper publisher William Callahan would seek the Liberal nomination for nearby Port au Port, saying, "There will be a large meeting in Corner Brook Saturday night to adopt, name, and endorse the candidates for these three districts. I will take a chance and go there in the hope of getting the nomination for Humber West."

Sure enough, on Saturday, August 20, what passed for a "nominating convention" in those days — naturally, nobody opposed any of the nominees — a few hundred local Liberals gathered in the old Palace Theatre on Broadway to rubber-stamp Smallwood's selections. Boasting that four of the six districts in western Newfoundland would be represented by cabinet ministers after the election, Smallwood said, "I would imagine that this is my last election. God help me. Four years from now I will be as old as Diefenbaker is now. Isn't that a distressing thing?"

For his part, Wells delivered a pedestrian speech, staying away from emotion and simply outlining his own history and qualifications. A column by Roger Simmons titled "Roamin' Round" in the Corner Brook newspaper *Western Star* reported that Wells "didn't fare nearly as well as did his running mate. . . . He felt it necessary to state his credentials including his college degrees and his campus political activities, and spent the remainder of his speech convincing his listeners why the job as an MHA and cabinet minister would be good for him, rather than vice versa."

(Wells was previously acquainted with Simmons, who was, at the time of Wells's speech, a high school principal moonlighting for the summer as interim editor of the paper. Wells had acted as his lawyer a year earlier in a straight real estate transaction and had also run into him through the Young Liberals Association.)

Besides writing the column, Simmons hired a local student to draw what is the first political cartoon featuring Wells, showing the new labor minister sitting on the stage next to Smallwood, dressed like a little boy in short pants, his right arm resting on Smallwood's left arm, looking up at the premier and asking, "And, daddy, what is a strike?"

Simmons also published an editorial three days before the meeting entitled "Sacrificial lamb?", saying that Wells, the youngest member of the cabinet, "may also shortly achieve another, though more dubious distinction — that of being the person who held a ministerial portfolio for the shortest period of time [four months]." Ironically, it was Simmons himself who set a federal record by sitting as Pierre Trudeau's mines minister from August 12 to 22, 1983, resigning over an income tax-evasion charge. Even more ironically, Simmons was convicted by the Crown, represented in court by lawyer Clyde Wells.

The editorial did concede that Wells could upset Noel Murphy, the Opposition leader, "with the melting charm of Canada's most expert politician [Smallwood] at his elbow" — which is exactly what happened. Murphy believes that had Smallwood not campaigned with Wells, he would have defeated the newly appointed minister. As it was, Wells won by just 379 votes (3652 to 3273).

"So I really had something going against me," Murphy recalls. "Joey went from door to door saying, 'I'm Joey Smallwood. I need you. You need me. You need Clyde Wells. This is Clyde Wells. Vote for him, will you?' And they all said, 'Yes sir, yes sir, three bags full.'

"But I didn't feel too badly. That's fair enough. Clyde was a serious campaigner. He did everything properly. He went from door to door. We both went on television and held public meetings. . . . Clyde has always been a gentleman, a hard campaigner, very firm principles, and I think one recognizes that." After Wells got out of politics, Murphy, who is president of Humber Valley Broadcasting, named him to his board of directors. "He was the most useful person on the board."

During the 1966 campaign, Murphy announced a major twenty-five-plank election policy manifesto, which included free education for all students up to grade eleven, a subsidized drug plan, removal of sales tax on children's clothing and footwear, salary increases for civil servants, teachers, nurses, hospital workers, police and firemen, a subsidized milk program, and a host of other things, including a royal commission to investigate patronage in the Smallwood regime. It didn't work. Smallwood's Liberals won thirty-nine seats, leaving only three Tories as the official Opposition, all of them in St. John's, where Gerald Ottenheimer would soon become their leader.

On election night, Murphy went to pay his respects to Wells and Smallwood, who were holding a victory party at the Orange Lodge. "The place was jammed," he recalls, "as it always was at these things, because they gave out free drinks. When I came in the door some started going, 'Yah, yah, yah, yah,' and Joey jumped up and said, 'No, don't be like that.' Joey was always very correct in what he did, and Clyde is the same. Very correct. Joey said, 'Let him come up. Bring him up to the stage.' So I got onto the stage and said, 'I've come to congratulate you,' and they both put their hands out at the same moment, so I took both of their hands at the same time, held them up, and turned to the crowd and said, 'You see, it took two of them to defeat me.' I don't know that it went over terribly well, but some people chuckled. And it was the truth."

Ninety non-professional workers at Corner Brook's Western Memorial Hospital were threatening to strike during the election campaign, but Smallwood didn't let his new labor minister handle things. Instead, he issued a proclamation prohibiting the strike, having declared a "state of emergency" under the powers of the Labor Relations Act. A week later, the hospital agreed to wage increases recommended two months earlier by a conciliation board. The board and the union had both accepted the report at the time, but the hospital hadn't had the money to pay the raises. However, with an election on, Smallwood suddenly helped the hospital find money, and a strike was averted. It would not be that easy the following January, when Wells was given his first opportunity to show his political mettle.

Life was looking pretty good for the poor kid from The Crossing. He had taken to wearing monogrammed shirts and expensively tailored suits, and zipping around town in a large Lincoln. He had bought a spacious, side-split house on a large, well-treed lot in an upscale Corner Brook neighborhood. He had taken up skiing seriously, particularly at nearby Marble Mountain, and his law business was prospering. On top of that, he was now an MHA and a cabinet minister to boot, giving him access to government planes to fly back and forth between Corner Brook and St. John's.

He delivered his maiden speech in the House of Assembly on December 9, opening by praising Bowater, "probably Newfoundland's greatest single industry." He was already beginning to do some legal work for the company and would soon win their corporate account. He then defended Smallwood's decision to go on television and announce that any Newfoundlander who wanted a job on the giant Churchill Falls project should write him directly, a plea criticized as blatant patronage by the Opposition. "I could have gone on television," he said, "and made the announcement and asked for applications and asked for letters . . . but I suggest the result would have been far, far different. I am certain, absolutely certain, we would not today have 14,000 letters, had I or any other honorable member of the house gone on television and made such a request."

Wells said that by campaigning with Smallwood in Corner Brook he knew "full well the high esteem and respect and admiration held for the premier. . . . I don't wish to get sentimental about this, but I would like to mention one thing that happened. I saw tears stream down the face of an eighty-five-year-old man who talked about the premier when I knocked on his door at suppertime.

"Now I have no illusions about the fact that I collected all of the votes I got. I would like to think that I did, but I must be honest. . . . No, although those votes were cast for me, they were not cast for me as a person. I like to think that a fair number might have been, but I know they were cast for me because I supported a party that was led by a man admired and respected and loved in this province."

Wells then launched into his criticisms of the school system and applauded the throne speech announcement that Newfoundland would soon have a provincial ombudsman. He said people "need and should have" such services available. "Citizens cannot always afford to go to court either in time or in money, and this parliamentary commissioner [ombudsman] will give further recognition to the principle that government exists to serve the people. . . ." (In 1991, as premier, Wells killed the ombudsman's office as a cost-cutting measure.)

Wells finished his lengthy speech on another subject, which was to become a favorite theme: the shortcomings in the province's legal system. During his time in office, he gave numerous speeches on this topic, calling for a Supreme Court judge for Corner Brook, more court officers, and making numerous other suggestions, which may have been fair enough, but which reflected a self-interest from somebody standing to benefit directly from such reforms.

The next time Wells rose for a major speech in the House of Assembly, on Thursday, January 26, 1967, the atmosphere was less congenial. On Monday of that week, Smallwood had declared a state of emergency to stop 125 non-professional hospital employees from walking out at the Central Newfoundland Hospital in Grand Falls. The circumstances paralleled exactly those of the previous summer in Corner Brook. Both the hospital management and the Canadian Union of Public Employees, Local 990, had accepted a conciliation board report, but because the hospital didn't have the money to pay, it had turned to the province for help. Smallwood had promised higher wages for provincial employees in his last throne speech, but when no specific word was forthcoming, the union voted to strike. Smallwood then ordered them to stay on the job under his legislation, which required compulsory arbitration within thirty-seven days. Tory leader Gerald Ottenheimer said there was no other solution other than the government's honoring the conciliation board findings. "The government should act without delay in order to protect the sick and hospitalized in Grand Falls," he declared.

The union said they needed to await an arbitration system, since they'd already agreed to the conciliation board, and during a wild meeting, they were told that Atlantic CUPE president John F. MacMillan advised them to strike in spite of the emergency order, offering the national union's full support. At 9 a.m. Tuesday, in temperatures of minus twenty degrees Celsius, the union workers walked off the job in defiance of Smallwood's order.

A few hours later Wells told the legislature he would introduce two bills to amend the Labor Relations Act and the Hospitals Act. The Opposition demanded an emergency debate, but Smallwood said there was no urgency for a debate, because Wells had made it clear government action was in the works. Ottenheimer called a news conference to announce his plan for a thirty-day back-to-work agreement, with the union agreeing to compulsory arbitration and the government rescinding its order and agreeing that the strikers would not lose financially or be prosecuted. Smallwood and Wells weren't interested. They had their own agenda to bring the union to its knees.

As the strike entered its fourth day, and national CUPE president Stanley Little announced in Ottawa that the 100,000-strong union planned to pour money and men into support for the strike, Wells introduced two pieces of legislation designed to end the strike, but no copies of either bill were made public or given to the members, so the contents of the legislation, like the cabinet decree earlier in the week outlawing the strike, remained secret. Wells told the assembly, "I never dreamed, I could not imagine that the first bill that I might ever introduce to this house would have to be such a bill . . ." After defending his government's actions, Wells attacked the strikers for "anarchy. That is just what it is, no law, no order, do as you please, everybody do as they please. . . . That is what this situation is called, anarchy. That has not existed in the British democratic system for a thousand years, and there has been a system of law, a democratic system of law in the British heritage, for a thousand years. That union seeks now to set us back to 958, before the Battle of Hastings. Can you imagine that? That is only the first step. They chose not to obey this law. Next week they may choose not to obey another law, if they are permitted to do it. . . . It is almost inconceivable that a union would strike against the sick and dying and that the hospital be told they have to send patients home."

During a five-hour debate the next day over the bill making all hospital strikes unlawful, backed up by threats of decertification and heavy fines, both Wells and Smallwood were muttering dark warnings about a conspiracy by "Upper Canada union leaders" to embarrass and undermine the Newfoundland government. Smallwood accused the unions of communist techniques and anarchist aims, and even invoked memories of the International Woodworkers' strike. "I see mainlanders, trade unions, wiring and telephoning down here, not even bothering to come down, but saying ignore Joey, that little government, ignore those jackasses up on the roof of the Confederation Building. We'll sling down the money and the men. Well, they flung down money and men," he said. "Where is the IWA now? We are still here on this side of the house and more numerous in number."

Wells, guiding the legislation through second reading, said it would ban hospital strikes "under any circumstances," and if seventy per cent of the employees did not return to their jobs within three days after the act became law, they would face union decertification and stiff fines of between $1000 and $4000 for the union, between $100 and $500 for union officers, and $10 a day for anyone else breaking the act. Wells said he had some sympathy for employees who were "led astray" by union leaders. "The members of the union in Grand Falls did not make the decision to go on strike," he said, echoing Smallwood's Upper Canadian conspiracy theory. "They followed what their irresponsible anarchists told them to follow. . . . We have had ample demonstration of where the fault lies, and this bill will take care of this. It provides for decertification of unions striking against hospitals."

On Friday, January 27, the first two bills ever introduced by Wells were passed into law by Smallwood's overwhelming majority Liberal government. On Sunday, hospital workers voted ninety per cent in favor of returning to their jobs to avoid decertification after being urged to do so by local and national CUPE officers. MacMillan told the workers that he hoped "never again in our lives, or in the history of our parliament, we will see this type of legislation again. There is no place in a democratic country for this type of legislation."

During the debate, Wells displayed his characteristic penchant for clinging to some minute technical detail to deny the practical effects of something he has just done or said. When Ottenheimer complained that the bill, in calling for decertification, was too harsh, Wells said, "We are not decertifying the union." It is just this kind of nit-picking mentality that drove the other premiers nuts during the closed-door Meech Lake session in 1990. In a strictly technical sense, Wells was correct. They were not decertifying the union. But if the union continued to act like a union and support its right to strike, then it would be decertified, so for all practical purposes, the bill was indeed a decertification bill.

While Smallwood and company were feeling pretty smug after ending the strike at Grand Falls, the first signs that people were beginning to tire of one-man rule came in October 1967, after Smallwood had convinced Prime Minister Lester Pearson to appoint his man Charlie Granger to the federal cabinet to take the place of veteran Jack Pickersgill, who had been Newfoundland's cabinet representative. This meant a byelection in Granger's Gander riding, which the Liberal had won easily over Tory Harold Collins the year before. But much to everybody's shock, Collins won the byelection, defeating Liberal Jack Robertson by 805 votes. True, it only gave the

Opposition four seats, but it turned out to be an omen of future shocks.

As for Wells, he was still defending his anti-union legislation during the budget debate in late March of the same year by ridiculing Opposition arguments defending the right to strike. One Tory MHA suggested the armed forces should have the right, an idea, Wells said, "just so ridiculous as to be inconceivable." And what about police? he then asked. "It is equally unthinkable and ridiculous. We don't even have to go that far — the ordinary civil servant. What about the department of justice? Should they go on strike and have a breakdown in law and order?" Wells added that there were "certain categories of people carrying out certain functions . . . hospital workers and nurses and civil servants" who should not be allowed to strike. And on the situation at Grand Falls, he said, the unions still had the right to be certified and represent their members. "We had not taken away any right, but only the right to strike" — which most labor unions would view as a rather serious loss.

After less than a year in cabinet, Wells was already beginning to get restless. In April he approached colleague Bill Rowe — who would become Liberal leader in the late 1970s and is now a well-known novelist, lawyer, and radio personality in St. John's — to say he was finding it difficult to run his law office in Corner Brook, where his family lived, while spending so much time in the capital. "Right from the start this was really eating at the man, driving him nuts," says Rowe. "He and his wife are very close. They like to do things together, and she didn't like it at all when he had to be in St. John's."

Rowe, twenty-four at the time, had returned from studying at Oxford in June 1966, been elected in September, and named to the Newfoundland bar in April 1967, when Wells offered him $13,000 to become an associate at his Corner Brook law firm. "In 1967 that was enormous amount of money. . . . For a young lawyer, fresh out of school, it was a measure to me of Wells's

desperation. . . . [Wells] had come in on Joey's coat-tails, as we
all had, plus [he had] a pretty high estimate of himself, which
I found out later. Joey put him into cabinet even before he was
elected, with John Crosbie and Alex Hickman, and here was
this young man suddenly lumped in with heavyweights."

Rowe claims that, even before Wells walked across the house
in May 1968, there was a feeling that he was the type who
couldn't stick to anything for very long, his law practice
excepted, because after all he had to make money. "Joey used
to talk about it. We all did. The example of going into the army,
then buying his way out. . . . He knew what he was getting into
when he accepted Joey's invitation to become minister of labor
and then to run. And in a year, he wants out of it."

Clearly, in his early years, Wells had a reputation as a
money-grubbing opportunist, more interested in both his
growing family and growing bank balance than in the pursuit
of public policy issues. While his image then may have been
flighty, his reputation now is the exact opposite, that of the
fabled English bulldog grabbing a bone and clinging to it for
life.

Rowe does recall one occasion in late 1967 when Bell Island
Liberal Steve Neary upset the St. John's legal establishment by
launching a public attack on legal fees charged people for such
routine transactions as buying a house. "Neary had turned it
into a real cause célèbre. He ended up debating it on TV with
the head of the law society. Every lawyer in town was cheesed
off at Neary. Naturally, they didn't think they were overcharg-
ing. What professional does?"

But the publicity generated by Neary's campaign put such
heat on the lawyers that the local law society called a special
meeting to deal with the issue. Wells didn't attend the meeting,
but he sent a long telegram from Corner Brook agreeing with
Neary. "He didn't say this publicly at the time, but to his fellow
lawyers he agreed that the fees were too high. It astounded the
people who were there. He was the only lawyer that I know of

who supported Neary's view, but I don't believe he was looking for publicity. Nobody else knew about it except the other lawyers. I think it was merely a missive to his confreres."

For even then Wells was beginning to get a reputation as one of Newfoundland's most high-priced lawyers. Asked how he would square his own practice with a call for lower fees, Rowe said that Wells "would separate that easily in his own mind. He would say, 'If you want me, Clyde Wells, you will have to pay accordingly. If you want me, you want the best, but you'll have to pay for it.' But for a clerical matter like a real estate transaction, which a lawyer is responsible for but many of which can be done by para-legals and secretaries, the fees shouldn't be that high. He would not have been doing that sort of thing anyway. It would have been done by juniors in his office. And because he wasn't doing it, he would have felt it was something for which the charge shouldn't be so high."

At any rate, Wells simply didn't want to be away from home so much, and Smallwood, wanting to keep him in cabinet, agreed in the spring of 1967 to let Wells drop his labor portfolio but stay in the cabinet as a minister without portfolio. Even that job, however, required attending cabinet meetings in St. John's, and it wasn't long before Wells began looking for a way to get out of cabinet altogether. In 1968, he would find one.

That wasn't a good year for Smallwood. His government admitted publicly for the first time it couldn't afford the mounting costs of education, and the fisheries were on the verge of economic collapse. Despite the large labor force required for the Churchill Falls hydro development, there was a net migration of 5000 people, as the young men went "down the road," mainly to Ontario. Smallwood would ultimately announce his resignation from active politics. It was the year the tide went out for the federal Liberals, too, as they lost all but one Newfoundland seat.

As minister without portfolio, Wells continued to pop up periodically to deliver speeches in defence of the government or on some of his favorite themes: education, law, the grandeur of Corner Brook and how it wasn't appreciated by St. John's, and the importance of Smallwood's plans to industrialize the province.

At Smallwood's request, he was in the House of Assembly on March 25, 1968, when Pierre Trudeau spoke at length on the Constitution, praising the premier's promise to extend some bilingual services to the island's tiny French-speaking minority. Wells, no doubt, applauded Trudeau's call for "the preservation of our unity, without the loss of our diversity . . . possible only in a federal state; for only a federal constitution can be sufficiently clear in its general goals to ensure unity, yet sufficiently flexible to ensure diversity. . . . The appeal of federalism is found not only in its political and cultural guarantees to individuals, but also in its promise of a better standard of living through the use of wealth-sharing devices. . . . We must seek to open Canada to all Canadians; no Canadian should be penalized if he chooses to live in Corner Brook or Glace Bay or Medicine Hat rather than in Toronto or Montreal or Vancouver." Trudeau added that the task ahead would require "the preservation of a central government equipped with the tools necessary for redistribution of this country's immense wealth . . . a federal government possessing the legislative competence necessary to ensure the efficient operation of our economy . . . a central government with the power and the will to create a climate for public and private investment that alone can ensure full employment of human resources and a better-balanced regional development of our economy."

Every now and then, Wells displayed his lifelong moral certitude about right and wrong. During a May 1968 debate on new liquor regulations, Wells scolded a St. John's Tory who had complained about seeing teenagers drinking in a local night club, demanding to know why he didn't do his "duty" and call the police. "If you see a crime you report it," he said.

While Wells was one of the bright Young Turks recruited by

Smallwood in 1966 to infuse the party with youth and vigor, by far the biggest star was John Crosbie, deputy mayor of St. John's when Smallwood recruited him and scion of one of Newfoundland's most successful and powerful family empires. Crosbie was everything that Wells aspired to. His grandfather, Sir John Chalker Crosbie, built the family fortune from a St. John's fish-exporting business and later became Newfoundland's finance minister. His father Chesley — Ches, as he was called — diversified the business, moving into construction, airlines, beer, and Coca-Cola distribution. John Crosbie once said his father "used to make money in Coca-Cola and beer and lose it in the fishery." Ches Crosbie was also prominent during the Confederation debates, but instead of wanting to join Canada, he wanted an economic union with the United States. Throughout school, John was consistently gold-medal material, and when he opened his law practice in St. John's in 1957, it immediately prospered.

Wells took to Crosbie right away. Among other things, the two men worked longer hours during that first term than any of the other ministers or MHAs. Liberal MP George Baker, who was chief clerk and Hansard editor when Crosbie and Wells first arrived on the scene, said the two "really had the work ethic. . . . I used to have to do the debates and everything else, so I'd be leaving late, and usually the only two guys still there working were Crosbie and Wells."

While Wells was articulate but passionless and lacking a sense of humor, Crosbie had lots of passion and even more humor, but wasn't very articulate. Former Newfoundland premier Brian Peckford, who worked for Crosbie in the late 1960s, says the early Crosbie was "a terrible speaker, simply unbelievable." But about the time Crosbie and Wells fell out with Smallwood, he hired the local Dale Carnegie representative, practised religiously, and made himself one of the better political orators in the country.

It was just this sort of determination, combined with unbridled ambition, that made it impossible for such strong personalities as Smallwood and Crosbie to coexist for long. Crosbie admits his father warned him not to run, figuring, correctly as it turned out, he wouldn't get along with the bombastic and overbearing Smallwood. But Crosbie, running as municipal affairs minister, easily won his St. John's riding in the September 1966 election.

"I was disturbed for some time by some of the crazy things Joey was doing," says Crosbie. "His dealings with John C. Doyle and his proposal for a linerboard mill at Stephenville, which required a lot of financial assistance from the province, was one major project which concerned me."

Dealings with Doyle, president of Canadian Javelin, concerned a lot of people in the mid-1960s. Doyle was involved in a series of political scandals in Quebec, and Revenue Canada was claiming $2.6 million in back taxes. In August 1966 the Montreal Stock Exchange delisted a Doyle subsidiary after it failed to file an annual report, and despite Doyle's becoming a bail jumper and fugitive from justice, in 1967 Smallwood, over Crosbie's objections, among others, arranged for the temporary acquisition of controlling interest in the troubled Canadian Javelin. Doyle served a short time in the Newfoundland penitentiary before he fled to Panama in 1974 to avoid a three-year prison term in the U.S., and fraud and breach-of-trust charges in Canada.

For a time, Doyle tried to direct Javelin through several Panamanian companies. Later, a six-year probe by the Restrictive Trade Practices Commission concluded that Javelin was "nothing more than a corporate vehicle devised, dominated and corrupted" by Doyle for his personal benefit. The 109-page report also questioned Smallwood's role in two major transactions: the purchase of timber concessions in Newfoundland, and to shares issued in connection with the purchase of buildings in Stephenville. A federal investigator uncovered four letters of grant for the timber concession on the premier's stationery signed, "Joseph R. Smallwood."

In 1986, Quebec's Superior Court ruled that the fugitive multimillionaire owed his former Newfoundland company $15.5 million in compensation. But in 1991 the Appeal Court cut that to $9.5 million, including an order to cancel more than one and a half million Javelin shares held by Doyle.

"The other major project Joe had under way at that time was the oil refinery at Come By Chance, which had started out to be a third pulp and paper mill in that area, but the emphasis had gone from that to this oil refinery," says Crosbie.

"The main problem was Smallwood did everything himself. It was a one-man government. He was completely dominant. All economic development matters, he looked after himself. He hated feasibility studies, because he didn't want something to be shown to be not feasible. He wanted development. He didn't want any trifling doubts being expressed by these feasibility studies. So I persuaded him we should have a cabinet committee to deal with John Shaheen [the oil man] and John Doyle and those two projects because they were so major."

Smallwood agreed, and appointed veteran cabinet minister Les Curtin to head the committee, joined by Alex Hickman, Wells, and Crosbie.

"That's where I first got to know Clyde well," says Crosbie. "He was intelligent, a good lawyer, alert. He was independent in nature, he wasn't kowtowing to Smallwood. He wasn't a kiss-ass."

Crosbie says the normal procedure in cabinet in those days was that "Smallwood would talk and everybody would listen, nod their heads, and look wise. There simply wasn't any dialogue. Smallwood would come in and he might talk for an hour, an hour and a half. . . . He was handling Brinco at the time, the great Churchill Falls project. Nobody else really knew what the details were, what the hell was going on. Smallwood did it all himself.

"Occasionally you might get a chance to ask something, and then Joey would speak another half hour. It was hard to believe this, but anyway, Clyde would speak up from time to time. So he took a more independent line. This went on for about two years."

Crosbie tells one anecdote from cabinet in early April 1968, the day before the Newfoundland Liberal delegation was to leave by chartered aircraft for Ottawa to attend the federal Liberal leadership convention (won by Trudeau):

"Joey was going on and on, and Clyde was getting more anxious because he wanted to get a flight back to the west coast [Corner Brook]. So Joe finally stopped for a moment, to get his breath or something, and Clyde said, 'Well sir, it's five o'clock. If you don't mind, I'd like to go now because if you get started again, I'll miss my plane.'

"The implication was that Joe was long-winded and not much was being done. We were just sitting there listening to Joe. And Joe, what a performance he put on. 'Gentlemen,' he said, 'have you heard what I have heard? One of my ministers is suggesting I'm wasting your time. Do you think I waste your time?'

"This went on for about ten minutes, and Joe was in a complete rage that somebody was suggesting he spoke too long, and the result of it all was that Clyde missed his plane, so we dropped him off the next day on our way to Ottawa."

Crosbie wasn't exactly toeing the line himself and hadn't been for some time. He had been openly bad-mouthing Smallwood around St. John's, and naturally word got back. The previous year, Crosbie had infuriated the premier by siding with the Opposition's call for a recorded vote. The Tories had only three MHAs at the time, and house rules say four are needed to force a vote. Crosbie later explained he did it because it was a "piece of tyranny" not to allow a vote.

In any event, the cabinet subcommittee was grinding along in its study of the Doyle and Shaheen projects, but every time they reached a stalemate dealing with the two promoters, Doyle and Shaheen would simply call Smallwood and get whatever they wanted. After months of bickering, they finally agreed to a $30 million guarantee from Newfoundland to Shaheen, but the financier also needed interim financing, and instead of raising it privately he arranged a sweetheart deal with Smallwood for $5 million. What it meant, in fact, was that Newfoundland was taking all the risks, putting up all the money, while Shaheen stood to enjoy the profits, assuming that there were some. As it turned out, there weren't.

For Smallwood, this kind of deal had become standard fare. In 1966, for example, Smallwood brought four Holiday Inns to Newfoundland by agreeing to pay the full $9 million cost of building them to the company's specifications. Holiday Inn would then manage the inns, pay the loans if they made any money, and after twenty-five years acquire the four hotels for a dollar each. Smallwood argued the province would lose millions in tourist revenue without the Holiday Inns.

When the Come By Chance deal came to cabinet, Smallwood wanted the interim financing supplied by Newfoundland increased to $10 million. Hickman, Wells, and Crosbie vigorously opposed the deal. Smallwood was doing his best to try to smooth things over temporarily at least, mainly because Trudeau had called a June election and Smallwood's Liberals had dominated federal ridings, as well as provincial ridings, since Confederation. In 1965, for example, the Liberals had won all seven federal seats in Newfoundland. Even in Diefenbaker's mammoth 1958 sweep, the Liberals won five out of seven on the Rock. This gave Smallwood mileage to play the big wheel in Ottawa, as well as St. John's. What's more, he had supported Trudeau and delivered the bulk of Newfoundland's eighty-four delegate votes to him — which earned him a seat in Trudeau's convention box — brazenly breaking his earlier pledge of support to Trade Minister Robert Winters. Smallwood did not want anything to jeopardize his position of prominence with

Trudeau. He had boasted to the new prime minister that he could deliver Newfoundland again, and he planned to do just that. He certainly didn't need serious internal divisions bursting into the open just weeks before the federal election.

This time, however, Smallwood didn't get his wish.

Sick of the dilly-dallying over the Shaheen deal, Crosbie and Wells told Smallwood that if he persisted with what they saw as an outright, unsecured gift to Shaheen, they would have to resign. What happened next has as many versions as there were players involved. After Wells and Crosbie had threatened to bolt cabinet, Smallwood said to wait a few days. "Now we didn't trust Smallwood," says Crosbie. "I certainly didn't. So we spent our time getting ready our letters of resignation. We made sure we had all the points covered. Naturally, this is not something you do lightly, decide to resign on an issue of policy. Alex Hickman was against the interim financing, as well, but he decided he wasn't going to resign.

"So Clyde and I went in to see Joe [May 14, 1968] to say we hadn't changed our position. . . . Joe handed me a letter telling me he was firing me. And luckily, I had my letter with me and I said, 'Like fuck you are, I'm resigning,' and I threw Smallwood my letter as he passed me his letter. His letter was nasty. He was a son of a bitch, you know. He really went after you in the gonads. Anyway, he alleged he was firing me for a conflict of interest. That's what he had in his letter. And when he left his office, by golly, he went out and had a press conference. He had the press all arranged out there. They were brought in ahead of time.

"He accepted Clyde's resignation. He was firing me. See, he knew that Clyde wasn't planning to carry on in politics. He was planning to go back to Corner Brook, so I guess he didn't consider him an immediate threat. But he knew I wasn't planning to get out of politics, and I think he had the view that I was out to get his job."

At his press conference, Smallwood claimed that Crosbie

had been asked to divest himself of all connection to the various family holdings, but said Crosbie had not done so. Reading from his letter to Crosbie, Smallwood said, "I was disturbed a short time after you went to the cabinet and came to my office and virtually demanded that your family's construction company be given the contract to erect the new Elizabeth Towers building." Smallwood also accused an unnamed member of the Crosbie family of demanding certain contracts in the Shaheen deal in return for John Crosbie's support. These allegations, and others, were completely false. By week's end, threatened with a lawsuit by the Crosbie family and challenged to produce evidence, Smallwood was forced to publicly retract his accusations.

(Wells, writing his version in the 1990 update of *Call Me Joey*, says that Smallwood was "domineering. But I have come to have more sympathy for that. Having the responsibility of heading cabinet and leading a caucus, I've come to recognize the extent to which a certain amount of it is necessary in order to hold together. You can't have a cabinet of 15 people going in different directions. There's got to be a strong, dominant direction." And there's no doubt that Wells, like Smallwood, is the one who determines that direction absolutely.)

Wells and Crosbie held their own press conference and returned late for the afternoon session. "We hadn't said we were resigning from the Liberal caucus, we were simply resigning from cabinet," says Crosbie. "But when we went into the house that afternoon, our chairs were moved across the house, nailed down on the other side of the house, so if we wanted to sit, we had to go across and sit. . . . Again, this was Joe."

Steve Neary says, "Wells always claimed he quit over a matter of principle. That's not what I was told by Joey. What principle was involved? Joey and I discussed this many times. It wasn't a matter of conscience, a matter of moral principles. It was a matter of bridge financing."

Neary recalls that the sergeant-at-arms didn't know what to

do, because he didn't know if they'd resigned from cabinet, from the Liberal party, or from the house itself. "I told him to go to the premier's office and ask. He did, but they didn't seem to know either. So what he did was put two extra seats on the opposite side of the house in case they wanted to cross. He left their seats there. They claim their seats were moved across the floor, but in actual fact, their seats were not moved. They went across the floor. It was Crosbie who walked in and saw the two new seats. I heard Wells reminiscing one day about this. He said Joey more or less forced him across the house. That's not true. Crosbie saw the two seats, and Wells toddled along behind Crosbie. It looked like he was being led by Crosbie."

In his 1985 book, *The Smallwood Era*, former senior cabinet minister Dr. Frederick Rowe writes that both Crosbie and Wells promised him they would not quit Smallwood's cabinet until after the June 1968 federal election. Their pre-election defection did "enormous damage to the Liberal cause."

And so, the two men did end up across the house with the four Opposition Tories. Smallwood told the assembly he had asked for Crosbie's resignation but that Wells had volunteered his. He added that, several times over the past eight months, he had told Wells "he would have to make up his mind soon as to what he proposed to do, whether to continue residing in Corner Brook and heading up a large and, I hope, profitable legal business, one of the most successful law firms in the province; whether he would concentrate on that and cease treating his membership in the cabinet as a sort of hobby or a sort of sideline, or give up the law practice and become a full-fledged member of the cabinet . . . he was fairly well aware. . . . I regarded his position as altogether anomalous and unsatisfactory, and it may be that he thought I would shortly be asking him for his resignation."

Smallwood said he was "thrilled and humbly grateful for a completely unanimous and enthusiastic endorsation" of him by his cabinet that morning. One reason for the lack of cabinet opposition was that Smallwood had invited *Globe and Mail* reporter Michael Gillan into the meeting in the hope that other ministers wouldn't raise hell with a reporter present.

It worked, despite the fact that several ministers, Hickman in particular, were not happy with the deal and were upset that a recent royal commission report on the province's economic prospects had been critical of Smallwood's pet economic development projects and the province's public debt. The latter was thought to be under $200 million, was in fact $509 million, and would rise to $1.3 billion by 1971-72, making it difficult for the province to borrow the money it needed without drastic cuts in service.

Over the years, Wells and Crosbie have been lumped together as men who confronted Smallwood on a point of principle. That all three men had giant egos is indisputable. And Crosbie, certainly, had his own leadership ambitions. But in 1968 he could not have believed that crossing Joey would enhance his chances, so it's fair to conclude his major concern was the Shaheen giveaway. When Wells became such a prominent figure during the Meech Lake debate, he came to be seen by some — although he has not claimed this himself — as the key player in the Shaheen dispute, rather than Crosbie. No doubt Wells genuinely opposed the Shaheen deal, but his actions may have had less to do with the province's balance sheet than with his personal desire to return to his law practice with its prospect of greater income and social status than could be earned by staying in St. John's as an MHA.

Crosbie recalls that Joey was a "dictator, and he could make life hell for anybody who opposed him," but it was Crosbie, not Wells, who suffered the brunt of Smallwood's ire. Wells certainly benefited politically in the long run and has done nothing to dissuade the public from the notion that he faced down Smallwood over a matter of great principle.

In his own May 14, 1968, speech in the house, Wells claimed

his actions involved more than the dispute over the oil refinery. He said he'd tried to hire lawyers for his Corner Brook firm and that, if he couldn't, Smallwood had agreed he had "no alternative but to resign as a minister without portfolio," which is why he had given up his labor portfolio in April 1967. What's more, Wells said that as a minister he thought he "would share equally with the premier and all other ministers full responsibility for all policies of the government," a remarkably naive view of how government power functions, and one from which he has deviated dramatically in his own administration. Wells, like Smallwood, is often accused of running a one-man show.

With Crosbie and Wells sitting as independent Liberals, joining the articulate Ottenheimer on the other side, Smallwood experienced for the first time serious opposition in the house.

Newfoundland broadcaster Rex Murphy, one of the organizers of the 1968 People and Pierre Movement, a failed attempt to stop anti-Smallwood feelings from hurting the federal effort, recalls inviting Wells as a guest speaker to a June rally in Grand Falls. But rather than a quick rah-rah partisan speech supporting Trudeau, Wells delivered a long "tedious, detailed rationale of why he left Joey. It was a bit extravagant in terms of what he thought was important and what the audience wanted to hear."

Murphy says Wells earned "an excessive reputation for standing up to Joey. It wasn't that hard to do at the time. Joey was beginning to lose it, clearly, but people weren't used to it." Murphy draws a parallel between Clyde Wells and John Turner during the 1970s and early 1980s, saying that "as long as the prince is in exile, his stock is increased. . . . [Wells's reputation] was press-generated and press-fed."

On June 25, 1968, Smallwood's worst fears were realized when all but one of the province's seven federal seats went to the Tories, despite the nationwide Trudeaumania that saw the

Liberals demolish Bob Stanfield and his Tories. Only Don Jamieson hung on in Burin-Burgeo, his winning margin substantially reduced. A headline in the St. John's *Daily News* announced, "The Smallwood Era is over in Newfoundland." Smallwood himself said, "The tide has gone out, but it will come back again."

Bill Rowe, who along with Steve Neary was elevated to cabinet after Crosbie and Wells split, said that after Wells left he "provided the most effective opposition that I'd ever seen. He did a tremendous job. He took on Joey Smallwood in a way that even showed the way for John Crosbie. . . . Clyde was making fun of Joey — that was never done before. . . . He worked hard and did his research. He was well prepared. Really, for the first time that I had seen, he kind of made mincemeat out of Joey Smallwood."

Neary said on several occasions after he'd crossed the house, Wells "became rather nasty with Joey, and on one occasion he threatened to divulge discussions of cabinet. But Joey gave him a great lecture and he backed down. . . . He really got under Clyde's skin. He does have a temper, you know. He's a very stubborn fellow."

George Baker, who was chief clerk and Hansard editor during some of this period, recalls that Wells's threats took place during "moments of anger. He tends to feel that nothing should be secret. Nothing. There should be no such thing as secret deals. If it pertains to the public or the public purse, then everything should be public, even what is in cabinet. He made reference to that a couple of times in the legislature, and Smallwood grew very angry."

On August 26, Crosbie, Wells, and Labrador West Liberal MHA Tom Burgess issued simultaneous press releases in St. John's and Corner Brook, announcing the formation of a new "Liberal democratic movement," calling for such things as district associations, a free and open Liberal leadership convention in the fall, and properly organized nominating conventions for future elections. The same day, Smallwood upstaged them, announcing that 1200 Liberals, thirty from each of the forty-one electoral districts, would meet Saturday, September 28, in the Grand Falls stadium to launch the "first step" in reorganizing the Liberal party. In addition, Smallwood said he would call a leadership convention before the end of the year to choose a new Liberal leader.

The next day, Smallwood said Crosbie had "less right in the [Liberal] party than a Tory," pointing out he had forfeited his right to advise the party when he crossed the floor with Wells to sit as an independent Liberal. Smallwood said that applied to Wells also, but added that Wells is of "no consequence whatsoever." He had no comment on Burgess.

In a prepared statement August 29, Crosbie said he and Wells had not resigned from the Liberal party. "It is my opinion that no man can determine . . . whether another is a Liberal or not. Who has given the premier the right to say that any person who disagrees with certain of his views is no longer a Liberal? Despite what the premier says, Mr. Wells and I consider that we are Liberals, though we differ from him with reference to some particular policy matters." Wells had nothing to say.

Smallwood sent both men a letter inviting them to the Grand Falls meeting if they would sign a declaration saying they were Liberals, and supporters of the party and the government. Crosbie said he would not rejoin if support meant "blind allegiance to the party and the government," but added he was still a Liberal and had no problems signing the declaration. Smallwood said Crosbie agreed to sign with no more than proper reservations, but Wells "refused point-blank to support the present Liberal government and he will not be accepted back into the Liberal party."

In a story from Corner Brook in the *Evening Telegram*, Wells said Crosbie was "quite right" in accepting Smallwood's invitation to attend the meeting. "I agree with the position he's taken. He has stated clearly that he does not support the government without reservation, and those are the exact words that were in my letter [to Smallwood]. Obviously, Mr. Smallwood's decision is based on something other than the letters. I can only assume that something is a desire not to have Mr. Crosbie and I together — unless there's some other reason, and only Mr. Smallwood can say." Wells said the incident shows that the convention is "very, very much a one-man party."

In a 1991 interview, Crosbie recalled the event. "Clyde [is] stubborn as hell. He was a Liberal, but he wasn't going to have anything to do with this new democratic Liberal party of Joe's. But for me, to join that party and run for the leadership, I couldn't continue to sit on the other side of the house, and I had to make a decision. . . . I decided that I would rejoin the Liberal ranks and become a member of the new party. Clyde said no. He was going to remain as an independent. So Clyde stayed on the other side. Once he makes his mind up, there is no turning back."

Wells showed up for the convention in Grand Falls wearing an "I am a Liberal" button on his lapel, but he was not allowed into the stadium and watched the proceedings on a local television station's video monitor. Richard Cashin, who had lost his bid for election in St. John's West in June, was elected party president, defeating Smallwood's candidate Grant Chalker. Cashin, now head of the fishermen's union, is one of Wells's strongest critics. Roger Simmons, who as president of the Newfoundland Teachers Association was an outspoken critic of Smallwood's education policy, was elected vice-president.

But the real fireworks were between Smallwood and Wells. Wells said the newly constituted association should "tear up and throw away" its constitution if the party "allows Mr. Smallwood to dictate to them" that he, Wells, was not allowed to be a member of the party. "Who is Mr. Wells?" retaliated Smallwood. "Who wants that kind of Liberal? We can do without him . . . and well afford it. . . . I dragged him into the

House. . . . I brought him in by the heels, didn't I?" Smallwood called Wells a "clever and brainy fellow," but said he only attended "about one in twelve" cabinet meetings. "I couldn't get him to attend . . . he wanted to build up a great law practice. Good luck to him . . . let him build up a great law practice . . . but he couldn't do that and be a regular and good cabinet minister." Wells said Smallwood was "completely and totally wrong . . . I rarely missed a cabinet meeting."

Smallwood had still not set a date for the leadership convention, although he often repeated his intention to retire, with the caveat that he would stay on if he felt the party would "fall into the wrong hands." The hands he wanted to succeed him belonged to Education Minister Dr. Frederick Rowe, who on January 31, announced he would be a leadership candidate.

It didn't take Cashin long to discover that despite Smallwood's claims about a new "democratic" Liberal party, it was business as usual. Cashin resigned and Roger Simmons became interim party president until Smallwood promoted his own man, MHA John Mahoney. Smallwood had boasted the new association would sign up 100,000 members, but it never went above 8000 in the whole province. Just before Rowe announced his candidacy, having consulted with Smallwood first, the premier sent his letter of resignation to Mahoney recommending the party hold a fall leadership convention.

By all accounts, Smallwood was shocked when Crosbie, just a few days later, announced that he, too, was a candidate. Smallwood had believed that Crosbie, having crossed the floor the year before, was now out of the running. But in March, the well-organized Crowds for Crosbie began to appear, turning the campaign into an almost religious crusade against the tyrannical leadership of Smallwood.

That was all Smallwood needed to convince him that the party would indeed fall into the wrong hands, so he announced that he would be a candidate for his own job after all at the October 30–November 1 convention at the St. John's Memorial

Stadium. Rowe immediately withdrew and threw his support over to Smallwood. Smallwood let it be known that Wells would not be allowed in to the convention but, according to Bill Rowe, "saner heads prevailed. Ed Roberts and I convinced Joey to let Clyde in to the convention. We just said let him in. Why take him on? He's going to win if you take him on in the battle for public opinion.

"But the real point is that Wells had a tremendous kind of moral courage. I don't know if it is based on the fact that God is with him, he's actually the Anglican Archbishop as Cashin says, or whether it's based on extreme self-confidence, a moral certainty that he's got to do the right thing come hell or high water, no matter what. I don't know."

Rowe thought Wells was interested in getting out of politics anyway, and was only waging a kind of rearguard action against Joey, putting himself in a position where all hell might break loose and he might be ignominiously banned. "Joey had the power to keep him out, and then he would be reduced to a guy shouting and screaming. He was prepared to do that. But people caved in. So he always has had that streak in him, whatever it is. He would stand up to the devil himself if he thinks he's right."

By the time the convention arrived, there were six formal candidates: Smallwood, Crosbie, Alex Hickman, and three fringe hopefuls, Vincent Spencer, Peter Cook, and Randy Joyce. But the contest was between Smallwood and Crosbie.

Wells was Crosbie's campaign manager for western Newfoundland. During the four months leading up to the October convention, there was intense campaigning around the province. Wells delivered numerous speeches for Crosbie. Lawyer Fred Stagg, who articled with Wells, says he could never understand why Wells went moose-hunting for ten days during the critical period just before the convention. Stagg, who ran successfully for the Tories in Stephenville in the 1971 campaign, says Wells was "inspiring, but he didn't do the grunt work." Stagg, who also had a young family at the time, says it still burns him that Wells walked away from politics when he was most needed.

On the eve of the convention, Wells arrived in town to considerable fanfare and media attention, and gave a statement likening Smallwood's tyranny of the party to the Russian invasion of Czechoslovakia. Smallwood had said earlier that, when the campaign was over, "we'll show them there is no room for rebels in the Liberal party." Wells said, "I want no part of this attitude — we must stand and fight, as John Crosbie has fought in the past six months or more, fight for the right of free expression of opinion." Wells accused the credentials committee, which at that point hadn't approved his credentials, of being "men of straw, both bent at the premier's will."

For all that, however, when it came time to vote on the Saturday night, Smallwood won a smashing victory, crushing Crosbie 1007 to 440, with Hickman at 187, Joyce, thirteen, Cook, three, and Spencer, one. The bitterness and anger of the anti-Smallwood forces, particularly the young Liberals supporting Crosbie, boiled over after the votes were announced, disrupting proceedings for about fifteen minutes.

Like most political junkies in Newfoundland, Patrick O'Flaherty, a MUN classmate of Clyde's, had gone to the arena to watch the show. "I was there as a bystander with my father, looking down on this demonstration, and I saw Clyde, his face red with anger, and I hesitate to use the word 'hatred,' arms raised in the Nazi salute, shouting, 'Sieg Heil! Sieg Heil!' at Smallwood, along with a group of young delegates."

Indeed, the angry demonstration almost got out of hand, as youths went from mimicking Hitler Youth to burning their Liberal membership cards, but after police surrounded the group, things eventually calmed down.

Even after Smallwood won his resounding victory, Wells, obviously smarting, told reporters he expected either Smallwood's resignation or an election very soon. "I don't suppose that anywhere in North American political history has a man won a leadership with such a large majority and still lost as Mr. Smallwood did. The demonstration for John Crosbie and the reaction particularly of the younger people, was almost incredible. Something is radically wrong when the man who loses on numbers wins so tremendously in the expression of support." Wells added he would continue to sit as an independent Liberal.

Not one to forgive his critics, Smallwood called a cabinet meeting four days after the convention and set about proving he meant it when he said rebels wouldn't be welcome in the party. Smallwood booted Hickman out of cabinet, along with Val Earle, the one minister who had supported Hickman. Both men quickly joined the opposition Tories. Crosbie, who also would eventually join the Tories, moved back across with Wells and, joined by former cabinet minister Beaton Abbot and Liberal backbencher Gerald Myrden, formed a Liberal Reform group.

After the leadership convention, Crosbie became far more prominent in the house than Wells, and in late 1970, Wells decided to leave politics altogether and spend all his time building up his law practice and looking after his family. Asked once why he didn't join the Tories as Crosbie later did, Wells said, "I told John I thought he was crazy. I couldn't see how anybody that had stood up and proclaimed the great virtues of the Liberal party and all that it meant to be Liberal, and talked about running for the leadership and reforming the party . . . could suddenly do a 180-degree switch and say the Liberal party is all wrong and the Conservatives all right. He wouldn't have credibility. I thought anyone like that would never be elected again. They would be snowed under in the next election. I wouldn't have anything to do with that. You either believe what you say or you don't. I believed what I said, so I got out [of politics] and went back to practising law."

Wells says that just before the 1971 election, Frank Moores, who captured Smallwood's old Humber West seat, tried to persuade him to run for the Tories in Humber East. Wells told journalist Tom Walkom that "Moores drank a whole bottle of whisky in my house trying to persuade me to run for the Tories. I couldn't see how I could stand one day and proclaim the virtue of the Liberals and the next day turn around."

Maybe not, but he didn't have any trouble encouraging the electorate to vote Tory. He made at least one radio commercial supporting the Conservatives, and his views were well known in Corner Brook, where the vote went to Tory Tom Farrell.

"Those of us who were in the trenches fighting for our survival were angry when we heard him telling the people of Newfoundland to vote Tory," says Steve Neary. "He himself helped Farrell, and a lot of us were angry at the time."

But politics, especially with a sniff of power in the offing, has a way of glossing over personal animosities. Years later, when Newfoundlanders were tiring of the pugilistic politics of Tory Brian Peckford and Liberals smelled their chance to regain power, Neary was one of those who went to Wells to plead with him to return.

5

Second City

Life was sweet in Corner Brook. And profitable. The Wells's third and last child, David, was born. The law firm of Barry, Wells, Monaghan, Seaborn, Marshall grew to become the biggest in western Newfoundland. Wells, though he was a workaholic, still had more time for his family, for his favorite pastimes — salmon fishing, sailing, golfing, alpine skiing — and for his church, St. John the Evangelist Anglican, and the Rotary Club. Between 1970 and 1972 he even built his own four-bedroom log "cabin" on a rocky point at Georges Lake, a few miles out of town.

His long-time partner, Mike Monaghan, said when Wells joined the firm in 1970, he was "zooming around town in a big Lincoln. He was really a Yuppie before his time. A guy who wanted the big job, the big car, and the big house on the hill. And he got it all."

Cabot Martin, who articled with Wells and later became Brian Peckford's senior adviser, told the *Globe*'s Jeffrey Simpson that Wells "is not a mysterious character. People have made some sort of a myth out of him. He's from a petit-bourgeois family whose measure of success was having a house on Highland Drive next to W. J. Lundrigan. And that's what he was concerned about.

"Jesus, half the population is like that. You can't fault a person for being like it. But it's ordinary. Very ordinary. He was a very ordinary person, extraordinarily ordinary. . . . There's nothing startling about his career at all. It's a straight line."

It certainly was straight ahead in Corner Brook, the island's Second City, where Wells was always more comfortable than he was in St. John's with its more obvious class consciousness. Time and again, as both a minister and an independent Liberal, he had chastised the St. John's crowd for what he saw as their superior attitude.

One long-time personal friend speculates that Wells "couldn't really escape his background, and he resented that. It's one of the things which on the one hand really drove him to excel, to succeed. On the other hand, it bothered him that he was never really accepted by the St. John's crowd. I think he felt more at ease in Corner Brook because it didn't have that long history of class structure. People here tend to be judged solely on what they'd accomplished, not what their birthright was.

"It's not something Clyde would talk about much. But I remember once when Crosbie was Moores's finance minister in the early 70s and we were watching him make some announcement on TV. I don't remember what the issue was, but I do remember Clyde saying, 'How would he know? He was born a Crosbie.' I remember he checked himself right away. He doesn't like to let his guard down. Ever. But there was something really visceral there. I've never forgotten that."

Corner Brook is a beautiful part of the province, sitting snugly in an amphitheatre-like bowl overlooking the Humber Arm, which flows into the Bay of Islands and from there into the Gulf of St. Lawrence, and surrounded by the Long Range Mountains.

About 9000 years ago, the Maritime Archaic Indians occupied the area. They were followed much later by the Beothuk, a now extinct tribe who were thought to number only about five hundred when John Cabot explored the island in 1497 and who were hunted down and eventually wiped out by the Europeans and Micmac hunters from Nova Scotia. When Captain James Cook surveyed the west coast of Newfoundland in 1768, there was no settlement at Corner Brook, largely because the Treaty of Paris had prohibited English or French settlers from year-round habitation. Even so, by the early 1800s, fishing, farming, and lumbering had begun to draw settlers to what was called Birchy Cove (later changed to Curling, and still later one of four communities amalgamated to form the current city, 681 highway kilometres from St. John's.)

The coniferous forests, laden with black spruce, have been the lifeblood of the city since Nova Scotian Gay Silver built a saw mill in 1864 on a stream named Corner Brook that flowed out of the hills and into the Humber Arm. By the turn of this century, there were churches, schools, and stores springing up in the area, and in 1923, after several false starts at major development, Newfoundland Prime Minister Sir Richard Squires — whom Smallwood campaigned for two years later in Corner Brook — helped set up the Newfoundland Power and Paper Company Limited, with the British firm of Armstrong, Whitworth and Company holding the majority of shares. The $51.8 million power plant and mill, which included the one-hundred-house Townsite for the workers, was built after both the Newfoundland and British governments guaranteed the interest on $20 million worth of bonds, a pattern of industrial giveaways, which Canadian academic Jay Goulding in his book *The Last Outport* called "institutionalized buccaneering." This pattern has characterized Newfoundland's entire industrial history and resulted in considerable benefits for the industrialists but few for the people or the province.

Former premier Frank Moores says that "the crazy thing . . . is that Newfoundland is richer in resources per capita than any other province in Canada. By quite a bit. It has hydro. It has mining. It has pulp and paper. It has fishing. It has oil. There aren't many provinces which have the resources that New-foundland has. But they've always been screwed up. They've given it away just for the development."

A classic example was the deal given near the turn of this century to Canadian engineer and capitalist R.G. Reid for building a narrow-gauge railway line between St. John's and Port-aux-Basques. The Railway Contract of 1898 gave Con-servative Prime Minister Sir James Winter $1 million to bail itself out of imminent collapse, but in return, Reid, for agreeing to operate the railway for fifty years, after which he would own it outright, was given three million acres of land (he had already received two million acres earlier), the right to buy the St. John's dry dock, a coastal steamship service (aided by a $100,000-a-year government subsidy), and the right to buy and operate the publicly owned telegraph net-work. That deal was so outrageous it led to the downfall of Winter's government. Even Winter's successor, Robert Bond, five years later struck a deal with the Anglo-Newfoundland Development Company for a pulp and paper mill in Grand Falls that exempted the company from municipal taxation and from paying duty on construction material and ma-chinery to be used in the project. Under the 1949 Terms of Union, Newfoundland gave away its right to control its most important resource, fishing. And, of course, in the 1960s and 1970s, in what has to rank as a world-class giveaway, the Smallwood government completed the Churchill Falls deal, a project, incidentally, that Wells, a Smallwood minister, en-thusiastically endorsed many times in the House of Assem-bly. Had a more reasonable profit-sharing arrangement been struck by Smallwood with Quebec and the developers, New-foundland, on the strength of this single project, would be a "have" province instead of the country's poorest "have not" province.

Local government did not come quickly to Newfoundland. Corner Brook West, Corner Brook East, and Curling weren't incorporated until the 1940s, and until 1951 Townsite was governed by six councillors appointed by Bowater. In 1949, representatives from the four councils met with Smallwood and formed the Humber Municipal Association. The association, and a report commissioned by Smallwood but financed by Bowater, recommended amalgamation, and in a 1955 plebiscite the residents voted seventy-five per cent in favor after Bowater agreed to pay $110,000 a year in lieu of property taxes and the government agreed to pay the city $125,000 during its inaugural year, $100,000 the second year, and $75,000 in the third. In April 1955 the Newfoundland House of Assembly passed the City of Corner Brook Act, and the next year Sir Eric Bowater, at the official opening of City Hall, gave the city a mayor's chain, the mace, and the Grant of Arms from the College of Heralds in England.

By the time Wells arrived to practise law in the city, the population had reached 25,000, and while Bowater was still far and away the major employer, the city also was home to a major cement plant, gypsum plant, construction company, and three fish-processing plants. As a minister in Smallwood's government, Wells took part in the opening ceremonies at the Arts and Culture Centre in 1967, a facility containing a four-hundred-seat theatre and an Olympic-size swimming pool.

In Corner Brook Wells attended the Church of St. John the Evangelist, a modest, white clapboard building just a block from his West Street law office. Like most things in Newfoundland, the Anglicans have a long history by North American standards. The first Church of England service on the island apparently was held on the beach at St. John's by Sir Humphrey Gilbert in 1583. In the early 1600s, the Reverend Erasmus Stourton became the first resident Church of England clergyman on the island, but he was expelled by Lord Baltimore in 1628 for his anti-Roman Catholic activities, and it wasn't until shortly after the 1697 French invasion of St. John's that William III ordered men-of-war to transport chaplains to the colony and the first church was built near Fort William in St. John's. During the three-month French occupation of St. John's in 1752, all Anglicans and other Protestants were expelled from the city and only Roman Catholic families were allowed to stay.

After that, the church gradually moved westward, arriving in the Bay of Islands area in the mid-1850s. The impetus behind the move came from the traditional feelings that because everything was centred in St. John's, the church hierarchy included, the western part of the province was being left out. After years of studies and meetings, as well as lobbying spearheaded by Wells, the Anglican Synod meeting in St. John's in 1976 resulted in a major restructuring: the single Newfoundland diocese of the church was split into three, and Wells became the Chancellor of the Diocese of Western Newfoundland, a position he held until moving to St. John's five years later.

Bill Rowe tells the story of a Tory MHA who attended the meeting and told him afterwards that "Clyde almost single-handedly persuaded the clerics to divide it into three. This guy was a political enemy of Wells, but he was totally amazed at the job [Wells] did, the persuasive ability he showed, taking the bit in his teeth, marshalling his arguments, appealing to fairness and balance, even back then, on a church matter. And, of course, he had this feeling going for him that the west coast was getting screwed. There aren't too many people who would go to that kind of effort on a church matter."

Archbishop Stewart Payne agrees that Wells "played a major role in the restructuring process." What's more, Wells got to write his first constitution as a result of this exercise, the constitution of the Diocese of Western Newfoundland.

As chancellor, the highest office for a lay person, Wells had the duty of advising the bishop and other church officials on all legal matters, sitting on the executive committee of the church, and attending the annual synod, which is the governing body of the diocese.

In a small way, as chancellor Wells got to play God, particularly in his role as a regular member of the Matrimonial Commission. In those years, the church didn't customarily marry people who'd been divorced. Those wanting to remarry in the church — at least ninety per cent of Newfoundlanders still get married in church — had to apply to the commission for permission. In the mid-70s, there was a detailed application process and the commission received between forty and fifty applications a year. It rarely turned one down. Archbishop Payne recalls that Wells showed "a great deal of compassion and fairness in dealing with people's private lives [and] would not only make legal decisions about whether these people could remarry, but also the moral decision. Our concern was not an inquisition, but to try to ensure a marriage was going to be a stable one."

By all accounts, Wells certainly has a stable marriage. While he is stiff and reserved, his wife, Eleanor, was described by writer Richard Gwyn in the January/February 1991 issue of *Saturday Night* magazine as "outgoing, self-possessed, uncomplicated, with rangy, outdoorsy good looks. Her defining quality is serenity. She's 'his best friend,' in the words of someone who is close to them both. He goes home to lunch with her every day. More socially adroit than he, Eleanor has views on social issues that are reportedly a good deal more liberal than her husband's; also more sense of humor. 'Clyde's idea of gardening is that everything should grow in straight lines,' she says, pointing to the soldierly rows of salvia and marigolds in front of their handsome but unpretentious white clapboard house in St. John's."

Eleanor herself stays completely in the background and has

little to say publicly. In a 1989 interview shortly after being sworn in as premier, Wells said his family is very supportive. "Eleanor, my wife, is a very stable and steady person. Her head doesn't get turned too easily. She's very practical-minded and she's not diverted from reality by any of the fuss made over the position."

His long-time law partner Michael Monaghan says Eleanor is "a lot of fun, livelier than him, no question. She was always the life of the party. . . . Clyde wasn't that type. He was always pretty guarded. . . . Now, he was a great host at parties. We'd go up there for a cocktail party or a booze-up, and Clyde would always give you the two-fingered drinks, pretty stiff drinks, but he would always make sure his own drinks were watered down. He had to be in control. All hands would get loaded, with the exception of Clyde."

He adds that Wells "had this little group of friends and they had this big feast every year on New Year's Eve. They'd start about seven o'clock and go on for seven or eight hours. They'd bring in the suckling pig and cases of champagne. I never attended one, but in a town this size you hear about it. . . . He has a number of friends or acquaintances, but I think really the friendships are more Eleanor's friendships. I mean, Bob Sexton and Bob MacLeod, they're friends. But I think the connection is more with the women. The women are closer."

MacLeod, a local dentist, has known Wells for thirty years. "He's been a good friend of mine, one of those fellows who would never let you down. If you called now and said 'Clyde, I have a problem,' I'm sure he'd respond positively. It may sound corny, but I have nothing but good to say about him. We've had a warm relationship. We had our disagreements. That's probably why we don't discuss politics."

So what does Wells discuss in social situations? "I can't say he's one of those fellows that hangs totally loose," says MacLeod. "He's not an extrovert, not the life of the party type, but he enjoys a sing-song." Problem is, he can't sing. MacLeod, an amateur musician, says Wells's "musical vocal limitations are legendary." His oldest son, Mark, says it was "funny standing up next to him in church and he'd be singing and you'd say that's terrible. It would sound awful. There's no particular music he really likes. He listens to opera music, some classical. He does not like rock'n'roll, never really did."

Mark Wells, twenty-eight, is an electrical engineer with Bell Northern Research, and he lives with his wife, Denise, also a Newfoundlander, and two children, Nicholas, eight, and Emily, four (who shares her November 9 birthdate with her grandfather), in a new development in Kanata, a few miles outside Ottawa. He says his father likes to keep "what is private, private, and what is public, public. . . . To dump your heart out in front of everybody . . . it's just not his style. It never was."

Mark's sister Heidi, twenty-seven, completed her masters in linguistics at Laval and is currently finishing her final year of law school, in French, at the University of New Brunswick. David, twenty-two, still lives at home and is studying political science at Memorial.

During the 1970s, as his law practice grew, business took Wells to St. John's and to the mainland far more than he liked. Certainly more than his family liked. In an April 1989 interview with Southam News reporter Julian Beltrame, Wells, in a rare open moment, recalled how he had been complaining that Brian Peckford should station a Supreme Court judge in Corner Brook so he could be home more often when "one day I intercepted a letter from my son David — he must have been nine — addressed to the premier. Maybe I shouldn't have opened it but I did, and he was asking Peckford to move a Supreme Court judge to Corner Brook so I would be home more."

Wells says David used to write letters all the time. "He was a very sensitive boy. He still is, although he puts on a gruff exterior and he's six foot two and 225 pounds, so you don't think of him as overly sensitive. But he was . . . and we had to be very careful about him as to discipline. If you were critical, then he would turn on himself. And his way of coping with these kinds of difficulties was not to talk to us, but by letter. David wrote letters constantly. I'd discipline David and send him upstairs to his room. Five minutes later he'd come down, reach around the corner, and hand me a note. He would tell me what he thought about what I did, and whether he thought it was right or wrong. As often as not, the letter acknowledged his responsibility and turned on himself."

One of Mark's favorite childhood memories is driving up to the cottage on Georges Lake. "I think of any material thing that he did, the cabin probably gave him the highest sense of satisfaction. He put a lot of thought and effort into that. I remember my younger brother's first birthday was out at the cabin, and at the time it was just partitions and two-by-fours, just open space, with trees all around and just this frame.

"Basically when school ended we moved out there and [dad] would come out there with us. In mid-August, he'd go back into Corner Brook. He'd commute to work, it was only a twenty-minute drive. He'd leave early and try to get back early and take a few days off here and there."

When he was building the cottage, Wells would pack his family in the car after supper and head for the lake. "He has always been a news junkie," says Mark. "He read a lot of newspapers and a lot of novels. A long time ago he read a lot of sailing novels. Then he invested in a series of books, 'the 100 greatest books ever written' — you'd collect them once a month or something, and he's working his way through those. He also reads a lot of political books, books on political people, political processes, and so on. He didn't have that many law books around, but he has a few on analysis of different types of law . . . but the vast majority of what he read were non-fiction political analyses and autobiographies or biographies, and fiction classical works."

The family kept a nineteen-foot sailboat named *Ellie B.* at the cottage. (Years later, having moved up to St. John's and up in status to a luxury thirty-eight-foot Hughes Columbia sailboat, Wells tried to name it *Ellie B. II,* but was outvoted by his children who opted instead for *Piper*, after the family pet, a Pembroke Welsh corgi.) "Georges Lake was where the whole family learned to sail," says Mark, and his father loves it. The family also swam constantly at the lake, but according to Mark his father's not a great swimmer. "So he took a course. I was really surprised when he did this, but one of the sons of a family friend was a swimming instructor, and a group of adults who were all friends, my father one of them, basically went through the survival level of swimming. I guess he figured that being out at Georges Lake sailing, he'd better learn to swim. He *could* swim, he just wanted to be a better swimmer."

Clyde also loved trout fishing in a small motorized runabout they had at the cottage, and once or twice a year went off with a group of men to Labrador or to Kaegudeck fishing lodge in south central Newfoundland, a place owned by entrepreneur Harry Steele, who later became one of Wells's major financial backers.

Mark says his father's work habits are the same now as when he was a lawyer. "I don't know how he does it. He starts at eight or eight-thirty at his office, comes back at six. Then there's a meeting at eight until whenever, and he comes home and does more work. And he does that all the time."

Daily life in the Wells household was, well, steady. "He was always very conservative. Our whole family is like that. No one ever got really mad, or shouted or jumped up and down happy or cried sadly. None of our family were like that. There were never peaks of emotions and then dips of depression. It was always very even."

When the children misbehaved, their father would "get upset, but not mad," says Mark. "He'd be disappointed. He'd say, 'I'm not very happy that you did this.' That was it. But it made me feel bad because, as a teenager, your parents' approval is really important. It was to me. I always respected my parents and I didn't like doing things that I knew they would strongly disapprove of. . . . There was lots of debate. I argued with him constantly. It was a very unfair situation, though. Being a very good lawyer, it was very difficult to argue with him. He'd always have a comeback for any point I made."

While Clyde worked long hours in the office and on the road, Eleanor worked hard at home. When David turned ten, she took a nursing refresher course and worked part-time for a couple of years, giving it up in 1981 when the family moved to St. John's. "She didn't need to work," says Mark. "It was just because she wanted to, and I think she really enjoyed doing that. The children were getting older and they didn't make such a mess in the house." But even working outside the home she still managed the house. "The meals were always made. The laundry was always done. The house was always clean. There was no difference in what happened at the house.

"My mom is a great cook. I wish she wouldn't cook her roasts so much, but other than that, she's terrific. She's a fairly adventurous cook. My father is also a great cook. He likes to do little fancy things. He's very patient."

Mark tells a story of when Clyde was on a business trip and had a dessert called peach flambé that really caught his fancy. "It was prepared in front of him so he wrote the recipe down. It is the best dessert you've ever had, made with vanilla ice cream, sugar, Grand Marnier, peaches. You caramelize the sugar and flambé it with Grand Marnier. Ah, it's incredible. You have to be very patient and very careful to make it. And he is."

Dinner at the Wells household, which began with Clyde saying grace, was a rather formal affair. "We all ate at the same time," says Mark. "Mom would prepare the dinner and dad would come home and we'd eat. It was shirt and tie for my father only because he'd walk in the door and still have his shirt and tie on. He was the only one well-dressed for dinner. It was always organized, unless there was some special event where one of the children had to go somewhere and would eat early. But our meals were never a free-for-all."

One thing Clyde didn't do at the dinner table was talk about his work. "He would just talk about normal family things, saying hello to everybody, asking what we did that day, how things were at school, that sort of thing."

Mark never saw his parents drunk. "Not ever. Even at big parties, they would get a cab home, but they'd never come in drunk. They weren't that kind of people. They didn't have any friends who were that kind of people, either. . . . They're always in control. He'd be very uncomfortable if he was out of control, but he'd never allow himself to get into that kind of situation. It rubbed off on me. I'm not like that either."

The other thing the family loved doing was skiing at Marble Mountain, just outside Corner Brook, which Wells and a host of the city's leading lights helped build into a major ski resort during the 1970s. At one time, he was president of the club, and over the years has become an accomplished skier. In an October 1991 interview on "The Inside Track" on CBC radio, Wells called the facility, with its 1700-foot vertical drop, "one of the best ski hills in the country." It has twenty-five trails featuring everything from intermediate to advanced, where Wells usually skis, to the OMJ ("Oh m' Jeezis!") trail, where he doesn't. Opened as a ski area in 1964, it was originally built up by local volunteers, Wells included, but during recent years considerable investment by the provincial government has turned it into a major resort, with future plans for all-season activities, including fishing, golf, tennis, and hiking. To Wells, that's public money well spent. "So you bring people in and that brings revenue and creates jobs, and the return to government on that kind of investment is in fact higher than it is on most other economic investment made by governments."

During the summer, in addition to fishing and cottaging, Wells used to play some golf at the Blomidon Club, but was never good at it. In 1973, the Blomidon clubhouse/curling rink complex was levelled by a $400,000 fire, and Wells was active in a major fund-raising drive, which saw construction of a new log facility in 1975. Wells was also Rotary Club president around that time, an all-round active pillar of the community.

In the 1979 provincial election, then premier Brian Peckford had convinced lawyer Tom Marshall, a partner in Wells's law firm, to run for the Tories. Wells, who maintained a mystique of a John Turneresque figure waiting in the wings to arrive and rescue the Liberals, was also asked to run for the Liberals that year. Peckford was furious when Marshall decided against running, blaming Wells for talking him out of it. Marshall says Wells didn't talk him out of it — at least, not exactly. He says he didn't want to run anyway, but was pressured by Peckford into saying yes. Then, after talking with Wells, he agreed that the firm came first and both men decided not to run. Two years later, when the firm's major client, Bowater, was about to announce what was to be either a closure or a major cutback — depending upon whether or not they could find a buyer for the operation — Wells packed his bags and headed for the green, green grass of St. John's.

One person who did run in Humber East in 1979 was Tory Lynn Verge, who over the years has been something of Wells's nemesis. In 1967 Verge had applied for a summer job at the law firm, then called Barry, Wells, and Kevin Barry hired her. She continued to work at the firm on a relief basis between 1967 and 1970, and part-time when she was in law school from 1970 to 1973. She was one of a group of people from the firm who went to Grand Falls to meet Wells on his way home after he'd left Smallwood's cabinet and crossed the floor to sit as an independent Liberal. After that, she articled at the firm and continued working there until 1975. The reason she left reveals a side of Wells his fans might charitably call old-fashioned and conservative, but what his detractors would call blatantly sexist.

Verge was the only woman lawyer in Corner Brook, and one

of only a half dozen in the entire province. Describing herself as a small "f" feminist, she had started a women's legal centre and was beginning to get more involved in the women's movement. As a junior in the firm, she didn't deal much with Wells. He was, after all, the firm's legal superstar. But one conversation from that time stands out. "He told me there was no place in the firm for me because I might have babies," Verge says. "I remember being shocked. It flashed in my mind being likened to a rabbit. It's one of those outrageous statements, if someone has that attitude. But at that point, I wasn't thinking," she said. Instead, she left the firm.

Marshall, who was in the room at the time, doesn't recall the precise words Wells used, but he does agree the conversation took place and remembers being "surprised" by what Wells said to her. As for Wells, he doesn't deny making the comment, although he attempts to put a more favorable spin on it. Asked about it by Tom Walkom in 1990, Wells bristled — as he typically does when he's not in control of the agenda — and said, "What I said to her was that a partnership depends on personal input. . . . If I'm going to expect to take a year off, or half a year off, or any time from a partnership, I can't expect my partners to pay me as if I were there working." Walkom concluded that his unapologetic version sounded much the same as Verge's. Supporters of Wells argue that times have changed, that back in the 1970s, such attitudes weren't unusual. Perhaps. But given Wells's explanation some fifteen years later, it appears doubtful his attitude has changed.

Verge backs this up when she points out that the Wells of much more recent vintage, as premier, refused to allow a moment of silence in the house to pay tribute to the fourteen women murdered by Marc Lepine in Montreal. At the time, Wells accused Verge of grandstanding, arguing he wouldn't mark the moment because women are no different from other groups, that is, everybody should be treated the same way, not singled out for special treatment, essentially the same philosophy he champions in the Triple-E Senate and elsewhere.

Just to complete the circle, Verge, whom Wells virtually advised to pursue another line of work, became justice minister and deputy premier in the Peckford-Rideout regime and took away some of the shine of Wells's April 20, 1989 majority election win by defeating him in Humber East by 138 votes, forcing him to bump Liberal MHA Eddy Joyce from an adjacent riding, then winning the subsequent byelection by acclamation.

Sometimes it seemed that the traits Clyde Wells displayed as a lawyer were the very ones that made some of his colleagues shun him at the polls. To quote one Corner Brook lawyer, who articled with Wells: "You'll notice that those of us who know him best didn't vote for him. What does that tell you?"

Monaghan describes Wells's legal style as being "like a dog with a bone. It's a good trait and a bad trait. The good trait is that you've got somebody who totally dedicates himself to a case, throws everything at it. The bad trait is that you lose objectivity and sometimes you lose a case, and sometimes if you don't cut a deal on the courthouse steps, your client loses.

"Clyde would appeal. If he lost, the lower-court judge was wrong. And then the appeal-court judge was wrong, and the Supreme Court of Canada was wrong. He'd just appeal, appeal, appeal. He loved to appeal."

Wells also had a way of stretching things out. What would take Monaghan or one of his other partners five minutes to advise a client on, Clyde could make last half an hour. Monaghan supposes that trait helped him politically.

Corner Brook lawyer Ed Poole, who faced Wells many times in court, calls Wells competent, but "stubborn as a pig. . . . There's not much humility in his soul. Not a goddamn bit of humor."

Both Poole and Monaghan remember one particular case where Clyde insisted on appealing up to the Newfoundland

Supreme Court, and the chief justice thought it was such a vexatious defence he damned him personally, saying he should never have brought the case this far and made him pay all the expenses. The case against Wells's client was open and shut. The man had borrowed money from a finance company, signed the promissory note, and hadn't paid up. Poole represented the company in the case. Wells tried to argue that the interest rates being charged were too high and shouldn't be allowed. Poole said the interest rates "may be an issue for Parliament to debate, but there was no legal issue in the case."

Monaghan says that was just like Clyde. He'd take it on and try to change black to white. He adds that Wells has a tendency to lecture. "You'd better agree with him, too. He doesn't like it when you don't agree with him. . . . He's right and you're wrong."

Even though he wasn't directly involved in many political events during the 1970s, Wells managed to keep his reputation as the heir apparent thanks largely, says Monaghan, to the media. "He was sure a sucker for a microphone. And if the press needed a comment, or the CBC needed a commentator, they'd come to him. For some reason he just had that mystique about him. I guess it was because he was an attractive fellow and a good speaker."

In the mid-70s, Tom Marshall first heard that a fledgling Newfoundland west coast TV company called Shelbird was trying to raise money from shareholders to get into the burgeoning cable market. Marshall researched the deal, figured it was a sure money-maker, and asked both Monaghan and Wells if they were interested in investing. They were. Wells immediately took on a leadership roll in preparing a case to sell the deal to the CRTC. The group invited a few other investors in — Wells's brother-in-law George Colbourne, his friends Bob Sexton and Cyril Vardy, and lawyer Dave Tizzard. The company didn't make any money for several years, and in the early

80s, Marshall and Monaghan wanted to fire the manager and run the company themselves. Wells disagreed. He had recently left Corner Brook to set up his private practice in St. John's. Colbourne had gone to Calgary with Petro Canada.

Two distinct sides emerged in the dispute, and Wells had a roaring fight with the shareholders one night at the Glynmill Inn. Marshall said Wells wanted to sell his shares for more than he'd pay for his partner's shares. It created some bitterness, but Wells wouldn't budge, and eventually the remaining partners paid him (Colbourne, siding with Wells, also sold his shares). Wells sold his shares in 1983, and the deal was completed in 1984.

"Clyde didn't lose anything on the deal. He made some money," says Monaghan. "But we signed a deal with Avalon Cable Vision in October 1986, and we sold our shares in June 1987. It was a very dramatic increase. If Clyde had waited, he would have gained over one million bucks for his share of the deal."

According to Monaghan, Wells has changed since he left Corner Brook in 1981. "He's much more dogmatic. He always was fairly dogmatic. When he took a position, it was his way and no other way. But I think he's become more dogmatic and more self-confident from the point of view that he's got confidence in himself and no confidence in anybody else. More so than he used to have . . . which is why he's running a one-man show. He's got all the confidence in himself, but not other people. And he's got himself convinced that he's the best man for Canada."

To Monaghan it seems there's only one thing holding Wells back. He's not competent, to use Wells's word, in the other official language. "He'll never speak French," says Monaghan. "Clyde has a terrible ear. You need that ear to be able to pick up a language. . . . Poor Crosbie in 1983. Getting him to learn six or seven words to say at the Tory leadership, Jesus, it was like pulling teeth. Clyde's the same way. A lot of us in Newfoundland are. We have enough trouble speaking one language. But Clyde has mastered that one."

The most sensational legal case handled by Wells during his Corner Brook years was fighting a libel action against the St. John's *Evening Telegram* and the CBC for Dr. Thomas C. Farrell, the prominent local physician who had won Wells's old Humber East seat for the Tories in 1971 and held several senior cabinet positions for the Moores government throughout the 1970s.

On April 25, 1978, Farrell was asleep in his apartment in the Elizabeth Towers in downtown St. John's when a fire broke out, causing extensive damage. The Royal Newfoundland Constabulary investigated the fire and in June turned their report in to the Department of Justice. On August 8, Farrell resigned from cabinet. On September 26, Liberal opposition leader Bill Rowe telephoned *Telegram* publisher Stephen Herder offering a copy of the report. Herder, thinking the report was being made available to others, agreed, and later that day two police reports arrived at the newspaper. The next day the *Telegram* headline was: "Report concludes blaze deliberately set by Farrell." On October 30, Farrell was arrested and charged with arson, but on December 21 Judge Joseph LeClair dismissed the charges because of insufficient evidence.

In January, acting for Farrell, whom he had helped get elected in 1971, Wells sued the newspaper and the CBC for libel. Farrell said the publicity had "severely injured his credit, character and reputation as a citizen as well as in his medical practice and as a member of the House of Assembly." At the same time, Justice Minister Gerald Ottenheimer appointed Judge P. Lloyd Soper to investigate the unauthorized release of the police reports. (The media refused to reveal the source, but Rowe admitted to Soper in April that he had leaked the reports.) Ottenheimer also appointed Judge A.S. LeGrow to investigate the cause of the fire, and on December 4, 1981, his report concluded that "by accident or design, the flame was applied by Dr. Farrell." During the hearings, anonymous telephone threats were made against both LeGrow and Wells. According to Detective Bob Hillier, the man who called Wells at home identified himself as a member of the Irish Republican Army and said Wells should quit the inquiry because the Irish-born Farrell owed thousands of dollars to the IRA. He also threatened to kidnap the Wells children if the case was not dropped.

Both Farrell and Wells were furious at LeGrow's conclusions, but exactly a month later, on January 4, 1982, Justice John Mahoney of the Newfoundland Supreme Court awarded Farrell $150,000 in his libel suit against the *Telegram,* at the time the highest amount ever awarded in a Canadian libel case. In May, the CBC broadcast an apology to Farrell on both radio and TV, saying it had no evidence its news stories linking Farrell to the fire were true. The province ordered yet another inquiry, this time by retired Chief Justice Robert S. Furlong, and he concluded in August 1982 that the available evidence would not substantiate charges against Farrell.

In February 1983, arguing before Mr. Justice Gerald Lang of the Newfoundland Supreme Court's trial division in an eleven-day hearing to assess damages against the CBC, Wells called it, "the worse libel in the history of Canadian and English law that I've ever seen [which should be] visited with the highest damages ever recorded." In November 1983, the court ordered the CBC to pay Farrell $80,000. Both sides appealed. The *Telegram* said the penalties were too high. Wells argued they were too low. In March 1986 the Newfoundland Court of Appeal reduced the $150,000 award to $35,000, finding the original award to be disproportionately high compared to awards in similar libel cases. Wells then sought leave to appeal before the Supreme Court of Canada, arguing in his written brief that the "sheer monstrosity of the libel [was] far more severe" than other cases. The court dismissed the application.

And so, at the end of all that, Farrell had his "victory," but he was broke. All the money he was awarded went to pay Wells's legal fees. Nevertheless, Farrell still considers Wells a friend. "These cases are very complicated, and it wasn't unusual for him to work until four or five in the morning and appear in court as fresh as a daisy. Of course, we were all a lot younger." Farrell, who suffers from lupus and is legally blind in one eye as a result, says, "While it didn't work out well financially for me, it was what I wanted to do." He adds Wells is "high-priced and he made plenty, but he didn't charge me for the appeal because I was broke."

One of the major cases Wells handled for Bowater, ironically, arose out of changes to the City of Corner Brook Act, which he had supported when he was the Liberal MHA in the late 1960s. Among the enormous concessions given to Bowater Newfoundland Ltd. by the province when the company bought the mill and power plant in Corner Brook was an exemption from municipal taxation, along with massive ninety-nine-year water and timber rights. In 1977, believing the City of Corner Brook Act had voided the pre-Confederation agreements, the city assessed the Bowater property, then sued the company for $873,000 in taxes. Bowater had already paid $255,000 as part of a $300,000 grant in lieu of taxes, and Wells, on the company's behalf, argued this amount should be subtracted from that bill. In March 1979, Justice Nathaniel Noel of the Supreme Court's trial division ruled that Bowater must pay the city $618,000 in taxes to the city. His main argument was that the Corner Brook Act had "altered the laws in force in Newfoundland at the date of union." Wells, having supported the act as a politician, immediately gave notice of appeal to the Newfoundland Court of Appeal, and a year later the court agreed with Wells that the pre-Confederation statutes still applied and the city's major industry didn't have to pay municipal taxes. The court also awarded costs for both the original case and the appeal to Bowater.

By the early 1980s, however, even tax exemptions weren't enough to keep Bowater in the black. High interest rates and diminishing foreign markets were beginning to take their toll. In 1982, Bowater announced a one-month shutdown. In late November the company announced it was in serious financial trouble, and in December said it planned to shut down its largest paper machine, which would represent a permanent loss of more than seven hundred jobs, a major blow to the city and the surrounding districts. As it ultimately turned out, Bowater got out and the government arranged a sale of the operation to Kruger, a European company, which operates it today under the name of the Corner Brook Pulp and Paper Ltd.

The question some people in the Corner Brook legal fraternity asked themselves when Wells decided to pack up and move to St. John's in June 1981 was how much of his departure from his beloved Corner Brook was related to the impending fiscal problems of his most important and most profitable client.

Wells said that two-thirds of his business was in St. John's, so it was "only practical" to move there. But critics argue that as the corporate lawyer, he must have known the company's plans. Monaghan says that "some people have suggested there was a connection, but I don't know. There're two stories. The story that he told us was that he was doing a lot of work in St. John's . . . there's no question he was away a lot. The other story is that he had advance warning and decided to bail out. Yes, there's no question if Corner Brook didn't have the mill back in those days, it would have been a real body blow to the town."

Fred Stagg says that, as a lawyer, Wells more than likely knew Bowater's position. Wells looked at leaving Corner Brook the way he'd look at a balance sheet; he left, selling his cable shares, his cabin, and his house.

During his throne speech reply on February 29, 1968, Wells had told the house that "without Bowater, Mr. Speaker, there is no doubt about it, there would be no Corner Brook . . . and as well, there would be fewer other towns prospering in the western part of Newfoundland."

Today, Wells flatly, and angrily, denies the Bowater situation had anything to do with his leaving Corner Brook. Quite the contrary. "Bowater's decision with respect to Corner Brook was made in 1984. I'd moved to St. John's three years earlier, in 1981. Now unquestionably it was prescient of me to foresee three years down the road. In 1981, Bowater was doing quite well, flat out."

It's true that 1981 was a good year for Bowater and the forest industry in general in Newfoundland. It's also true the final deal with Kruger wasn't settled until 1984. However, by 1982 Newfoundland's print industry was struggling with softer markets and tougher competition. It may be that Wells was not aware of this looming downturn, but whatever his prophetic skills, things began going downhill for Bowater much sooner than 1984.

Wells says the reason he actually left Corner Brook was the same reason he left politics in 1970: the work kept him away from home too much. In the late 70s, his law practice started to change. He'd built a comfortable life in Corner Brook but began to find he was spending about two-thirds of his time in St. John's, solely because of legal work, no connection with politics at all. "So the problem I'd had in the late 60s," he says, "came back again, only this time caused by legal work rather than politics."

The turning point, he says, was just before Christmas 1980. "I'll never forget it. The plane had been cancelled and I had to drive eight hours from St. John's to get home and then go back

Sunday to St. John's to be in court on Monday morning. I arrived home about 3 a.m. and on my desk in the study was a letter David had written. I still have it. And my recollection of it is: 'Dear Dad: You've been away twenty-three days so far this month. We think that's too much. You should try to cut it down to no more than fifteen days each month. You've got to think of the rest of us, you know.' And he signed everybody's name on it, including the dog, Piper.

"That's pretty hard to take. So I had to make a decision. Either I gave up the legal work I was doing and did legal work that would keep me in Corner Brook, or I kept up the work I was doing and moved to St. John's. Either I was going to work where I lived, or live where I worked. And that was essentially the choice I had to make."

His son Mark, who was happy with the move because it coincided with his attendance at Memorial University, also recalls David's letter. "That's a true story, and one of the memorable moments of childhood. And someone once accused him of fabricating that story and he was very offended by it, because it was true. . . . It's one of the odd things, that he shared such a personal story to begin with."

Because of David's letter, Wells sat down and mapped out the previous three years of his life, did a complete assessment of where he did the work and where the work originated. "Only a portion of it originated in Corner Brook, and an even smaller portion of it was being done in Corner Brook," he says. "So it didn't make much sense to continue to carry on that kind of work or, alternatively, to live in Corner Brook if I was doing that kind of work.

"At the time, there were major cases I was doing. The offshore, the federal constitutional challenge, the Churchill Falls case, and other major cases. And in professional terms, it's pretty hard to walk away from that kind of work. So I made the decision. I would move to St. John's. And I did.

"That had absolutely nothing to do with Bowater. In fact, if anything, the Bowater situation was pressure to keep me in Corner Brook . . . it was a major client. . . . People will say that because they want to say it. But it isn't true."

Whatever the motive, the next step in his inexorable march to fame and fortune had been taken. The Bayman had arrived again to battle the Townies, only by this time, he wasn't a wide-eyed kid from the boonies. He was a star.

6

Capturing the Capital

BY THE TIME Wells moved to St. John's he was in the top echelon of the Newfoundland legal fraternity. Not only was he among the best paid, making around $250,000 a year, but his successful handling of several major, high-profile cases, combined with his status as a former cabinet minister, contributed substantially to his reputation as a first-rate lawyer.

Because of his established practice and political connections, Wells would soon be handling major constitutional cases, fighting the federal side in the 1981-82 constitutional battles. His elevated status as a lawyer was confirmed in 1977 when he was chosen by the Canadian Bar Association to sit on a high-powered committee on the Constitution. The CBA chose one lawyer to represent each province — though three for Quebec and two for Ontario — and Wells joined the Montreal meeting with such well-known lawyers as Yves Fortier, recently retired as Canada's United Nations ambassador; George Finlayson, a big-name Toronto lawyer since appointed to the Ontario Court of Appeal; social activist David Matas of Winnipeg; and a young

Prince Edward Island lawyer named Joe Ghiz who later, as the island's premier, would become one of Wells's severest critics during the failed Meech Lake discussions in 1990. The group's executive vice-chairman and director of research was Gérard La Forest, now a Supreme Court of Canada justice.

The committee sprang from the general panic felt by federalists after the 1976 election victory of separatist leader René Lévesque in Quebec. At its 1977 annual meeting the CBA struck the committee to "search for a definition of the essential constitutional attributes of a Canadian federalism. . . ." The committee's report, "Towards a New Canada," was released with much fanfare and considerable publicity in spring 1978.

Among other things, the committee called for recognition of the "equal partnership" between the English- and French-speaking communities, an entrenched Bill of Rights, the right of each province "to choose its own official language or languages," the right to use either official language in all federal and provincial legislatures, recognition of the Queen as head of the Commonwealth but replacing her with a Canadian as head of state, major changes in the judicial system, a guarantee that three of the nine Supreme Court justices be Quebecers, and myriad proposals affecting the division of powers, taxing and spending power, social security, trade, telecommunications, marriage and divorce, and resources.

The report avoided publishing specific positions of the committee members. Instead, it used such references as "a majority agreed," or "a consensus was found." There was, however, one exception to this rule — the Senate. While no names were mentioned, the report referred specifically to Wells's fixation even then with the Triple-E Senate:

One member of the Committee is of the view that the essential role of an Upper House in a federation is to provide a means of recognizing the equal status of the constituent parts of the federation at the federal level. Each of these parts must be given an equal voice in the Upper House, the principle of equality of the individual through representation by population being given expression in the Lower House. Thus federal legislative power could only be exercised after weighing national opinion, both on the basis of the majority of the population and of the constituent parts of the federations, as is the case in Australia, Switzerland and the United States [the three countries Wells studied in Wheare's analysis at Memorial University].

Such a proposal would avoid the inequities that may occur in Upper Houses, such as the existing Senate, where representation is based upon a variety of factors or groupings of provinces. For with changing circumstances, the weight originally attached to these factors may result in anomalous and inequitable situations.

The report went on to say that the current arrangement gave the four western provinces six fewer senators than the four Atlantic provinces, even though the West has three times the population, a situation Wells still continues to point out. But while the report contained Wells's argument for an equal Senate, the other members did not concur. Its formal recommendations on Senate reform concluded that regional, linguistic, and population factors should be accommodated, and one way of doing that would be to give "considerably more members to Quebec and Ontario while ensuring regional balance by giving an overall majority to members from the rest of the country, and by giving somewhat greater weight to the western and northern regions than to the Atlantic region."

Yves Fortier says he met Wells a few times at CBA functions and that during the constitutional exercise the two of them became "quite friendly. I remember him as one of the most knowledgeable lawyers . . . one could never fault the logic of his interventions. He was a superb constitutional lawyer. He knew his stuff. Others around the table were not as authoritative on the Constitution as Clyde. . . . I remember him as a very pleasant debater, but not one who was given to any yielding on issues. When he had an opinion, and he reached that opinion laboriously by studying the cases and all the opinions of the judges, that would be it. There was very little give in the argument."

Fortier recalls that he and his wife spent a pleasant evening at dinner with Clyde and Eleanor during that time in Montreal. "I'm a hundred per cent certain we didn't talk only about the Constitution. Lévesque was premier then, and [Wells] was extremely interested in hearing whatever information I could convey to him about what was happening in Quebec City. He was always very hungry for information about things political. . . . He was a very intense person . . . but it was certainly possible to have a pleasant social evening with him." Nor did Fortier ever detect any anti-Quebec views in Wells.

Although David Matas found Wells personable and very friendly, he was dismayed by his stubbornness. Wells, he says, "had very strong opinions, particularly on Senate reform. We spent a lot of time on that, to my mind a disproportionate amount. We did try to work out a joint point of view on the Senate, but he was on his own and wouldn't budge. He was a difficult person to work with in the sense of a group of people who were trying to get a consensus. . . . He was just impossible. He argued it well enough to keep himself convinced, but not well enough to convince anybody else. On other issues, I wouldn't say he was more amenable or more movable. He tended to just stake out positions and stick to them. It frustrated the exercise of trying to get a consensus. . . . Being lawyers, we're used to taking a position and arguing it, but all the rest of us at least attempted to play the game the way it was designed."

Halifax lawyer Joel Fichaud, who was La Forest's assistant

for the study, finds it "ironic" that Wells's approach to solving problems is closer to the Civil Code methodology used in Quebec than the Common Law approach used in English Canada. "He's ideological, and he deduces . . . more the Trudeau approach. . . . The important thing for him is that his principles are symmetrical, rather than the English approach where you fix problems as they come up and the principles are sometimes not as important as the problem-solving.

"The most important thing for him back then was the Senate. That was his number-one concern . . . hearing him now is almost like going back in time. The same arguments, the same principles. He was a pleasure to work with, but at times he should have bent a little bit in the spirit of compromise . . . and he still made it known he was a dissenter. That was always important to him.

"Intellectually he had more to contribute than most of the committee did. He thought things out beforehand, rather than just jumping into the soup and mixing it up."

While Wells and Ghiz both served on the committee, they did not become friends, a reality that has become more apparent since the Meech Lake dispute, when their mutual hostility was almost palpable. Michael Monaghan knows both men well. He was a partner with Wells in Corner Brook for eleven years, and he went to Dalhousie Law School with Ghiz and spent time skiing in Europe with him. "Joe's got a bigger constitutional background than Clyde," says Monaghan. "He has his masters from the Harvard Law School, and at Dal he won the main prize in constitutional law. He sure hauled a lot of us through conlaw [constitutional law]. We'd be there wallowing in the stuff the night before the exams, the last-minute cramming, and Joe would come down to our room and would tell us the easiest way to do it. Joe's got a great mind. He's a very impressive fellow.

"Right in the middle of this Meech stuff I used to talk to Ghiz about it, and he'd say, 'Jesus, what is he [Wells]?' Trudeau gave him a couple of cases to argue. That's basically the sum and substance of it. . . . He acted for the federal government on the offshore case and a constitutional case in 1982. . . . I would think Joe probably feels he's a superior constitutional lawyer to Clyde . . . and there's no question, he is. I mean, I don't know the rest of those guys, but I know Clyde and I know Joe, and Joe's the best."

With the constitutional debate growing in both importance and intensity in the early 1980s, Trudeau appointed Senator Michael Kirby as secretary to the cabinet for federal-provincial relations. Kirby was born in Montreal, but both his parents were Newfoundlanders (his father was an Anglican priest), with the family going back several generations as inshore fishermen there. He had heard of Wells both through Liberal circles and his work in the bar association's constitutional committee.

At the time, Manitoba, Quebec, and Newfoundland had all launched legal challenges against Trudeau's constitutional package. Only Ontario's Bill Davis and New Brunswick's Richard Hatfield supported it. The other eight provinces were opposed. Kirby was looking around for a Liberal lawyer in Newfoundland on whom to bestow some considerable patronage in return for representing the federal interest against Newfoundland's legal challenge.

"We had concluded we would use local lawyers," says Kirby. "We would be clearly killed if we went in there, say, with lawyers from Ottawa or Toronto. So we looked for the brightest guy we could find, and we settled on Clyde in the Newfoundland court. He also worked on the appeal for us to the Supreme Court of Canada, when a whole battery of lawyers were there under the direction of J. J. Robinette."

The first case to be heard was that of the Manitoba Supreme Court in December 1980. Manitoba, supported by several other provinces, including Newfoundland, as well as the Four Nations confederacy, representing Manitoba Indians, asked the court to rule on three questions:

1) If the amendments to the Constitution of Canada sought . . . [by Ottawa] . . . were enacted, would federal-provincial relationships or the powers, rights or privileges granted or secured by the Constitution of Canada to the provinces, their legislatures, or governments be affected, and if so, in what respect or respects?

2) Is it a constitutional convention that the House of Commons and Senate of Canada will not request Her Majesty the Queen to lay before the Parliament of the United Kingdom . . . a measure to amend the Constitution of Canada affecting federal-provincial relationships or the powers, rights or privileges granted or secured by the Constitution of Canada . . . without first obtaining the agreement of the provinces?

3) Is the agreement of the provinces of Canada constitutionally required for amendment to the Constitution of Canada . . . affecting federal-provincial relationships or alters the powers, rights or privileges granted or secured by the Constitution of Canada . . . ?

On February 3, 1981, the court rejected three to two the province's argument.

A week later, Wells went before Chief Justice Arthur Mifflin, Mr. Justice Herbert Morgan, and Mr. Justice James Gushue of the Newfoundland Supreme Court's appeal division to argue the case of Ottawa against St. John's lawyer John O'Neill, representing the province. To the aforementioned three legal questions — which were later put in the Quebec challenge — Newfoundland added a fourth, asking if the Terms of Union could be changed under Trudeau's proposals in a way that could affect the Quebec-Labrador boundary dispute or the denominational education system.

O'Neill argued that under the current system the provinces were not required to justify legislation they passed, as long as it was under their jurisdiction, but under the proposed charter of rights, he said, the courts would be allowed to examine and interpret provincial laws relating to such things as preferential hiring practices, age limits, and Newfoundland's unique denominational system. "Are we now to have two classes of provinces?" he asked. "Is this what the great Canadian confederacy is all about?" (Ironically, Wells argued the other side in this case, but ten years later, his major objection to Meech Lake was that by giving Quebec "distinct" status, two classes of provinces are set up.)

While the provinces argued that Trudeau couldn't change the Constitution without the consent of all ten provinces, Wells told the court, "It is not an inherent characteristic of a federal state that all provinces agree on an amending formula, although it can affect all concerned. Is it reasonable that 100,000 people on Prince Edward Island should hold up an amending formula because they won't give their consent? I submit that is not reasonable."

Wells argued that Ottawa didn't need provincial consent to ask the British parliament to amend the Constitution. "An examination of the law, the BNA Act, and the normal principles of law does not justify the provinces' claim to sovereignty," he said, except for areas specifically assigned them under the BNA Act. Wells said an amending formula requiring unanimous consent of Ottawa and the provinces would put the country in a "virtual straitjacket," an analogy that would become ironic when Wells turned out to be the only real holdout among the premiers in the Meech Lake accord, a deal that died because it required unanimous consent.

Kirby says he dealt with Wells on an almost daily basis during that period. "He is very bright. What impressed me were his analytical skills, his ability to take an argument and dissect it on the one hand and then counter it on the other hand."

Maybe so. But it didn't impress Newfoundland's Supreme Court. The judges voted three to nothing on March 31 to side with the provincial argument, the only Ottawa loss in the three provincial challenges. On April 15, the Quebec Supreme Court also ruled four to one in favor of the provinces. Two weeks after that, the whole scene shifted to Ottawa and the Supreme Court of Canada, with Wells playing a minor supporting role. But on May 4, the final day of arguments in the Supreme Court, Wells showed he could handle himself well during a brief exchange with then chief justice Bora Laskin, Justice Brian Dickson, who followed Laskin as chief justice, and Justice Willard Estey.

Laskin asked Wells, speaking for the federal government, to lead off the Newfoundland appeal case. Wells cited former justice Ivan Rand in support of the federal claim that "Dominion" does not mean Ottawa and the provinces together, but only Ottawa, a reference to the 1931 British law, the Statute of Westminster, giving the "Dominion" the power to make amending requests to the British Parliament.

"Are you saying that the federal status of Canada is irrelevant?" Dickson asked Wells.

"That's a political matter to be decided in politics," he said.

"Is the federal status irrelevant to legal discussion?"

"The request of Ottawa is in accordance with the federal status of Canada," he replied.

Estey then asked if Wells was "backing off" the claim of Quebec lawyer Michel Robert, who carried the bulk of the federal argument in the case, that Ottawa could abolish the provinces.

"No," said Wells. "In effect, it can."

On September 28, in a complex, 115-page ruling, the Supreme Court essentially sided with the federal government.

Kirby says it was "not just another court case" to Wells. "He was very passionate about the Constitution. He was obviously good on his feet. . . . We [Ottawa] knew we were going to lose the minute our people reported back on how the judges were asking the questions. The sense I had was that the judges had already decided to rule in favor of Newfoundland, so we fully expected to lose. It was no reflection on Clyde that we did."

While the Constitution may not have been of great concern to the average Newfoundlander, Premier Brian Peckford's battle to get more for the province in the Churchill Falls deal certainly was.

In his book *The Past in the Present*, Peckford argues that the hydro development of the Upper Churchill River is the deal "contemporary Newfoundlanders find the most appalling betrayal of their interests. . . . It seemed that nobody realized what was happening at the time. It was such a large project — filled with romance and courage. Dare anyone object to seeing one of Labrador's great resources being developed for all Newfoundlanders and Labradorians? Dare anyone object to this great company, Brinco, and the Rothschild family with all the great financiers of the world, flocking to Newfoundland and Labrador to help us? It would be utter madness! Smallwood's oratory instilled in the people his own pride and delight in the sheer size of the project. Who was to say him nay?"

Certainly not Wells, who, from his very first speech in the House of Assembly in 1966, defended the project consistently. While the deal has proved to be enormously profitable for Quebec, it has been a disaster for Newfoundland because of the poor terms Smallwood negotiated. It is difficult to overstate the animosity many Newfoundlanders feel toward Quebec, feelings that burst out into the House of Assembly in 1990 when Dr. Hubert Kitchen, Newfoundland's finance minister, no less, debating the Meech Lake accord, blurted out that the province finally had Quebec "by the short hairs." While Wells made him apologize later, Newfoundlanders across the island and in Labrador were applauding.

Nothing better illustrates Newfoundland's tragic history of economic hari-kari than the saga of Churchill Falls. It began in 1952 when Smallwood, after several visits to England, enlisted the support of Prime Minister Winston Churchill and Canadian-born Lord Beaverbrook in forming the British Newfoundland Corporation (Brinco Ltd.) a modern-day Hudson's

Bay Company designed to explore and develop the resources of the province. Other major players were Sir Eric Bowater and Edmund de Rothschild. Originally called Grand Falls, then Hamilton Falls, Smallwood changed the name to Churchill Falls in 1965 in honor of the former British prime minister.

In March 1953, Smallwood's government passed legislation handing the Brinco consortium exploration and development rights to most of the Crown lands and water power in the province, including all mineral and forest rights on the 60,000 square miles of leased land, all but 10,000 of it in Labrador. In return, Brinco agreed to give Newfoundland eight per cent of its profits before taxes and fifty cents per horsepower of hydro energy developed. Negotiations with Brinco and Quebec continued throughout the 1950s, with Newfoundland and Quebec growing increasingly hostile because of Quebec's churlish decision not to allow Newfoundland to transport electricity from the project through lines across its territory to sell to the energy-starved northeastern United States. Former cabinet minister Frederick Rowe, in his book *The Smallwood Era*, writes that he was with Smallwood when he suggested to Quebec Premier Jean Lesage that he might ask Ottawa to have the transmission line declared "in the national interest," to which Lesage pointedly asked how he would deal with the problem of sabotage. Talks broke down several times as the two premiers hammered each other, often in public; but among the series of demands being made by Lesage, the one that most upset Newfoundlanders was a demand for an adjustment to the Quebec-Labrador border, an attempt to reverse the 1927 Privy Council decision that gave Labrador to Newfoundland.

The deal that finally emerged was that Brinco would develop Churchill Falls, provide Newfoundland with a small amount of power to serve its needs, and sell the rest to Hydro-Québec, which in turn would sell half to Consolidated Edison through power lines at the New York–Quebec border. In 1966, when Daniel Johnson defeated Lesage, he took only a few months to sign a deal with Brinco to purchase Churchill Falls power, ending fourteen years of political feuding and leading to an official sod-turning ceremony in June 1967, around the time Wells entered Smallwood's cabinet as labor minister. Newfoundland's problem, of course, was it didn't have any money and had to rely on Quebec and the private investors to put up the funds, settling, as usual, for a few thousand construction jobs to build the project. The real sore point came in 1969 when the Churchill Falls (Labrador) Corp. — which had been given a ninety-nine-year lease by Smallwood in 1961 to develop the project — signed a sixty-five-year deal with Hydro-Québec to sell it power at a fixed rate, power that would then be sold at an enormous profit to the New England states. Power didn't actually begin to flow from the project until December 12, 1971 — ironically, about six weeks after Smallwood's final election campaign — and the problem with the contract exploded three years later when energy prices skyrocketed, giving Quebec even more profits from the deal and leaving Newfoundland with mere droppings. The province began trying to renegotiate the deal in 1976, but Quebec was consistently unco-operative, and there was no hope the federal government would side with Newfoundland against Quebec. In fact, two years earlier, against Newfoundland's strong intervention, federal Energy Minister Jean Chrétien announced that the cabinet had approved the sale of electricity by Hydro-Québec to New York state, and as if to rub Newfoundland's nose in it, the province was notified of the decision by a secretary from the National Energy Board.

Even at the 1967 opening ceremony, Smallwood, who viewed the project as his crowning glory, still couldn't mask his concern about just how much Newfoundland would get out of it when he pointedly told the 450 guests that "this is our river, this is our waterfall, this is our land. . . . We are developing it mainly, chiefly, principally for the benefit of Newfoundland. Newfoundland first, Quebec second, the rest of the world last." In reality, it was Quebec first, the rest of the world second, and Newfoundland last.

An infuriated Brian Peckford hired a team of lawyers to study the Churchill Falls contract and to advise the government how to get out of it. It took them over a year of study, but the result of their report was the 1980 Upper Churchill Water Rights Reversion Act, which essentially expropriated Churchill Falls (Labrador) Corp.'s interest in the hydroelectric facility on behalf of the Crown. It was during the period of study that Wells had telephoned and asked for a meeting.

"He was advancing the notion that there were ways and actions the government could pursue under the existing Constitution of Canada which were better than those recommended by this committee of lawyers I'd had looking at it for a year," Peckford recalls. "He was very clear and precise and adamant in his view that his was a better approach to take. I don't remember the technical details, but I remember the approach he was suggesting had already been looked at by this team and by the Justice Department and wasn't found to be one of the more probable or likely approaches that could achieve success. But I do recall that he had a point of view and he thought that point of view was *the* point of view, period."

When the case went to the Newfoundland Supreme Court of Appeal in March 1982, the main player for the company was Toronto lawyer John Sopinka, now a Supreme Court justice. But among the cast of fifteen lawyers was Clyde Wells, this time representing Royal Trust, whose shareholders had put up $550 million to finance the project. Wells, again finding himself fighting against the provincial position, argued that if the effect of Peckford's act was to find the financial agreements repealed, it should be declared invalid.

Wells told the court he was "quite happy with the act . . . if it is executed properly," but added that if the act were approved the government could turn around a year later and declare fifty cents payment for each dollar owed. "Where does Royal Trust go then?" he asked, saying that if the province nationalized the project, all financial documents would have to remain in effect until full payment was forthcoming.

On March 5, 1982, the court ruled in Peckford's favor, in effect giving Newfoundland the right to take back the water rights the Churchill Falls (Labrador) Corp. was selling to Hydro-Québec, and Peckford, claiming Quebec was getting $500 million a year in profits out of the deal, about the same amount Newfoundland received from Ottawa in equalization payments, immediately referred the matter to the Supreme Court of Canada for a final decision. In 1984, the court ruled eight to nothing that Newfoundland did not have the right to break the deal giving Hydro-Québec cheap power until the year 2034. By this time, Quebec was making $800 million a year from the deal, compared to Newfoundland's approximately $8 million, even though the project is on its territory.

Wells found himself back in court on behalf of Royal Trust in October 1984 on a separate appeal by Newfoundland of a June 1983 ruling by the Newfoundland Supreme Court Trial Division that the province wasn't entitled to the extra energy it was demanding from the project. Here again, Newfoundland lost, but Wells's clients were protected, with the province ordered to pay his costs, as well as those of the other lawyers involved.

In the next major dispute between Peckford and the federal government — the battle over who owned and controlled the offshore resources, primarily large deposits of oil on the sea-bed — Wells once again became the federal Liberals' hired gun, working against Newfoundland's position.

Like the other major disputes, the offshore battle had its roots in the economic disparity between Newfoundland and mainland Canada, and the feeling that Newfoundlanders consistently got the short end. Between 1965 and 1969 seismic testing and exploratory drilling off the coast led to predictions of significant reserves of oil and gas. In 1967 in a ruling that would later hurt Newfoundland's case, the Supreme Court of Canada ruled that British Columbia did not own sub-sea resources, prompting Ottawa to claim that East Coast resources were also federal property. In 1977 the province established Newfoundland and Labrador Petroleum Ltd., a new provincial corporation to control offshore development. In 1978, Newfoundland formally claimed ownership of the offshore, and tests in the Hibernia field in 1979-80 showed larger reserves than previously thought.

Peckford came close to a formal agreement with Joe Clark during his short term as prime minister in 1979, but when Trudeau and the Liberals returned, negotiations eventually fell apart. Even though Ottawa and Nova Scotia signed an offshore pact, Newfoundland claimed it had a special case legally, because it had entered Canada as an independent dominion within the British Commonwealth and therefore had the same rights to offshore reserves as any coastal state, including Canada. Peckford argued that Newfoundland did not surrender those rights when it joined Confederation on March 31, 1949.

Finally, in February 1982 Peckford referred the dispute to Newfoundland's Court of Appeal, and Trudeau warned he planned to do the same thing before the Supreme Court of Canada. On March 15 Peckford called a snap election asking for a "mandate to negotiate" with Ottawa, and won forty-four of the fifty-two seats. In May Trudeau announced a federal reference to the Supreme Court, which would bypass the case pending in the Newfoundland court. Peckford declared an official day of mourning for the province.

It was in this climate, then, with Newfoundlanders feeling deeply aggrieved by Ottawa, that Wells walked into the Newfoundland Supreme Court of Appeal in October 1982, to argue the federal government's case. Newfoundland's lawyer James Greene argued there was no doubt Newfoundland had the legal right to ownership of seabed resources when it joined Canada in 1949. Montreal lawyer Colin K. Irving, a specialist in international and marine law, also appearing for Newfoundland, argued the B.C. decision had no bearing on the Newfoundland case because, among other things, B.C. had entered Confederation as a colony, while Newfoundland had been a separate dominion with its self-government suspended since 1934.

Wells argued Newfoundland's boundaries ended at the low-water mark when it joined Canada in 1949 and did not extend to the deep seabed offshore. According to Wells, Newfoundland didn't even enjoy the traditional three-mile territorial sea, but its seaward limit ended at its internal waters, such as bays and estuaries. Wells said that even if international law had developed to the point where seabed resource rights were generally recognized for coastal states before the 1958 Geneva Convention, Newfoundland did not have sufficient international status before 1949 to claim such rights. He pointed out that Britain's foreign office told other government departments in 1934, just after Britain had installed the Commission of Government to run Newfoundland, not to refer to His Majesty's Government in Newfoundland, but simply to the Government of Newfoundland. Wells said that was another indication Newfoundland did not enjoy full status as a separate country.

Continuing to downgrade Newfoundland's pre-Confederation status, Wells said it never joined the League of Nations or the United Nations, never made a separate declaration of war, had no diplomatic representatives abroad, didn't enjoy complete autonomy in either foreign or domestic affairs and, in short, remained a British colony.

In February 1983, in a sixty-nine-page opinion, the Newfoundland court ruled three to nothing that Canada, not Newfoundland, owns the mineral rights off the province's continental shelf, concluding that what holds true for West Coast resources also applies to East Coast resources. While Wells was on the winning side, the court disagreed with three of his major arguments: that Newfoundland ended at the low-water mark in 1949; that it did not have constitutional status prior to Confederation to have full rights to continental-shelf resources; and that it was reduced to the status of a Crown colony during the Commission of Government years.

It was around this time that Roger Simmons once again entered Clyde Wells's life. Simmons was first elected for the Liberals in a provincial byelection in November 1973, when Tory cabinet minister Roy Cheeseman resigned. In 1979, when Don Jamieson decided to leave Ottawa and become Newfoundland Liberal leader, Simmons again won in the resulting by-election. Because of technical delays in returning the writs to Ottawa, Simmons spent only six sitting days in Ottawa. Joe Clark's minority government was defeated on a confidence vote over John Crosbie's budget.

Simmons was re-elected in 1980, and in August 1983, after Trudeau bumped Newfoundlander Bill Rompkey in a major cabinet shuffle, Simmons was made minister of state for mines, and once more he set a record, this time for the shortest cabinet career, resigning just ten days later. For several days, both Simmons and Trudeau refused to say why the minister had resigned, Simmons arguing his reasons "far outweigh the public's need to know" and saying he was "most determined" his reasons for quitting cabinet never be made public. Well, he didn't get his wish. It didn't take long for journalists to discover that Simmons was having problems with the tax man and finally, in mid-September he admitted that was why he'd quit. The next day, Simmons was charged in St. John's with five counts of income tax evasion, totalling $5,148.78, by failing to declare $28,013 in income from 1975 to 1978, while he was a member of the Newfoundland legislature. Trudeau was forced to apologize publicly for failing to have a complete security check done on Simmons before appointing him to cabinet.

On September 28, 1983, Simmons entered a plea of not guilty before Judge J. A. Woodrow in St. John's provincial court. Trial was set for late October before Judge John P. Trahey. Simmons was represented by lawyers Norm Whalen of

St. John's and John Sopinka of Toronto. Again, Clyde Wells worked for the federal government, acting as Crown prosecutor in the case.

The issue revolved around a contract Simmons had signed with Bruce Pardy of Project Management and Design Ltd. in 1974 to help the company get school construction contracts in the province. Simmons had been president of the Newfoundland Teachers Federation, and under the agreement he was paid $400 a month for expenses plus one-half of one per cent of the total of projects he helped the company obtain.

Simmons testified he wasn't deliberately trying to avoid taxes; he was just inept at keeping track of his income. He said it was a "miracle" he was only caught once and cited several examples of his "abysmally" negligent attitude toward his personal affairs, including telegrams from the Newfoundland Motor Vehicle department giving him authority "to drive a car for a week" because he forgot to renew his licence, how his insurance policy was cancelled because he forgot to pay the premiums, and how he finally "bit the bullet" and went to the dentist in pain only to learn he needed three wisdom teeth pulled and ten cavities filled.

None of this impressed Wells. While many lawyers shun prosecuting a personal acquaintance to avoid the possible appearance of a conflict, Wells set about prosecuting Simmons with a vengeance, particularly considering that the amount of money was the smallest ever to reach tax court. (The same week the tax department decided to prosecute Simmons, they wrote to a Montreal businessman who owed $167,000 in taxes giving him more time to pay.)

Wells subpoenaed everything, even the expense reports Simmons had filed when he was a Liberal MHA. He told the court it is "beyond coincidence" that Simmons failed to report income he had included in his personal income projection sheets for four straight years. Simmons testified it was "beyond my moral capability" to deliberately avoid paying taxes, but

Wells countered that, as an MHA, Simmons had submitted illegitimate travel claims between St. John's and Kona Beach, a campground Simmons owned in South Brook. During his lengthy summation speech, Wells said Simmons "knew that he did not report the extra income. . . . The evidence is overwhelming, and nothing would be more conclusive other than a confession."

On December 2, 1983, the court agreed with Wells and found Simmons guilty on one charge of tax evasion. Wells told the court the Crown was withdrawing four other charges of making false statements on his 1975 to 1978 income tax returns. Simmons was fined $3500 or three months in jail. He paid. In September 1984, he lost his Burin-St. George's seat to Tory Joe Price by 240 votes. A year later, he ran again for the provincial Liberals and was re-elected. Simmons was serving as interim leader of the Opposition after the Liberals dumped Leo Barry (a former Tory minister who'd had some marital problems) when Wells returned to politics and won the leadership in June 1987. Simmons continued in that role, working with Wells daily, until Wells won a byelection in December 1987. In 1988 Simmons re-entered federal politics, winning the Burin-St. George's seat back from the Tories.

Asked in a 1991 interview what he thought of Wells as a prosecutor, Simmons said, "Well, of course, he's a good lawyer and I knew that before. In 1965 I had him as my lawyer. When you're on the other side, when you're placed in that position, well, you have your thoughts, disappointments, that kind of stuff. But in retrospect, I feel that from his standpoint he was only doing his job. I don't bear grudges very easily anyway, and in this case I'm not sure I have very much to bear a grudge about. On that one, I made my own bed in the sense that I had been negligent in looking after my own affairs. I learned a very valuable lesson, but I brought that on myself."

Asked about his relationship with Wells later in the provincial Liberal caucus, Simmons said it was good. "I don't believe anyone in his caucus, either then or now, has a warm cosy relationship with him. . . . The relationship that Clyde has with his members would have been a fairly proper relationship, a working relationship, but I don't think a personal relationship. I would think I was as close to him in that caucus as anybody was."

Wells's record of attracting major corporate clients continued apace. In late 1982 he represented Newfoundland entrepreneur Harry Steele, president of Newfoundland Capital Corp., in a legal action launched against him by Harold Wareham, former vice-president of Eastern Provincial Airways, of which Steele was a director and major investor. In 1987 Steele would also become a major investor in the new Newfoundland Liberal leader, Clyde Wells. The former commanding officer of the Canadian Forces Base in Gander from 1969 until retiring in 1974, Steele has become one of Newfoundland's most successful entrepreneurs, owning a string of hotels — including the Glynmill in Corner Brook where Smallwood first convinced Wells to enter politics — various resorts, media outlets, and offshore industrial interests.

Wareham claimed that Steele had not honored an irrevocable option Wareham had acquired to purchase 213,774 common shares of EPA in an April 1979 agreement. At the time, Steele borrowed $4.5 million from the Bank of Montreal to buy nearly 600,000 shares of EPA from Andrew Crosbie (John's brother) and two other men, and Wareham claimed he and Steele were to be equal partners in the deal, which would give them a controlling interest in the airline.

But Steele testified he had borrowed the money at his sole risk after Wareham's bank, the Royal Bank of Canada, was not willing to lend more than $3.2 million. He said he only bought the shares because Wareham, vice-president of finance at the time, assured him each share would return a $1 per share annual dividend, enough to cover the cost of servicing the debt.

Instead, in 1979 they returned only 32.5 cents and in 1980 no dividend at all. Steele said he could afford to carry his own part of the deal, but not Wareham's, and he asked Wareham several times to exercise his option and sell his shares, but he refused.

In its ruling on the case on March 3, 1983, the Newfoundland Supreme Court Trial Division dismissed Wareham's claim against Steele. Wareham appealed, and on August 14, 1985, the Appeal Court again dismissed his claim and sided with Steele.

Throughout the 1980s, Wells did not have a partner, only some junior associates to help him out. One reason for that, as a former legal colleague has been quoted as saying, is that "nobody could stand working with him."

Bill Rowe recalls two run-ins he had with Wells during that time, which were unlike any disputes he has ever had with any other lawyer. "I don't remember the specifics now, but on two occasions in my office in St. John's on Water Street, I found myself, Clyde and I, toe-to-toe, standing up in my office, faces six inches apart, shouting at each other, to such an extent that when we left, there was a pall, a quiet over the whole law office, and everybody wondered what was going on. Twice. It's never happened to me before with any other lawyers. It's never happened to me since."

Wells, it seemed, had refused to budge on an offer and, of course, it ended up in court. "He was just so adamant," Rowe says. "I've been in some pretty hard cases with other lawyers . . . but during breaks we would have coffee, just two professionals doing a job. I have never found myself in the position where I was yelling at another lawyer and he was yelling at me."

By the mid-1980s, Wells was earning more than $300,000 and was reputed to be Newfoundland's best-paid lawyer. The Liberals continued to devour their provincial leaders and Wells remained the focus of considerable speculation each time there was a leadership change. In addition to his law practice,

Wells served on the boards of a host of Newfoundland companies. He was appointed to the board of Newfoundland Light and Power in 1978 and elevated to chairman of the board in 1985.

Wells owned his large, two-storey, mortgage-free home on Glenridge Crescent in one of St. John's most prestigious areas, drove a charcoal-grey Audi 5000, had his sailboat moored at the yacht club, and at the time, was supporting his three children who were all in school.

In a 1987 article in the *Evening Telegram*, his stately home was said to "exude an old-world charm that is enhanced by stands of century-old maples and elms which fringe the property. Its well-manicured front lawn overlooks the heart of one of the capital city's most notable 'old money' neighborhoods.

"The interior of the house is equally impressive, with wide hallways and high ceilings adding to the spacious feel of the tastefully decorated rooms," one of those described as a den "dominated by long shelves of leather-bound law books."

Clyde Wells had arrived in the capital, no doubt about it. And now, with money in the bank and Peckford's pugnaciousness wearing thin even on Newfoundlanders, he was ready to ascend the throne.

7

King Clyde

DURING THE 1980S in St. John's, Wells concentrated on building his law firm and solidifying his own social and economic standing in the community. Wells, like John Turner federally, was automatically mentioned as a potential candidate whenever the Liberals dumped one leader for another. But except for offering periodic advice to the Liberals, Wells stayed out of active politics.

But Newfoundlanders were becoming disenchanted with the Tories, in power since Smallwood's defeat. Brian Peckford, popular at the beginning of the decade, was beginning to self-destruct politically by 1987, a year that would mark the beginning of the end for Peckford and deeply influence the life of Wells.

The year began with violent labor protests at the newly reopened Come By Chance oil refinery when Marco Construction, the chief contractor, announced it wouldn't pay union-scale wages. During the same month, the federal government signed the Canada-France Fisheries Agreement, which the Newfoundland government saw as "a secret sellout of northern cod," setting the tone for much of the year in federal-provincial relations. Premier Peckford got into the cucumber business, which was to be his ultimate undoing. He agreed to subsidize what was a proposed $18.7 million joint venture called Sprung, which by means of a hydroponic greenhouse in Mount Pearl was supposed to create tons of fresh veggies and 150 permanent jobs, but ended up costing several million dollars more and creating political and fiscal headaches that haven't yet been completely cured.

On the plus side, even though the inshore fishery suffered its worst season in thirty years, the fisheries overall enjoyed total landings of 500,000 metric tonnes valued at $250 million — $750 million export value — with prices paid for cod up thirty per cent from 1986. Unemployment was "only" 17.1 per cent, the lowest rate in five years, and the provincial budget, forecasting a record deficit of $172.67 million, contained no major tax increases. It was a record year for mineral exploration — 21,000 claims staked, up 6000 from a year earlier — and even the forestry industry made a strong comeback.

Early in the year, in a well-organized campaign, assorted Liberals began to call or gather either at the Wells home or his office to talk about the possibility of the former cabinet minister's going back into politics. Support for Wells had continued strong over the years. A significant block of sitting Liberal MHAs preferring Wells to Leo Barry — latest in a long line of Liberal leaders who followed Smallwood — began to organize a caucus revolt designed to get Barry out and Wells in. Two other prominent Liberals, former leader Ed Roberts and former provincial party president Phil Warren, were also approached. But Wells was the main target.

The campaign wasn't something Clyde was directly involved in, one MHA explained. "He would say, I'm certain, he didn't even know about it. And officially, that's probably true. But I must say I'd be shocked if he hadn't known about it, or suspected it, at least unofficially. It wasn't exactly a state secret. This isn't that big a place, you know."

Leo Barry's marital problems were unearthed in March, giving the pro-Wells conspirators the opportunity they needed to turn up the heat and bring their campaign out into the open. Barry, who as Peckford's energy minister had bolted cabinet and caucus over the offshore dispute, announced March 21 he was stepping down as Liberal leader. He didn't have much choice; after all, his own caucus had publicly called for a leadership convention. But he said he would be a candidate at that June convention for his own job.

Wells decided he would get back into politics. His only problem was the job didn't pay enough. That was the main reason he got out in 1970 and why he stayed out all those years. Veteran Liberal Steve Neary, who also served a term as Liberal leader, says that during the 1970s he twice went to Corner Brook to ask Wells if he planned to run. "The first time he told me no, he'd lose too much, and I got the impression he wouldn't come back into politics until he made his first million. So the second time, I said facetiously, 'Have you made your first million yet?' and he said, 'No, I'm still working on it.'"

This time, however, smelling power, the Liberals were able to raise the money privately that Wells needed to keep himself in the clover, and on April 13 he told the *Evening Telegram* he was "seriously considering" seeking the Liberal leadership. Three weeks earlier, when Barry stepped down, Wells had told the newspaper he would not run. Asked then if he would change his mind, he said, "Not bloody likely."

The real reason Wells changed his mind had nothing to do with ideology and everything to do with the fact that a tight group of wealthy entrepreneurs had fashioned a scheme to supplement the leader's income. On April 15 Wells announced he would resign as chairman of Newfoundland Light and Power at the company's annual general meeting later that month and run for the Liberal leadership. "Many people in the province have come to me and said I have an obligation to run," he pointed out, adding that he'd asked himself why he should make the financial sacrifice. "There's no question there will be a substantial reduction in my income."

Wells said he had been assured by the Liberal party there was enough money in party coffers to supplement his income if he won the leadership and was elected to the house, although, "it wouldn't come close to what I would be able to earn as a practising lawyer." Wells decided once he became leader he would have to close down his private firm, Wells and Co.

All sorts of rumors were flying around St. John's at the time, one claiming the Liberals had a $1 million fund to attract Wells. "I am sure that isn't true," he said. "If it is true, that would come as a complete surprise to me."

Wells flat out denied rumors he was getting financial backing from entrepreneur Harry Steele and Corner Brook construction magnate Harold Lundrigan. On the other hand, he consistently claimed he didn't know who was donating and didn't want to know, which raises the question of which version is correct: if he really didn't know where the money came from, how, for example, did he know whether Steele contributed or not?

Wells said then, "I feel this is the appropriate time for me to run. I know the party does not have a good public image now. But I also considered the economic state of the province, the present government's attitude, which promotes stagnation, and its philosophy that it is immoral for anyone but Newfoundlanders to make a profit in Newfoundland."

Wells insisted that before he took the job as Liberal leader he would have to earn a total of $125,000, the same pay as a Newfoundland Supreme Court justice. At the time, the Liberal leader's salary was $33,888, but because Wells wasn't elected, he would not get paid as an MHA and leader of the Opposition. The Liberal party agreed to supplement his income to the $125,000 level. They would reduce the supplement accordingly once he got elected, and drop it completely when he became premier.

Wells denies there was any private trust find set up to meet his demands, saying that the money came straight from the party's general funds and was paid in equal monthly instalments by cheques issued by party treasurer J. Douglas Cook. "Remember," Wells says, "Peckford got a salary from the Conservative party while he was premier. Oh, he used to say it's only $6000 or $7000 a year, but he did, and he was premier. Yet he could stand in the house and be critical of me. I made the thing public. Everybody knew it was a supplementary salary."

In most quarters, Wells received high praise for being upfront about the supplement. His supporters point to his forthrightness on this issue as one example that proves Wells is a new kind of politician. "I think Clyde Wells is so different from other politicians, so far removed from political reality that it's really impressive," says colorful Newfoundland Liberal MP George Baker, whose brother, Winston, contested the leadership against Wells and is now deputy premier. "I have never met in all my years a politician like Clyde Wells and I never will again. I don't know how long he'll survive, but we will never meet him again. There will never be another person as straightforward as Clyde Wells is. That is a fact."

Nevertheless, while Wells has always said he accepted the extra money, he has never said where it came from, despite several requests from journalists and from Opposition politicians. He hasn't, says Baker, "because he doesn't know. I suggest to you if somebody were to speak to Harry Steele, they could find out."

But Steele also flatly denied it at the time. In an April 1989 interview with journalist Barbara Yaffe in the *Sunday Express* (which Steele owned) she quoted the businessman as saying, "Clyde and I have been friends for a long time, but I have not committed a nickel to him. . . . I don't have any plans [to supplement his income] right now. I might consider supporting anybody, even the NDP, sometime down the road."

Steve Neary, who was Liberal leader between 1982 and 1985, says Wells's statement that the party itself had the funds to supplement his income is not true. "When I was leader of the party, we didn't have a pot to piss in. We owed $400,000 to $500,000. And suddenly, within a couple of years, they can pay him an extra $50,000, plus expenses? He says it came from a general fund of the party. It didn't. We didn't have a general fund. It came from a special fund this board of trustees handled. We as a party didn't have any money. We were trying to keep our creditors off our backs."

Even when Wells won the leadership, Norm Whalen, president of the party's executive board and the defence lawyer in the Simmons case Wells had prosecuted, said the party was about $100,000 in debt. "All political parties in Opposition are like that," Whalen says. "If an election is called we'll have no difficulty raising the funds to fight in an election."

When a reporter asked him about Whalen's comments, Wells testily replied, "I'm not sure that kind of thing should even be discussed in public," an odd reaction for somebody who claims to bring a new openness to the process.

So who did put up the money?

Neary says it was Steele, Lundrigan, and Labrador millionaire Mel Woodward, a former MHA himself. Lundrigan says it wasn't him. He says he's given money to both major parties, but knew nothing about a trust fund for Wells. Neary also says that prominent St. John's lawyer Jim Chalker, a senior partner in the firm of Chalker, Green and Rowe, was named by Wells as trustee of the fund. Chalker, who often opposed Wells in major court cases in the past, concedes that Wells asked him, along with an unnamed businessman and an accountant, to act as one of three trustees with respect to a fund that would be used to supplement his income to $125,000 — a figure arrived at by Wells. Their responsibilities were primarily to look after collection of the money to make sure it was handled properly. As things turned out, says Chalker, the group never really had to do anything, because the money was raised through general Liberal Party funds. He said the turstees did have one meeting, but they never handled or received any money. Wells has since elevated Chalker to chairman of the board of Newfoundland Power and Light Company Ltd., and Cook, the former Liberal treasurer who used to write the cheques for Wells, now works in Chalker's firm, something Chalker insists is a coincidence, with no connection at all to the supplementary-fund issue. Another wealthy traditional Liberal supporter was contractor Tom Hickman, who later became a central figure in the controversial awarding of a $24 million government contract to build three medical centres in Newfoundland, which the Opposition claimed was based on patronage. Hickman says, "I gave nothing to Clyde Wells." Perhaps not, but the answer is ambiguous. Nobody actually handed money directly to Wells to fatten his salary. It was channelled through the party and *then* sent to Wells.

Harry Steele seems quite open about the subject now. "Well, sure, I contributed something," he says. "I know Mel [Woodward] did, too. I don't know how many others did. Why not? When are you going to get a man with the talent Clyde Wells has in Newfoundland?. . . . I've never been involved in partisan politics [but] I'm not going to deny this. I guess there are only a few politicians in Newfoundland I haven't supported, including Frank Moores, Brian Peckford, and Steve Neary.

"Clyde is not one of those . . . fellows like John Lundrigan or Moores or Crosbie. He's different. He wouldn't blink if the hydrogen bomb was going off in his pocket. Clyde made a terrifically large financial sacrifice to go back into politics. He was the highest-paid lawyer in Newfoundland."

Mel Woodward isn't quite as direct as Steele, but he certainly doesn't deny contributing to the special fund for Wells. "He's the one greatest politician we have in Canada," says Woodward, a former Smallwood minister and long-time Liberal backer. "I've known him since 1966. I'm a great supporter of the man himself. He has great principles, an enormous amount of integrity. I was pleased when he came back to run for the leadership. I saw a winner and was very active in getting him to run. I've always contributed to the Liberal party but never to Clyde Wells directly. If it did go to Clyde Wells it had to come out of the Liberal party. You know what I'm saying," Woodward says, laughing. "That's all I'm going to say. Be happy with that."

One Liberal who isn't happy is Neary. "Clyde got a substantial expense account on top of the $50,000 supplement," he says. "We call people like him the original beggars on horseback. During the summer, when the province was falling down around our ears, he was out yachting. He gave himself a $20,000 allowance for entertainment in his house and for fixing up the grounds. His argument was that he didn't take a house from the government. He said he was the only premier who didn't. Joey didn't. As bad as Moores was, at least he paid rent. Clyde took the limos from the cabinet ministers but gave them an $8000-a-year allowance so they can buy a car on instalment, and when they leave, the car is theirs.

"He says about that supplement, because I'm upfront I'm pure. Because [Nova Scotia Premier John] Buchanan wasn't upfront, he got into trouble. But I say, so you're only half a whore. If you disclose the sources of it, then I'd say you're upfront. But if you don't disclose them, you're being a bit hypocritical."

One Newfoundland Liberal said the money raised for this purpose, much of it in $5000 instalments from major contributors, was in fact channelled through the Liberal party instead of into a separate trust fund so that the contributors would be eligible for the generous tax writeoffs for political contributions.

Newfoundland Federation of Labor boss Dave Curtis says that Wells "has had this reputation for honesty and integrity built up to such a high level, mainly by the media, that if anybody else in Canada was getting $50,000 from supposedly unknown sources it would be a scandal. Here, because he announced it, it's seen as yet another example of his integrity. He said he had no idea where the money was coming from. Well, it seems to me the agenda he's brought to this province since becoming premier has been aimed at those Newfoundlanders who could afford to donate $50,000. It didn't come from the local fishermen sending in $5 and $10 in envelopes, I'll tell you that."

When Wells won the leadership in June 1987, a sitting Liberal resigned to make room for him, but Peckford petulantly refused to call a byelection until December. "He wanted to keep me out of the house," says Wells. "Keep me without income. Because the other decision I took, I had to discontinue and terminate my law practice . . . so I had no income during that period . . . so the party paid me a salary. After I became leader of the Opposition, that was significantly reduced because I got paid as leader of the Opposition and they supplemented it. . . . The standard they used, and I'll never forget it, is he should be paid at least as much as what a Supreme Court judge is paid. That's a proper standard. But that was still only a portion of what I was making as a private practitioner. But this became an issue politically at the time, and I believe it was before the election I announced that, if I were elected, that salary supplement would cease. And it did."

Wells insists that to the best of his knowledge a trust fund was never created for him, and that he was paid out of the party's general funds. He thinks it's a sad commentary that this kind of political pressure exists, and politicians are not sufficiently straightforward and honest in dealing with it upfront "where it's somehow unacceptable to pay responsible people who offer for public office a reasonable salary, something even partially comparable to what people in reasonable positions in the private sector earn.

"The head of the Public Service Workers Union in New-foundland makes substantially more than I do as premier, and yet people say there's something wrong with my getting this salary that I did and I have to supplement my living out of my savings," says Wells. "Now if that bothers people, then they should turf me out in the next election. If that makes me unacceptable to operate in that way, then vote against me. I have no problem with that. I have no regrets about that, There was nothing improper about it."

(Actually, union chief Fraser March earned about the same as Wells did last year. Including overtime and perqs, the union paid March $169,000, considerably more than the $103,000 paid to Canadian Labor Congress head Shirley Carr, but about the same as paid to Wells — roughly $140,000, $119,014 of that tax-free, including his $20,000 housing allowance, but not including the cost of his chauffeur-driven limousine. March's salary, of course, is fully taxable.)

Throughout the controversy, Wells displayed an attitude of overwhelming self-absorption. Growing increasingly irritated when reporters asked about the money, he began to snap that he was sick of talking about it. "I'm not going to be a martyr," he once said. "If people don't like that, they can vote against me." Anyway, he insisted, nobody cared about the issue except all those meddling reporters, and he wasn't going to talk about it anymore. So there.

One journalist who was covering Wells regularly at that time was CBC reporter Brian Dubreuil. He said Wells "genuinely didn't get it. He couldn't understand why it was an issue. From his point of view, he needed the money for his house, his boat, his cottage, that kind of thing. And on one level, that's understandable. And honest. But when you're in the poorest province in Canada and you're saying how difficult it is to get by on $125,000, you have to wonder what the unemployed fisherman in Bay de Verde thinks of that. I don't blame the guy for what he did. It's just that he didn't appear to have any understanding of how that attitude would play out there."

Newfoundland is, after all, the poorest province in Canada. It is also the most class-structured, with little middle class to speak of, particularly outside St. John's. The latest Revenue Canada review of tax returns, for example, showed Newfoundlanders had an average 1989 personal income of $17,156, a full $10,000 behind Ontarians, and about $6700 below the Canadian average. In St. John's itself, the average personal income was a relatively heady $22,056 — which was less than half the $48,506 enjoyed by West Vancouver residents — and in one rural area toward Fogo Island, the average personal income was only $13,450.

Typically, Wells turned his decision to seek the Liberal leadership into a moral duty rather than a partisan power play, saying he felt obligated to run because so many people were asking him to. "You can't ignore all that," he said, forgetting that Liberals had been asking him to run since 1971. "If you have some ability and people perceive that you have some ability and are prepared to ask you to be involved and make a contribution, anybody who is in that position does have some obligation to make a contribution in whatever field he can do it."

The outcome was never in doubt. Shortly after he entered the race, Barry got out. At the June 5-6 convention, Wells received 564 of the 643 ballots cast, easily defeating two other candidates, Winston Baker and Ted Noseworthy, prompting a front-page headline in the *Evening Telegram*: King Clyde Crowned.

Later that month, Windsor-Buchans MHA Graham Flight announced he was stepping down so that Wells could gain a seat in a byelection (Flight was rewarded with a cabinet post after the election). When Peckford finally called the byelection for December 17, 1987, Wells won by 428 votes over Tory candidate Sean Power, with New Democrat Helen Joe a distant third.

And so, after nearly seventeen years, the prodigal son of the Liberal party returned to the scene of his first political adventures, only this time he was no longer the prince-in-waiting. He was the new king, come to rescue his subjects from the dreaded Tories.

Peckford, who stayed on as premier for a little over a year with Wells leading the Opposition, says, "The whole thread of rigidity seems to flow through most of the things that I know about the man. . . . He spent more time attacking my style than the substance of what I said, but that's politics. . . . Still, there's an irony in all those speeches he made saying that all Peckford wants to do is fight, you won't get anywhere fighting, you have to be conciliatory. . . . Well, he sure wasn't conciliatory in Meech Lake, was he?

"In watching him perform, I don't question his integrity and the fact he means what he says. But there seems to be a throwback to the 60s in the sense that, and Smallwood took this narrow view, too, on a whole range of issues they take very narrow views of their responsibilities and obligations as a provincial government. It's all thrown over to the federal government. He is not a provincialist at all, and in that way he's more like Smallwood, who believed in an extremely strong central government, almost the 'Uncle Ottawa' idea that Moores attacked when he won his first election. . . . You almost get that impression, that his whole vision of Canada and the relationship between Ottawa and St. John's as being far more similar to the way Smallwood performed in the 1960s, as opposed to the way Moores or myself performed during the 70s and 80s."

When former fisheries minister Tom Rideout won the Conservative leadership in early 1989 (Peckford resigned to enter the private consulting business on the offshore), the first thing he did was commission Toronto pollster Allan Gregg of Decima to tap the mood of the electorate. According to Gregg, now was the time to strike. Wells, essentially, had built a reputation in the house as somebody who droned on at great length with dull, unimaginative, statistically laden speeches more wooden even than Rideout's. Based on the Decima finding that the Tories enjoyed a fifty-one to thirty per cent lead over Wells and the Liberals, Rideout called a snap election for April 20, a decision that would make him Canada's shortest-reigning premier ever, and set the scene for Wells to become a national household name.

Going into the campaign, the Tories held thirty-four of the fifty-two seats in the house, the Liberals, fourteen, the NDP, two. Early in the campaign, Wells displayed his stiff, impersonal style, the antithesis of Newfoundland politicians on the stump, or anywhere else for that matter. The historical isolation of Newfoundlanders, particularly those outside the few major centres, has reared a people with some unique characteristics. The challenge of survival has imbued in them a remarkable resilience to constant hardships, along with deeply ingrained values of familial kinship, a striking level of unselfish warmth and hospitality, and yes, a fatalistic sense of humor, qualities that Wells, at least externally, seems to lack. He is, or seems to be, a most unNewfoundlandish Newfoundlander. The fishermen's union boss Richard Cashin, who has known him since the early 1960s, once said of Wells, "He's not of this place."

Life on the Rock has never been easy. But for all its hardship, nothing tears at the hearts of Newfoundlanders more than the need for so many of their sons to go down the road looking for work. Nothing. In her book, *Outport*, author Candace Cochrane quotes the poignant experiences of one rural Newfoundlander: "We misses the young feller now. We reared him. Took him when he wasn't a year old. His mother had a big family out to the Grey Islands. I went out and brought him in and he was here then until he was twenty. That fall he went away. He won't be back. I don't imagine he'll leave his job now. He's making good money. So I don't believe he'll come back for fishing. I thinks some hard of it. I wouldn't wish for him to be gone, not for all that's in the world today."

Even Wells, it seems, was not immune to the scourge of what is bureaucratically referred to as out-migration, although at the beginning of the campaign, you wouldn't have known it. But in mid-campaign, at a rally in Corner Brook, his attitude suddenly changed. *Globe and Mail* reporter Kevin Cox recalls that he and some other reporters were chatting with Cliff Wells, Clyde's brother, who was working as a driver in the campaign — the Liberal campaign bus was dubbed the Wells Express. "I said to him that Clyde comes across as a bit boring. He said, 'Oh, I'm sure Clyde wouldn't agree with that.' So I said, 'Well, he doesn't shown any compassion, any feelings.' That was the night, whether there's a direct connection or not, he went to the arena and gave his passionate 'Let's bring the boys home' speech. He had little old ladies in tears that night, and he used that theme over and over again in the campaign. We were all flabbergasted he showed so much emotion. He rarely does."

Wells told the Liberals that night his son had to take his grandson away from his doting grandfather because "there's no work here. There's not a person here who doesn't have a brother or a sister or a son or a daughter who had to leave because there hasn't been any opportunity in this province to make a living in the last ten years."

For the rest of the campaign Wells used the example of his own son and grandson to promise that when he became premier, he'd bring the boys home — "every mother's son" he used to say. Clearly, Wells had struck a chord. People began showing up at Liberal rallies with signs saying BRING OUR CHILDREN HOME.

Wells used the theme to great advantage during the televised leaders' debate when he attacked the Tory record. "They've driven 35,000 people out of the province since 1981 to Toronto, or Calgary, or Edmonton to find work. . . . They've failed their fundamental responsibility to provide an opportunity for our young people to come out of school and expect to find a job here with their family and relatives." Never mind that has always been the case in Newfoundland, and has continued since Wells has been premier. The theme pulled at the heartstrings of all Newfoundlanders.

While the tactic clearly worked for Wells, his son Mark's version of his own departure from the Rock is not quite as heart-wrenching as the version Wells offered voters. "I came to Ottawa in 1988 for Bell Northern Research. I had arranged a job a few months before graduating. After I graduated, I came up here to work. No, there are jobs in Newfoundland, but no jobs that I was interested in. I'm interested in designing electronic circuits, a very high-end, high-tech industry, and there isn't anything in Newfoundland that can come close to BNR in terms of resources and expertise and that kind of thing."

And Wells himself, in an Canadian Press interview late in the campaign, admitted that it was all part of a deliberate plan: "Quite a number of people felt I was too quiet as leader, and they expected a lot of ranting and raving all the time," he said. "We decided as a deliberate policy and a deliberate tactic not to do that, but to wait and hold it for the campaign."

Since the election, out-migration has continued. Granted, it has slowed down, but that's mainly because Ontario, the traditional destination for most Newfoundlanders, has been so ravaged by the recession that there are no jobs to go down the road to. Even so, in 1990 there was a total out-migration of 4500. For all this, however, Wells says accusations by the Opposition that he has failed in his campaign to bring home "every mother's son" are false because "there never was any such campaign . . . it wasn't real."

That assertion may come as a surprise to many who heard his campaign speeches, or those who read the following quote in his campaign literature: "This election is about change. We must change direction in Newfoundland and Labrador. We must stop our downward economic slide and growing unemployment. We must stop the draining of our people to other parts of Canada. We must keep our young people and their talents and energies here at home to build our province's future. Now is the time for a real change."

Today, Wells insists his words are being deliberately misconstrued by his critics, both the Opposition politicians and the unions.

"The position I took was, look, we've got to try to rebuild the economy of this province so that it is capable of generating employment opportunities for our people without having to leave the province, and there's lots of others who have left in the past, who, if we get the economy moving to that degree, would in all probability want to come home. If they do, fine. If they want to stay where they are, fine. At least give them the choice. At least we have a responsibility to try and create a circumstance where they will have the option to choose to stay in Newfoundland where there's reasonable economic opportunity.

"But I made it quite clear that you can't achieve this overnight. This takes time to do. It may not even be possible to achieve it in any event, but nonetheless you have to try. That was my position during the campaign, because we had deteriorated over the years far worse than people really ever understood."

He goes on to say the province's once significant population growth stopped through the 80s right along with the economy. "The [Peckford] policy was to get as much help and money as you could out of the federal government. That was the way to deal with Newfoundland's economic problems. Instead of generating economic activity in the private sector, the focus was on getting more from the federal government, more support and UI and other forms of payment. This is why I felt that whole approach had to stop."

And so, economic development to provide economic opportunities without having to rely on federal economic support was the focus of his campaign. But after the election, the Opposition cast the focus in the form of a campaign promise. "It now became a political promise to bring every mother's son home. . . . There never was any such thing. That was a fabrication of the Opposition. The campaign position was clear. It's on the record. There are all kinds of tapes about what I said and what I didn't say. . . . There never was a campaign to bring every mother's son home."

During the campaign interviews, Wells also bristled at the suggestion that his appearance of wealth and privilege made it difficult for him to relate to outport Newfoundlanders. "I went to a one-room school with a potbelly stove. I was the second oldest of nine children and my father worked in the freight shed on the railway. I went to the beach for my mother in the morning and bought codfish for five cents a pound for our dinner."

Liberal MP George Baker argues that Wells doesn't like to campaign at all. Nor does he see any point in spending too much money campaigning and advertising or making campaign promises he can't keep. Baker tells of campaigning for Wells in several ridings where the Tories had promised to build an indoor ice rink, but Wells wouldn't promise them anything. "This was getting really serious. Each of our candidates was saying to me, 'Look, I'm going to lose. What are we going to do? We don't have a platform. Wells is going around and he's talking about being responsible and he doesn't promise anything.' His philosophy was, you judge me during the end of my term, I'm not going to promise a thing, and I'm not going to treat Liberal districts any different than the Tory districts or the NDP districts. This was unheard of in Newfoundland politics. . . . One of the main reasons so many people cross the floor in Newfoundland is to get on the government side so they can deliver more to their riding.

"And a stadium! My goodness, all they've ever watched is CBC and CTV. They haven't got cable in most of these small communities. All they can ever get is this faraway signal on the CBC's remote coverage plan. So they watch hockey, and this would be a big thing to have a stadium. So when a fellow says he's going to cross the floor to get this, that's a great push. And that's the odd thing. We had the Tories going all over the province promising stadiums. We were joking that if they built them all, we could skate around the entire province."

So where, then, Baker asks, was the attractiveness of Clyde Wells, who was saying the province had to retain its fiscal credibility, couldn't overspend, couldn't borrow money, couldn't make promises, and couldn't do major capital works? This was the great dichotomy in the political scene in Newfoundland.

Baker had never got involved in provincial politics before, even when his brother Winston ran against Wells for the leadership. But the reason he campaigned for Clyde Wells was the man's attraction, coupled with the knowledge that it wasn't going to do Baker any harm in his riding after the election, "because he wasn't promising anything. I wouldn't have to go to the community after and have the community say, well, all right, Baker, where's the arena, where's the water, where's the pavement? Because every meeting [Wells] was at he made it clear that you're not getting anything nobody else is getting.

"I think Clyde Wells is not a politician at all in the traditional sense. He's apolitical, and I believe that in the majority of people's minds, that's what makes him more attractive as an individual." Baker is not sure how many terms Wells will get elected by being that way, because Newfoundlanders are an extremely political bunch. "I mean, the elections prior to Clyde Wells are based on who could outpromise whom, and the elections were always timed with major events. Smallwood was a master at it.

"But with Clyde, I think it goes back to this thing about being a breath of fresh air. It's almost like he's there only for a short time to clean house, to change the perception of people that they get everything from politicians. In Newfoundland, I can't overstress that. I had the largest phone bill in Ottawa for ten years, and that's because everybody comes to you for everything. I spent the last three weeks filling out applications for medical school and applications for law school for people. I will spend at least three weeks doing income tax for people each year in March. I appear before the tax board of Canada on a regular basis with appeals against Revenue Canada. I appear before federal judges appealing Unemployment Insurance cases. Everything you want in Newfoundland, you go to the politician. I mean everything. About your divorce, about your house being lost, your credit company calling you, your marriage, everything. Your politician is supposed to be there."

And then, says Baker, along came Clyde Wells, who didn't operate that way. "If you've got a problem, he says you go try to fix it first, and if you don't have any success, then we'll look into it for you."

Wells did, however, unveil an $87 million program to help out in education, health, and water and sewage between rural and urban areas, which was $10 million more than the program announced by Rideout. Wells was helped, one assumes inadvertently, by the federal Tories who, among other things, messed up the Canada-France fishing treaty by giving away northern cod to placate the French, changed the rules for Unemployment Insurance, making it tougher for seasonal workers to get, and announced a delay in the Hibernia offshore oil project during the campaign.

Then, of course, there was Sprung, Peckford's pet $22 million scheme to grow cucumbers, which went into receivership just as the campaign was getting organized. At a university debate just over a week from election day, Rideout seemed to be winning points with the audience by calling Wells "the man of the 60s," but he lost the momentum when students began chanting, "Mr. Cucumber, Mr. Cucumber."

Ironically, Wells sought and received campaign advice and workers from two other Liberals — Ontario's David Peterson and New Brunswick's Frank McKenna — both of whom, along with PEI's Joe Ghiz, would develop a visceral dislike for Wells during the Meech Lake process.

Yet for all the outside help and the province-wide disenchantment with the Tories, both the provincial and federal varieties, Wells was lucky to win, especially by such a solid majority. It was one of those victories, like Bob Rae's in Ontario, where the votes just happen to split the right way and electoral purists point to as an example of the flaws in our system. He won, yes. But Newfoundlanders didn't exactly take him warmly into their hearts and minds. The Tories actually received one per cent more of the popular vote, forty-eight to forty-seven per cent.

Rex Murphy, who had worked for Leo Barry and briefly for Wells when he first won the leadership, says it wasn't a matter of the Liberals winning the campaign but rather of the Tories losing. "Peckford burnt himself out and became egregiously vulgar. The Liberals were due back. It's as simple as that. Anyone who thinks the Liberals won the election is wrong. The PCs lost. They strangled themselves. Peckford was smoking cigars on the elevators, going off to the Cayman Islands. He had simply run the gambit . . . and Tom Rideout had the intuition of a beach rock. There was no way this man was going to win, and no way, barring a mass rape on the beach, that the Liberals were going to lose." Clyde Wells's getting in had been no great triumph. The only thing he'd offered was a contrast in style and he'd benefited from a nascent discontent with politics in general.

In addition, says Murphy, Barry had made great inroads into Tory strength in the 1985 election. "That election looked like a Tory sweep. They won thirty-seven to fourteen, but it was really a lot closer than that. Some 1100 votes spread over twelve seats would have given the Liberals a solid majority, so even before Clyde, they were already close to unseating Peckford. In Peckford's last three years, he was doing everything possible to make people angry at him. He was brilliant at it. And the Liberals had Clyde, who was clean. He came from a distance. He had a fairly good slate of candidates, which wasn't completely infested by lawyers. By Newfoundland standards, it was about as good as you're going to get."

Even though by the end of the campaign, Wells seemed to be catching on with the electorate, or was at least seen as a lesser evil than another term with the Tories, the Liberal campaign got a jolt just five days before the April 20 election when the *Evening Telegram* published an Omnifacts poll giving Rideout an eleven-point lead over Wells. The next day, the *Sunday Express* published another poll by Research Associates (RASE) that gave the Tories a six-point edge.

Wells has publicly denied what happened next, events first reported in the author's 1989 book *Margin of Error*, on public opinion polling. Despite his denials, the story has been confirmed by someone who has first-hand knowledge of it.

The day the RASE poll was published, Wells was campaigning in Renews, a small community on the southeastern shore of the Avalon Peninsula where the *Mayflower* stopped off for supplies during her sixty-six-day journey from Plymouth to the New World in 1620. Wells and his officials were debating how to respond to the polls. As one person who witnessed the event tells it, Wells "was saying, 'We didn't get a God damned poll done, but we're going to get some people on the phone to do one.' Then an aide said, 'Does it make any difference?' and everybody agreed it didn't, so we just decided to make one up."

Which is exactly what they did. That night, four senior Liberals, two from Gander and two from St. John's, made up their own poll over a conference telephone call. The main argument was "whether it should show us way ahead or show us in a tight battle with the Tories. We were convinced we were going to win, but we wanted to invent a poll just to balance things out in case too many people believed the published polls."

The next day, the *Evening Telegram*'s main front-page story was "Poll Politics: Who Has the Momentum?" in which it reported a Liberal poll released that morning gave them a 3.5 per cent edge, 49.1 to 45.6 over the Tories. It said 421 Newfoundlanders were polled by telephone the night before by "research professionals within the Liberal campaign organization," supplemented with data from an unnamed "major national polling organization." The Liberal insider says, "The whole thing was bullshit. The figures were just pulled out of the air. Clyde knew about it. We told him it was concocted when we gave him the numbers. Hell, as it turned out, we were a lot closer than the so-called legitimate polls anyway. At least we picked the right winner."

Wells won thirty-one seats, although he lost Humber East to Tory deputy premier Lynn Verge by 138 votes. The Tories were reduced to twenty-one seats. The NDP, which had expected to make a major breakthrough, lost the only seat it had.

Wells subsequently claimed the polling story was a "lie. . . . I can say to you with complete certainty that if anybody concocted any polls, I know nothing about it; but to the best of my knowledge, the poll was a real and valid poll" conducted by the Liberal party. That, of course, was the point. It was conducted by some of his senior Liberal supporters, not by a polling firm, and Wells has never suggested the name of a pollster or produced any evidence to show there actually was a poll conducted. Journalist Michael Harris was telephoned after the publication of *Margin of Error* by a "very senior Liberal" and grilled about the author's source for this story. "Obviously they wanted to find out who spilled the beans," said Harris. "At the time, Clyde was setting up his own political advisory group, and he didn't want the guy who leaked the story to be part of it. This guy told me he wasn't calling on

Clyde's instructions, he was just calling on his own. Yeah, well, if you believe that. . . ."

Much to the delight of two hundred party faithful at his Corner Brook headquarters on election night, Wells lifted his five-year-old grandson Nicholas into the air and said, "My favorite Liberal," and he later dismissed his loss to Verge as "a minor detail," saying he'd ask one of his colleagues to step down "very quickly" so he could win a seat in a byelection.

A few days later Liberal MHA Eddy Joyce stepped aside for Wells and was hired to run his Corner Brook office. Wells was elected by acclamation in the Bay of Islands district adjacent to Corner Brook after Rideout announced the Tories were unable to convince a "credible" candidate to run against Wells and the NDP, which had practically disappeared in the election, and said it was more important for them to direct their energies at long-term party objectives.

On May 5 Rideout arrived at Government House and informed Lieutenant-Governor James McGrath he was stepping down as premier in forty-four days. Two hours later, Wells arrived to say he was stepping up. And not just Newfoundlanders, but Canadians coast to coast, were about to sit up and take notice.

8

The Gathering Storm

THE HAMLET OF Port Saunders, tucked neatly alongside Ingornachoix Bay on the rugged coastline of Newfoundland's Great Northern Peninsula, is a powerful magnet for sports fishermen, drawn to the place by its nearby ponds and two major salmon rivers — East and Torrent.

On May 1, 1987, Clyde Wells was in the tiny community, but he wasn't fishing for salmon. He was attempting to lure delegates in his campaign for the June 6 Liberal leadership contest. That's when he heard the news on CBC radio that Brian Mulroney and the ten provincial premiers had signed the Meech Lake accord.

After a phone call to his office in St. John's, Wells was faxed the highlights of the accord, and he immediately sat down at the desk in his modest motel room and made eight pages of handwritten notes outlining what he saw as the flaws in the deal.

Mulroney had called it "a good day for Canada." Quebec's Robert Bourassa said it was "a historic breakthrough for Quebec as a Canadian partner." Clyde Wells didn't agree. And never would.

Indeed, before he had spoken to anyone about the deal — and that includes Pierre Trudeau — Wells immediately zeroed in on what, for him, would become an insurmountable problem: "Is it intended that this will permit total veto power in Quebec? How will this affect Charter rights in Quebec?" And he wrote that the unanimity requirement in the new amending formula would "render virtually impossible fair and proper Senate reform."

Unlike Peckford, the passionate provincialist, Wells is a strident centralist, a leader of the poorest province in the land who, instead of seeking more powers for his province, has sought less; and a man who has asked aloud many times what use is power when there is no money to pay for the things you have jurisdiction over. "We now have complete power over eduction but no money, complete power over hospitals and we're having to close wards," he says.

For the majority of English Canadians, Wells would become not only a hero, but a man with the courage of his convictions, a politician prepared to put principle before power. As Richard Gwyn describes it, Wells became to most English Canadians "a populist bard — a constitutional Milton Acorn of Canadianism, of the idea of a community larger than the sum of its parts."

Mind you, not all the support he garnered sprung from such noble ideals. Some of it, certainly, was because Wells was seen as sticking it to the French. And while he consistently disavowed supporting such views himself — and, on one level may even have meant it — when he got to the point of waving his letters of support around, he didn't distinguish between those writers who were genuinely troubled by the accord, as many were, and the bigots who adopted Wells as their only chance to screw Quebec.

Meech boosters such as Mulroney and erstwhile Ontario Premier David Peterson didn't help by going around the country telling everyone that a rejection of Meech would be a rejection of Quebec, a scenario based on the false notion that Canada had turned its back on René Lévesque in 1981 rather than that Lévesque had turned his back on a deal with the rest of Canada.

Mulroney conveniently forgot the fact that when he publicly congratulated Trudeau after the constitutional deal, he said only a fool would believe that Lévesque, the separatist, had wanted to sign a pact with Canada. This is what Mulroney wrote in 1981: "Should we have been surprised with the results? . . . René Lévesque's mission in life is the dismemberment of Canada . . . why should we be surprised because Mr. Lévesque has refused to agree with a concrete gesture that would prove Canadian federalism is, in effect, flexible and can work? To do this would be to demolish all of his beliefs and vitiate his entire political action."

And Lévesque himself, in his May 19, 1981 opening address to Quebec's thirty-second legislature, called Ottawa's constitutional proposals "unjustifiable and immoral," and pledged to do everything in his power to block Trudeau's plan to patriate the British North America Act. Does this sound like a man who was bargaining in good faith, only to be betrayed by Trudeau and English Canada?

Nevertheless, politicians of all stripes, federal and provincial, spent the three years between the birth and the death of Meech preaching the spiteful gospel that a "no" to Meech was a "no" to Quebec. No wonder then, that when Meech died in June 1990, polls showed that most English Canadians did not see the failure of the accord as a rejection of Quebec, while almost every Quebecer did.

But Wells, at least in the beginning, was strictly his own man expressing his own views. Instantly, in that motel room in Port Saunders, all the teachings of K.C. Wheare and Mose Morgan, reinforced by his own constitutional experiences and buoyed by his remarkable self-confidence, came flooding back to him. He couldn't have known then whether or not his stand would be popular. Nor could he have known those who opposed him would accuse him of being Trudeau's stalking horse, or that Mulroney, Peterson, McKenna, and Ghiz in particular would come to despise him, or that the majority of Quebecers would see him as their mortal enemy. What he knew at that moment, or at least believed — which for Wells is the same thing — was that the deal was flawed and needed to be fixed. And he intended to dedicate himself to fixing it. The fact that he wasn't yet Liberal leader, let alone premier, was a technicality. He knew his destiny had been set.

In 1983, the year he won the federal Tory leadership, Mulroney published a book called *Where I Stand*. In light of what happened at Meech — and what is happening even now — it is well worth remembering what Mulroney had to say about the 1980 resolution that led to the patriated Constitution and the Charter of Rights and Freedoms.

First, he praised the amending formula requiring approval of seven provinces with at least fifty per cent of the Canadian population, writing, "After all, unanimity has never been an evident characteristic of the history of our country. And it seems to be even less so today." It was, of course, the unanimity required for approval of Meech that was its ultimate undoing.

And this is how Mulroney said the constitutional resolution should be handled by parliamentarians: "I suggest that the Resolution be referred to the Special Committee of the House, a Committee enlarged to include the Premiers of the provinces or their special delegates. If they wished, the Premiers could consult their legislatures prior to attendance, and the time-frames in the Resolution could be adjusted to accommodate this.

"The debate would be *entirely open to the public at all times* [author's emphasis]. There would be no sessions behind closed doors. Canadians could see and judge those who have been elected to serve them and determine if, in the interest of a more generous country, they have really answered an urgent and irresistible call to grandeur."

That was before Mulroney locked the premiers in a room at Meech Lake, and later at the Langevin Block, and kept them there, away from public view, until they hammered out a deal; before he repeated the same techniques in June 1990; before he rolled the dice on Canada's future and came up snake's eyes.

On March 3, 1985, Quebec Liberals had set five conditions that had to be met before they would sign the 1982 Constitution Act. Bourassa won the Quebec election December 2, and on May 9, 1986, Quebec's Intergovernmental Affairs Minister Gil Rémillard outlined the five specific Quebec demands at a conference at Mont Gabriel. Quebec wanted a veto over all future amendments, recognition of Quebec as a "distinct society," limits on federal powers to spend in areas of provincial jurisdiction, a role in the appointment of Supreme Court judges, and more constitutional power over immigration.

That, of course, set the wheels in motion, prompting Mulroney in July to appoint Senator Lowell Murray to begin a new round of talks with Quebec. In August the premiers issued the Edmonton Declaration, agreeing to deal only with Quebec issues at the next constitutional conference, and on March 5-6, 1987, the first full federal-provincial meeting on the demands was held in Ottawa. Talks continued throughout the spring, and on April 30, at Meech Lake, they reached agreement to amend the Constitution.

On May 27 Trudeau launched a detailed attack on the deal in newspapers in Quebec and Toronto, but in a late-night session at the Langevin Block across Wellington Street from Parliament Hill, the eleven first ministers reached a unanimous agreement on the accord. Three weeks later, the Quebec National Assembly ratified it, and a month after that, Trudeau once again attacked the deal before a joint Senate-Commons committee. The next day, August 28, the premiers agreed not to reopen the accord, and the next month, the Senate-Commons committee recommended adoption with no changes. One by one, the players began ratifying the accord: Saskatchewan, September 23; Alberta, December 7; Prince Edward Island, May 13; Nova Scotia, May 25; the House of Commons, June 22; British Columbia and Ontario, June 29; and finally, Newfoundland, July 7.

The Meech Lake accord gave Bourassa all he had asked for and more. First and foremost, it recognized that Quebec "constitutes within Canada a distinct society." It gave Quebec greater control over both immigration and discretionary spending powers, as well as giving the provinces a voice in Supreme Court appointments. The eleven leaders also pledged to hold an annual constitutional conference, commit themselves to Senate reform — just what sort of reform was not delineated — and at Peckford's insistence, later dropped at Wells's insistence, a pledge to deal with serious problems in the fishing industry.

One thing it didn't do, which would also come back in the end to haunt the deal, is offer anything to Canada's native community. A constitutional conference in March 1987 on native issues ended in complete failure when four premiers rejected its proposals and Bourassa boycotted the meeting, sending one of his ministers instead.

By the time Wells took power April 20, 1989, the only provinces that hadn't ratified the accord were New Brunswick and Manitoba. On October 13, 1987, Liberal Frank McKenna had demolished Richard Hatfield's Tories, winning every single seat in New Brunswick. The next fall, McKenna opened public hearings on the accord and in March 1989 he announced details of a companion resolution, which Mulroney said would be studied by a special Commons committee.

In Manitoba, the situation was far more tenuous. Tory Gary Filmon had won a minority in the April 26, 1988, election, but

Halifax-born Liberal Leader Sharon Carstairs had stormed from obscurity to a strong second place, largely on the strength of her anti-Meech campaign, leaving New Democrat Gary Doer, who had been stuck with the collapsing remnants of Howard Pawley's regime, in third place. Among the few NDP members who did survive was a soft-spoken native from Red Sucker Lake named Elijah Harper. In the end, Harper and Wells would come to share much of the blame — or the credit — for the death of the accord.

Mulroney was certainly doing his best to pressure both McKenna and Filmon to approve the accord. At a four-hour first ministers' meeting on February 27, 1989, Filmon said, "We in Manitoba cannot approve the Meech Lake accord unless we have certain understandings and accommodations." McKenna said, "Did they convince us? I guess the answer is no."

A sombre-looking Mulroney once again raised the spectre of Quebec separatism if the accord failed. "This is very serious business," he said. "There are realities ongoing in the province of Quebec and elsewhere that would be ignored only at very considerable risk and peril."

Peckford, as premier, left the meeting without comment. He resigned the next month and Rideout took over.

While the accord was a major issue during the Manitoba election, it was not raised at all during the Newfoundland campaign, although Wells consistently made his views known to anybody who asked, mainly mainland journalists. As Opposition leader, Wells had spoken in the house against Peckford's motion to approve the accord and announced then that, if he became premier before the rest of the provinces had approved it, he would take steps to rescind it.

For those who still hadn't noticed what his view was, Wells launched an attack on the accord April 21, 1989, at his first press conference as premier-elect, at the Glynmill Inn in Corner Brook just one day after winning the election. Announcing that the government he leads "will do what is right and proper," Wells left no doubt what he thought of Meech. "I don't want to be difficult to get along with, I don't want to create any problems, but I will not shirk from doing whatever is necessary to protect the long-term interests of this province and . . . Canada," he said. "I'm not creating a bargaining chip. We're not talking about cabbage, or kilowatts of power, or barrels of oil. We're talking about the Constitution of this country for the next century."

He said the accord's "distinct society" clause would give Quebec the "special status the whole country, including Quebec, rejected in the early 1980s." In addition, he said small provinces would never gain economic justice within Canada unless the Senate was reformed to redress the domination of Central Canada in the Commons, and Meech's unanimity requirements rendered Senate reform "practically impossible."

From the outset, Wells had three major concerns with Meech: the impact of the distinct society clause; what he saw as the threat to meaningful Senate reform; and what he saw as the disadvantage for poorer provinces, such as his own, from what he called "the unrestricted limitation of the federal government's spending powers" in the accord.

It wasn't that federal authorities didn't know what Wells was saying. Reacting to Wells's initial news conference as premier-elect, for example, Mulroney's Quebec lieutenant Lucien Bouchard — who later bolted from the Tory benches and headed up the separatist Bloc Québécois — angrily rejected Wells's views and said that failure to approve the deal would rekindle Quebec separatism. Nor was Wells cowed by obvious threats from both Ottawa and Quebec City. Bourassa, for example, told reporters the day after Wells won the election that Newfoundland's current unemployment rate was sixteen per cent. "Newfoundland needs a great deal of economic development, and I think that one way of favoring that development is by having good relations with its neighbor — Quebec — and with the federal government in Ottawa, which is also very attached to the Meech Lake agreement."

At the same time, Crosbie, who'd joined the Tories after losing the leadership to Smallwood in 1968 and won a federal byelection in 1976, set the tone for what was to become a growing animosity between the two former friends and colleagues, saying that if Wells revoked Newfoundland's approval of the accord, the move would certainly affect his party's relationship with the Newfoundland government. "We'll play ball with them [Liberals] if they'll play ball with us. However, if they want . . . to reopen old issues like Meech Lake and so on, then we'll have to reassess the situation." Wells, of course, had no intention of playing ball with anyone, or at least not by their rules. One would not expect a premier of such a poor province to be prepared to risk economic reprisals to hold on to what he saw as the principles of a constitutional deal. Many in Ottawa thought Wells was bluffing, that when it came down to the short strokes, he would trade off his support for a federal program.

Looking back, Crosbie says the federal government underestimated Wells's determination, even though he kept telling them they should respond. Crosbie said if the island were sinking and the only way for Clyde to save the island was to agree to Meech Lake, "he'd go down with the island. . . . He's a strange bird to be in politics, because he's not prepared to compromise. I mean, it's very difficult to have a dialogue with Clyde. Personally I think that politicians who are too principled are a real bloody menace. You know, they're fanatics and they endanger the system. That's how I'd categorize Clyde, a bloody fanatic.

"The day he got elected," Crosbie continues, "I called him and told him not to go buggering around with the Meech Lake accord because I knew how important it was to Mulroney and to the federal government, that we should work together and see what we could get for Newfoundland, that this was not the way to get anything out of Ottawa by starting to interfere with Meech Lake. I told him we had to be practical, but Clyde wouldn't go along with that at all. He said there was nothing more important than the Constitution, that it would go on for a thousand years whether Newfoundland got X, Y, or Z in programs for the present day. That's a very short-term matter, he told me.

"I tried to warn all the geniuses [in Ottawa] who were in charge of Meech Lake that he was going to be trouble, that it was serious, and then a few months later he had the bloody House of Assembly revoke the Meech Lake resolution. So there was certainly enough warning," says Crosbie. "They underestimated him. The theory was that Clyde would have to fall in line, that Clyde can't stand up by himself. They didn't appreciate the nature of the beast they were up against.

"Mind you, Clyde's a hard one to deal with. My experience is that most of his fellow premiers hate his guts. They get puce in the face if you mention Clyde to them. So whether it would have done any good or not to try to make peace with him earlier, who knows? But it couldn't have done any harm."

On May 25, during his first throne speech. Wells promised to push for changes in the accord and ask the house to rescind its earlier resolution ratifying the agreement. Wells said he was prepared to meet other governments to discuss the deal openly, but would not barter Newfoundland's future. "I'm not prepared to 'agree to it or you won't get regional development dollars,'" he said. "I'm prepared to deal with it honestly."

In an interview with the *Toronto Star* in June he said Meech Lake would doom the have-not areas. "I want us to have a fair opportunity to be a full participating province of this country. Meech Lake would stop that dead in its tracks." He said the other nine provinces should "bend over backwards wherever possible" to get Quebec to return to the constitutional fold, but "in my opinion the economic consequences [of passing the accord] are worse, infinitely worse, and more certain [than the consequences of rejecting it]. It may not be adverse economic consequences to either Ontario or Quebec. But it is certainly adverse economic consequences to smaller provinces like Newfoundland that would keep us forever in a state of have-not, begging for handouts."

And so it went throughout that summer and fall, Ottawa and many premiers attacking Wells, and Wells attacking back. While he wasn't gaining any support among the politicians, Wells appeared to be winning over the public. He received a standing ovation at a Liberal luncheon in downtown Toronto when he attacked Mulroney, Bourassa, and Peterson for "scare mongering" to save the accord. He said he was tired of Mulroney and others accusing critics of the accord of trying to break up the country. "All that says to me is that there is a lack of confidence in the merits of their position, and they're dealing with it behind this mask. Set aside that mask and deal with it on the issues."

At the annual summer meeting of eastern premiers chaired by Robert Bourassa at the Quebec resort of Montebello Wells at one point was refused entry by a Québec Sûreté officer because he was not wearing the special lapel pin that would have given him access. Why wasn't he wearing it? Because it featured a map of Quebec that included Labrador, a rather thoughtless gesture that not only underscored the historic boundary grievance between the two provinces, but served as a visual reminder to Wells that Quebec had aspirations to include Labrador within its boundaries. When Wells did get into the room, he told his fellow premiers they had too much power already. "Premiers should not be involved in the exercise of national legislative power in a federal state," he said, a unique message to a group whose raison d'être has been to gang up on Ottawa to gain more power for themselves. "Provincial premiers should be exercising provincial powers. They shouldn't be transferring over and exercising the national powers, because their focus, their way of thinking, and their obligations are to the confined provincial interest."

Then, moving into his favorite theme, Wells said, "That's why we should be electing senators to a national institution that will exercise the national legislative power." According to him, a Triple-E (elected, effective, and equal) Senate would "diminish the level of dissension and differences in the country."

In addition to his opposition to Meech itself, Wells was furious that neither Mulroney nor Federal-Provincial Relations Minister Senator Lowell Murray had attempted to meet with him since his election to discuss the accord. Mulroney didn't even make the customary congratulatory call when Wells won the April provincial election. One close friend said that Wells was both "hurt and furious" that he was being "deliberately ignored" by Mulroney. Asked about the federal government's attitude to Wells by *Globe and Mail* reporter Susan Delacourt in a late September interview, Murray got caught with his arrogance showing when he said he expected to see Wells "soon — but on a whole range of federal-provincial issues. . . . I'm certainly not going to send a signal to other provinces that have ratified the accord that I'm down there renegotiating it with Clyde Wells."

Wells was left to fire verbal volleys at Ottawa, and in that regard he resembled an entire heavy artillery battalion with his relentless campaign to blast the accord. He told an Osgoode Hall law school audience in October that Mulroney was guilty of paternalism in his attitude toward Newfoundland, and that unless the accord was substantially changed, Newfoundland would soon pull out of the deal. He said Mulroney "has not addressed the merits of the issue and has not even expressed any concern about whether Newfoundland has any basis for its position. He hasn't even deigned to consider it.

"His latest comment that Newfoundland should be grateful that she was welcomed into Canada in 1949 and should now

reciprocate that welcome by welcoming Quebec, without regard for the impact on Newfoundland, is paternalistic tripe that
is hardly worthy of response — quite apart from the historical
inaccuracy of it," Wells said. "All the prime minister or the civil
servants are talking about is dire threats to anybody who dares
to speak against Meech Lake. And the suggestion that if you
oppose Meech Lake you are somehow against Canada, you
want Canada to fall apart, and you're unpatriotic, well, I'm as
patriotic as the prime minister. I care as passionately about
Canada as he does. And I expect him to accord me the same
rights to express those feelings as I accord to him. I don't
appreciate him telling me I am insensitive to the future and
the security of Canada."

By this time, Mulroney, while still refusing to speak to Wells
directly, had announced that a November 9 first ministers'
conference would be held in Ottawa, an event that would
propel Wells from a regional irritant to a national figure.

In an early October speech to law students at York University, Wells called on New Brunswick and Manitoba to join him
in a common front to demand changes in the accord, saying
he wanted a pledge from Ottawa at that meeting that there
would be significant changes made or he'd pull the provincial
plug on the deal. He said it wasn't just the deal, but the whole
process that was wrong. "It was wrong to have the ten premiers
and the prime minister sit in a room and hammer at one
another, and have the ten premiers pressured by the prime
minister to say, 'If you don't do this, Canada is going to fall
apart.' It was wrong to deprive ordinary citizens of input into
the process before committed positions were taken."

Wells would rail about this process many times, but when
Meech got down to the crunch in June 1990 in Ottawa, he
joined Mulroney and the other premiers in a lengthy, closed-
door pressure-packed session.

By this time, Crosbie was accusing Wells of having "lost his
senses" by opposing Meech, and much of the national media,

particularly the *Globe* and the CBC, which marched in complete lock-step with the pro-Meechers, were beginning to panic as they saw Wells growing in both stature and popularity. In an October 9 editorial, for example, the *Globe* accused Wells of "a stunning bit of revisionism" for saying, "This country can no longer carry on doing things because it will be acceptable to Quebec."

"For twenty years, federalist Quebecers have been battling separatism with promises of change," the *Globe* wrote. "Mr. Wells will strip them even of that weapon. By rescinding Newfoundland's support for Meech Lake, he will empty the promises of most Quebec federalists and impose upon all Quebecers his vision of the rightful evolution of their province."

That was essentially the only argument the pro-Meechers offered — it can't be changed, because we owe it to Quebec to keep the province in Confederation. While Wells, whether the people agreed with him or not, consistently offered a detailed critique of what he saw as the flaws in the accord — even the accord's backers freely admitted it was seriously flawed — none of that was supposed to matter in the face of the "greater good" of satisfying Quebec's demands.

Finally, tired of waiting to hear from Mulroney or Murray, Wells dramatically upped the ante by firing off a strongly worded ten-page letter to the prime minister and the other premiers dated October 18, 1989, writing, "In the absence of a commitment from the federal and provincial governments to address Newfoundland's concerns, the government of this province will have no alternative but to seek the recision of Newfoundland's earlier approval of the accord," adding that the deal "goes far beyond what is necessary to accommodate the legitimate concerns of Quebec and would prevent forever the kind of Canada the vast majority of its people espouse and desire."

Wells said Newfoundland did not object to the principle of

recognizing Quebec as a distinct society, but the way it was recognized in the accord would undermine the Charter of Rights and Freedoms, create a special legislative status for Quebec, and pave the way for laws restricting the anglophone minority in Quebec.

The letter was drafted with the help of Wells's new senior constitutional adviser, Deborah Coyne, a gold medallist at Osgoode Hall law school, holder of a master's degree from Oxford, and, like Wells, a disciple of Trudeau's vision of the country. She once described herself in an interview as "good friends" with Trudeau, but it turned out she was more than that. She eventually gave birth to a baby girl and named Trudeau as the father. As the Meech deadline drew nearer, those increasingly desperate pro-Meechers who saw the evil hand of Trudeau in every action were convinced that Coyne was also part of the Trudeau plot.

The story in Newfoundland was that Wells had read some anti-Meech articles Coyne had written in some academic journals and been impressed. She had been on the tenure track at the University of Toronto but quickly tired of it and was looking for something else. Later, during the fabled Meech week in June, Ontario officials were whispering to reporters that Coyne had been the first professor ever fired by the university for incompetence. She wasn't fired. She quit. At the same time, senior New Brunswick officials were also trying to smear her by telling reporters that Coyne couldn't be trusted because she was having an affair with Trudeau.

In a January 1991 *Saturday Night* magazine interview with Richard Gwyn, Coyne, who had just returned from a rigorous backpacking trip through Peru, said it was not her connection with Trudeau that brought her to Wells's attention, but her anti-Meech articles. "If you come all out against Meech, you'll be a national hero," she told Wells. "I don't want to be a national hero," he replied, which is why she decided to work for him, joining famed constitutional authority the late Newfoundland-born Senator Eugene Forsey, who also acted as a key adviser to Wells until quitting when he felt Wells was caving into pressure from the other leaders.

Wells was flattered by the comparisons to Trudeau. In an April 1990 interview with the *Evening Telegram*, he said he only hoped Trudeau was not offended by the comparisons. "He is a man of great intellectual integrity and very substantial intellectual capability. However, I don't think I measure up. It is a greater honor than I deserve."

Former Newfoundland premier Frank Moores said he believes there was something to the charges of Trudeau's influencing Wells, even if it wasn't that direct. "Clyde first got into politics as a young Liberal just before Trudeaumania was at its zenith, and he quickly became a disciple. The blemishes of Trudeau had not emerged. There was total blindness and support from young budding politicians, Clyde being in the front row . . . but Clyde left politics and went back to Corner Brook . . . and all those years he wasn't involved with the failings of his hero.

"I think that's why Deborah Coyne was his adviser on Meech Lake, because she was a good friend of Trudeau's. I think it's why he still took the Trudeau line and enlarged on it. It was almost like a guy returning from the grave politically. He did it, and he did it without the impediment of having been exposed to everything that happened between when he left and when he returned.

"I'm not saying Clyde was holding meetings with Trudeau or anything like that. There are a lot of declared Christians around here, but they never met Christ. . . . And this whole idea that Trudeau could almost do no wrong, in his own mind I think it was still there. I mean, Debbie Coyne didn't arrive accidentally. Someone had to recommend her, and it sure as hell wasn't the Canadian Bar Association. . . . I believe in coincidences, but I'm damned if I do to the degree that Coyne/Trudeau/Wells all happened for any other reason but that there was at least an intellectual tie-in among the three of them. To me, of all the constitutional experts in Canada, to pick the one closest to Trudeau, I don't think it was accidental."

The standard procedure in serious federal-provincial matters would have been for officials from Ottawa's Federal-Provincial Relations office to have studied the Wells letter in search of common ground, attempting to find ways to accommodate his concerns while still pressing ahead with Meech Lake. But they didn't do that. Instead, in a letter dated November 2, 1989, just one week before the Ottawa conference, Mulroney sent Wells what essentially was a glorified form letter, using all the standard buzz words and simply dismissing Wells's concerns, offering the standard pro-Meech argument that the accord had to be approved or the country would be in jeopardy.

Wells immediately shot back a three-page response saying he did not share Mulroney's view that "the terms of the patriation agreed upon in 1981 did not address Quebec's concerns." Wells wrote, "Every matter addressed in the Constitution Act of 1982 was as much a concern of Quebec as it was of any other province." He also dismissed some of Mulroney's points as "clearly unfounded," and "specious," and enclosed a copy of a nineteen-page Newfoundland report called "An Alternative to the Meech Lake Accord," which was consistent with Wells's argument that it wasn't good enough just to knock the accord, the prime minister and premiers had to come up with constructive alternatives to satisfy the legitimate aspirations of Quebec and the rest of the country.

These actions set the stage for the first public showdown between Wells and Mulroney. Meanwhile, Filmon and McKenna still hadn't come on-side. Filmon, like Wells, was demanding a major overhaul of the accord, while Bourassa, Mulroney and Peterson were sticking to their view that the accord was a "seamless web," not to be tampered with for fear the whole thing would fall apart. McKenna, whose province still hadn't approved the deal, was trying desperately to find a middle ground through a companion resolution or parallel accord that would allow the Meech Lake accord to go ahead and resolve outstanding differences in the other accord. Bourassa, even if he were inclined to soften his position, didn't dare do so in the face of a resurgent Parti Québécois. Filmon, with anti-Meech Sharon Carstairs and Gary Doer both ready to precipitate a provincial election on the issue, was in a similar political straitjacket.

Mulroney had become so pessimistic about the chances of Meech — and so cynical — he had senior advisers telling reporters that if it failed, it shouldn't be seen as a failure for Mulroney, since it was not a federal initiative per se, but rather an agreement among all eleven first ministers. "The problem isn't between the federal government and the provinces," one prime ministerial adviser privately told the *Toronto Star*'s Ottawa bureau chief Rosemary Speirs. "Any agreement is between premiers, with the prime minister acting as mediator."

Wells tabled in the House of Assembly the constitutional package of alternatives he had sent to Mulroney in his second letter, repeating his intention to rescind the 1987 approval by Newfoundland if there was no willingness from the prime minister and other premiers to discuss changes in the accord at the Ottawa meeting. Wells said he didn't expect a great breakthrough to solve differences over the accord, only an indication of a willingness to change it. "The maximum I'd expect would be some agreement on putting a future process of negotiation in place."

On his way to Ottawa for a pre-conference dinner hosted by Mulroney, Wells heard that Bourassa was still refusing even to discuss the possibility of reopening Meech. Ignoring his previous pledge to see if there was a willingness for change at the conference, he stepped off the plane and promptly told waiting reporters that "the Meech Lake accord as it is now is not acceptable to Newfoundland, so we will have to rescind it. . . .

You can't have a compromise on [Quebec's] terms. That's not a compromise, that's blackmail." This attack prompted Ontario's David Peterson to accuse him of "poisoning the well" of Confederation and promoting "a very destructive act" by withdrawing Newfoundland's support.

Even McKenna, whom one senior Newfoundland official dismissed derisively as "being under Peterson's thumb," said Wells should adopt a more "constructive" approach. Mulroney, visibly annoyed, simply brushed past reporters without replying to the shouted question about Wells's remarks. McKenna, in fact, was one of the big losers in this whole debate. Since New Brunswick, unlike any other province, has a substantial English-French split, roughly sixty-forty in favor of English, he was initially seen as one leader who could bridge the gap between the two solitudes. He began the process by adopting a tough negotiating stance, calling for changes in the accord, but by the end, after he'd pleaded for a parallel accord and then finally come on-side completely, under pressure from Mulroney and Peterson, he looked like a Boy Scout waiting for his pack leader to tell him where to set up his tent.

For most of the opening day at the November 9-10 first ministers' conference, Mulroney had managed to keep Meech off the agenda, with the leaders offering up their set speeches about the economy. The plan was that, in the afternoon, the leaders would all give their opening remarks in public and then, as had become the custom over the years — despite Mulroney's continued criticism of the process — they were to go behind closed doors to do the real work of constitutional bickering and bartering.

But Mulroney, despite warnings from Crosbie and others, hadn't counted on Wells.

Bourassa opened the debate with a low-key defence of Meech, saying that for most Quebecers "Canada is the first choice and they would like it to remain that way," but adding that "reopening the accord is tantamount to destroying it. How could we take such a decision when we have the opportunity to . . . permit our country to be more united than ever?"

Peterson, displaying the patronizing arrogance that would ultimately cause him to lose what appeared to be a Liberal dynasty-in-the-making in Ontario, offered less of a defence of his own position and more of a professorial lecture to those, Wells in particular, who dared to disagree. "I hope desperately that when we leave this conference, none of us will do anything to deepen the wound," he said. "I have seen the atmosphere of this country change quite dramatically in the last couple of years."

Indeed the atmosphere in the room changed quite dramatically a few minutes later when Wells began to speak. Apparently he had not been at all cowed either by the pressure put on him by the pro-Meech premiers at a private dinner the night before at the National Gallery of Canada, or by the public speeches from the other leaders preceding him.

Wells jumped on an argument Mulroney had used to defend Meech, that it was impossible to imagine a Constitution without, say, Ontario, supporting it. Wells, sparking an electrifying exchange between himself, Mulroney, and Peterson, said, "To say that failure to accept the Meech Lake accord as it is now is a rejection of Quebec is a political misrepresentation that does great disservice to the nation as a whole and particular disservice to the people of Quebec. . . . I believe the comment serves only to foster and promote separatism in Quebec, not to diminish it," at which point Bourassa gathered his papers and stomped out of the room. He claimed later he was simply leaving to prepare for a private session, but nobody believed that.

Wells, his face flushed with anger, went on to say he was not rejecting Quebec. "I am rejecting Canada with a class-A province, a class-B province, and eight class-C provinces," he said. "I believe that is what the vast majority of the people of this nation are rejecting. At the very least I can say with certainty that is what the people of Newfoundland and Labrador are rejecting, and we resent greatly the implied allegation of prejudice by those who suggest we are rejecting Quebec."

Wells made a passionate plea for Senate reform, arguing that it was the only way to offset the overwhelming power of Ontario and Quebec in the Commons. He said that in 1961, earned income per person in Newfoundland was fifty-three per cent of the Canadian average, and by 1987, it had risen to just fifty-six per cent. "We have failed miserably," he said. "That is not the Canada that was promised. That is not the Canada that was written into our Constitution in 1982," and Meech Lake, Wells argued, would make Senate reform impossible: "The effect will be to constitutionally entrench the regional disparities that now exist."

In one sense, Wells seemed caught on the extension of his own logic. When he was asked later by reporters what he would do if he believed, as he said he did, that no one province should be allowed to impose constitutional amendments on everybody else and he found himself the only holdout against Meech, Wells replied, "I will have a great deal to think about." He then countered dramatically by challenging Mulroney to call a national referendum on the accord.

Obviously, the pro-Meech forces did not want to chance a referendum, knowing it would likely be rejected by voters, certainly in English Canada by this point. Bourassa immediately pooh-poohed the suggestion. "So why should we have a national referendum and why was that not mentioned in [Wells's] speech?"

Mulroney was also quick to dismiss the idea, saying, "Referendums are not the Canadian way." He said it was to avoid a referendum that the accord was negotiated in the first place.

Public reaction to the Mulroney-Wells exchange was swift and direct: an overwhelming vote of confidence for Wells. Within minutes, his office in St. John's and hotel in Ottawa were deluged with calls, fax messages, telexes, and telegrams from all over Canada. Within four days of the meeting, Wells had received more than 2500 letters of support from across the country. University of Toronto historian Michael Bliss, a prominent opponent of the accord, said Wells had proven himself to be "the true heir of Trudeau in understanding the essence of our constitutional quarrelling."

Despite the testy exchange ending the first day of the conference, however, the eleven leaders met privately the next morning and managed to agree that Lowell Murray would travel across Canada to quietly seek grounds for compromise among the premiers, presumably leading up to a full-fledged constitutional meeting before the June 23, 1990, deadline for approval of Meech expired.

Both Peterson and Bourassa threatened to walk out of the meeting if Wells stuck with his decision to ask his legislature to rescind support for Meech the next week. Moments before Wells was to speak, Mulroney, who had been told by his officials that Wells had intended to pull the plug on Meech, called a coffee break. It was during that break that Ontario's Attorney-General Ian Scott persuaded Wells it would be a disaster if he didn't at least give the process another chance to work. In return, Wells got a federal agreement that Murray would attempt to see if the impasse couldn't be broken by accelerating the issue of Senate reform.

Murray finally arrived in St. John's December 8 as part of his cross-country tour to promote the idea that Meech could be saved with a separate, parallel act, an idea Wells immediately dismissed.

Controversy broke out again, this time from an unexpected source. Retiring Governor General Jeanne Sauvé, in her farewell speech to the nation at year's end, waded into the political arena by urging the country to ratify the Meech Lake accord. During her brief fireside chat, Sauvé, in a plea for national unity, said, "That unity is an illusion if it is not based on defined foundations that promise to be durable and whose durability is not beyond testing of the building's material and organization. Such testing cannot be undertaken unless we accept, once and for all, the inevitable compromises, and unless the parties involved ratify their pact and do not let Canada drift into an unforeseeable future." She went on to defend the idea of Quebec as a distinct society.

Sauvé's press secretary, Marie Bender, denied Sauvé was attempting to meddle in politics, pointing out that the term "Meech Lake" was not used in the speech and claiming that the "pact" referred to was the historical pact between French and English Canadians to live together. Wells was unconvinced and told the governor general bluntly to butt out.

As the deadline drew nearer and Wells still wouldn't bend, the pro-Meech forces became desperate. In January they dragged out two veteran politicians, Robert Stanfield and Jack Pickersgill, to write a highly publicized letter to Wells accusing him of not understanding the accord and of placing the entire Atlantic region in grave jeopardy. "It is almost beyond belief that any Atlantic premier would, for no reason based on fact, expose Atlantic Canada to even greater difficulties than its people already face, much less give encouragement to those who would break up Canada," the two wrote.

Wells stated he found their comments "offensive," adding that the letter "demonstrates clearly a lack of confidence in the accord, where they don't deal with the real issues but base their position on this kind of unfounded fear-mongering. . . . The only thing that causes Quebec separatism on this issue is irresponsible statements such as those being made by Mr. Stanfield, Mr. Pickersgill, and Mr. Mulroney. If the accord is so good, they should argue for its merits."

Wells launched his own nationwide speaking tour to promote the evils of the accord — or, as some critics suggest, to promote himself as a future prime minister, noting he had begun taking French lessons — carrying his message directly into Quebec on January 19 at a Canadian Club luncheon in

Montreal, attended by Trudeau. He argued, "To say that failure to accept the Meech Lake accord as it is now is a rejection of Quebec . . . is an offensive insult to the majority of Canadians [and] does great disservice to the nation as a whole and particular disservice to the people of Quebec. I believe the comment serves only to foster and promote dissension and perhaps even separatism in Quebec."

Asked by reporters how he thought the speech would fly in Quebec, Trudeau said, "I think the nationalists will hate it, but the people will love it. . . . The campaign has only started."

In addition to news conferences, editorial board meetings, and another speech at McGill University, Wells also met for an hour with Bourassa, after which Wells said, "If anything, I'm probably more confident" a solution to the impasse could be reached before the June deadline, and Bourassa quipped sardonically, "I'm not less optimistic."

In early January, Ottawa writer Robert Lee flew by helicopter with Wells to the fishing village of Grand Bank southwest of St. John's, where Wells delivered a speech. Lee, an Alberta native, told Wells that his situation reminded him of former Alberta premier Peter Lougheed's during the National Energy Program dispute in the early 1980s. He said Lougheed had become adept at explaining the complex issue in simple metaphors, such as it was bad enough to have the federal government arrive as an uninvited guest on the porch, but they'd just walked into the house with the NEP. Wells's task was to make a link between the economy and Senate reform.

Wells, who told Lee it wasn't an easy connection to make, did his best. "I'll be goddamned," said Lee, "if he wasn't up there in Trepassey saying that the economic problems in the fishery are directly tied in to the Constitution." Indeed, Wells told the audience that Newfoundland's fishery crisis is what the NEP was to Alberta, and received a standing ovation when he said a Triple-E Senate "directly affects the situation here in

Trepassey — today, and ten, twenty, and forty years from now."

In the early spring of 1990, with the Meech clock running down, Wells called the ratification deadline artificial. "I don't think there is any magic to June 23. That's being imposed by the proponents of the accord as though the guillotine is going to fall on June 24."

In January, Wells dropped by Queen's Park for a meeting with Peterson, but the two men didn't resolve any of their differences. One person who witnessed the meeting first-hand described Peterson as "a very glib, superficial kind of guy. A nice guy. But you walk in and it's 'Hi, Clyde. How are you doing?' Red tie and all. And you could just see the discomfort between the two of them. The two of them just don't operate on the same plane."

On February 12, during a visit with British Columbia Premier Bill Vander Zalm, whose attempts at compromise Wells also dismissed, Wells said he was tired of waiting for somebody to make a move. "Newfoundland is not prepared to accept the accord as it is, and in due course, the Newfoundland legislature will be asked to rescind its approval."

On March 8, as the House of Assembly began its spring sitting, Wells formalized what he'd been saying, announcing unequivocally in his throne speech that Newfoundland's ratification of the Meech Lake accord would be rescinded in the current sitting, which was scheduled to end in May or June.

Murray chided Wells for having promised in November not to rescind it while negotiations on the stalemate were continuing. "Discussions are continuing between the federal government and the various provinces and among the provincial political leaders and officials all the time," said Murray. "The dialogue continues. Meech Lake is not dead. The process is going on and naturally we expect that Premier Wells will honor the commitment he made." Mulroney said, "This kind of action is needless. . . . [Wells] knows we're all trying to get an arrangement," and Crosbie accused Wells of "an appalling display of fanaticism."

Quebec Tory MP François Gérin was prompted to say that Wells's actions made it easier for him to give up on Confederation. "Each day, it will be easier and easier for us Quebecers to make up our minds. I'm going home this afternoon very happy, and if the other provinces of Canada don't want me as a Canadian, I'll go back home and I'll stay there and I'll be very happy. And tell that to Mr. Wells." His Quebec colleague Louis Plamondon predicted, "It's the end of this country." Both men subsequently left the Tory caucus and helped start the Bloc Québécois.

Wells promptly contradicted Murray's claim that talks were continuing. Rumors had been circulating in Ottawa that federal officials were holding secret talks with New Brunswick and Manitoba, and shutting out Newfoundland, but Wells telephoned both Filmon and McKenna, and both said they weren't aware of any negotiations. But Wells said if talks were going on, he should be involved, to which Mulroney shot back, "I'm entitled to speak to whomever I want," adding that Wells should "mind his own business." Wells retorted, "The future of Canada is my business."

By mid-March, Wells was still complaining that neither Mulroney nor Murray were talking to him about concrete steps to resolve the deadlock. "In my judgment, that's shocking treatment," he said. In total there were only six exchanges to that point between Wells and either officials in the prime minister's office or the federal-provincial relations ministry. Mulroney had spoken to Wells three times, once in October after Wells released his critique of the accord, once during the heated exchange at the November conference, and the third time right after the throne speech when Wells called him to say he was going to rescind Newfoundland's endorsement of Meech Lake. Wells had never even met Lowell Murray or Norman Spector, the two men most responsible, next to Mulroney, for the accord, until the November conference in Ottawa.

In November 1991 Murray said he "was under no illusions — none of us were about [Wells]. He is nothing if not very clear with his statements . . . but we could not put ourselves in the position of negotiating on his grounds. . . . We knew if he persisted in his position that the accord would probably fail, but if there was anything worse than failure, it was a failure in which Quebec had been isolated by the rest of Canada, in which the federal government had been seen to connive against Quebec's interest.

"Once we had a deal, and Quebec was the first province to ratify, the federal government could not be seen to be involved in something which meant renegotiating or reopening Meech. I mean, things are bad enough now in the aftermath of the failure of Meech. But if Meech had failed and the people of Quebec and their government had been able to point the finger at the federal government as having betrayed them, that would have been the worst possible scenario for the country and," he added, chuckling slightly, "not very good for the future of this government either."

Murray said federal officials believed from the outset that New Brunswick would get back on-side "and we were hopeful we'd be able to put together enough votes in the Manitoba legislature [to approve it]. The one government that was opposed to Meech chapter and verse, body and soul, opposed to the essence of Meech, was Clyde Wells in Newfoundland. That wasn't true in New Brunswick and it wasn't true in Manitoba . . . and I think in the end, events showed our assessment to be correct."

On March 22, Murray flew to St. John's to meet Wells, only to come away "with no feeling whatsoever that there was much room for change in his essential position. But we wanted to keep the process going. Others were talking to him — Ghiz, McKenna, Buchanan . . . but there was almost no give on important matters of substance because he regarded them as more than that. He always regarded them as matters of principle, almost dogma. Now I mean no offence, but it was like speaking with the man who is in charge of the Society for the Propagation of Faith, the Cardinal in Rome who has the last word on dogma. His mind was made up on these matters.

"His opposition to Meech Lake was not on one or two or even three items. He was opposed to it in principle because it did not conform to his view, not of Canada, but of federalism. He has a theory of federalism. He treats federalism as a dogma outside of which there is no salvation. [For Wells] there aren't different kinds of federalism. There are certain principles of federalism he believes are immutable and cannot be compromised. For that reason he believes strongly in what we call the Triple-E Senate, that the Senate must have powers equal to those of the House of Commons, equal in every respect, and that the representation from each state or province must be equal. And of course, it must be elected. . . .

"Most of the scholars of federalism will tell you there are all kinds of federalism, and there are some scholars who will even argue whether ours is really a federation at all . . . but he had no doubt what federalism was, and if it didn't conform to his view, then it wasn't federalism.

"So I went down there knowing I was dealing with a fellow who (a) had his view of federalism, and I was prepared to discuss that because it's a political issue, and (b) had some rather refined view as to the legal implications of this or that clause in the Constitution. I was always prepared to discuss the political implications. I'm not a lawyer and I'm certainly not a constitutional expert, so I brought Mary Dawson, the associate deputy minister of justice with me, as well as Norman Spector, precisely so we could discuss the finer legal points. And they did exhaustively in my present. It was a very substantive discussion. It always is with him. He was always very forthcoming about process."

On March 22 Wells formally introduced the motion in the house to rescind the earlier approval of the accord. The move came one day after McKenna had introduced a companion resolution to the accord in his legislature, which Wells said dealt with some of the "less major issues" and wouldn't solve the bigger problems.

Wells called for the clause recognizing Quebec as a distinct society be put in the preamble instead of in the body of the Constitution. He also wanted to add recognition of aboriginals, delete the clause affirming the special role of Quebec's legislature, remove the amendment allowing the provinces to help appoint senators, and obtain assurances that provinces opting out of federal spending programs and getting compensation for it would meet national objectives so that the poorer regions wouldn't suffer.

He also said he would go along with the Meech Lake accord if Newfoundlanders supported it in a provincial referendum, but he would call the referendum only if both New Brunswick and Manitoba decided to accept the accord as it was written.

On March 27, the three Maritime premiers — McKenna, Ghiz, and Buchanan — met with Wells in Corner Brook, but failed to convince him to support McKenna's idea for a companion accord. Wells flew back to St. John's that same day and opened debate on his motion to rescind, saying, "I won't sell the dignity and self-respect of the people of this province for any sum of money. We may end up as paupers, but we will maintain our self-respect. . . . I don't want this province to be doomed forever to accept what I was told by the premier of Quebec last week when he said that Ontario and Quebec paid sixty-eight per cent of the support of Newfoundland."

During the debate, Newfoundland Finance Minister Hubert Kitchen linked the province's opposition to Meech to the Churchill Falls deal. Kitchen chose the first day of live television broadcast of the house to say that the province would remain a colony of Central Canada if the accord were passed as written. "They got us by the short hairs on Upper Churchill," he said. "We've got them in the same place on Meech Lake," a comment greeted by loud desk-thumping approval from his Liberal colleagues. Wells immediately called Kitchen's comment "unfortunate, inappropriate, unacceptable, and offensive. I think Newfoundland has been embarrassed by it and I greatly regret that. Clearly [our Meech policy] is not developed by this government as an act of vengeance."

Wells apparently forgot that, a couple of weeks earlier, he himself had linked the two subjects in an interview with Southam News. While he didn't use Kitchen's rather graphic analogy, he did complain bitterly that Quebec was taking $500 million a year from the Newfoundland economy because of Churchill Falls, and the situation would never be corrected if the accord was passed.

Wells may also have forgotten his April 24, 1989, reaction to Bourassa's statement that the newly elected Newfoundland premier should worry more about his province's unemployment and do less grandstanding on Meech Lake.

Wells, absolutely furious, described Bourassa's comments as demeaning and unworthy. "Newfoundland has seventeen per cent unemployment partly and maybe greatly, because Quebec deprived Newfoundland of its constitutional right twenty years ago," preventing the province from getting its hydroelectricity to market. Wells said Newfoundland was "blackmailed and pressured" in the Churchill Falls deal, and he declared that accepting the accord as it was would make Newfoundland subject to such blackmail again.

On April 6, despite heated opposition from the Tories, the house voted to rescind the 1988 approval of the accord, prompting Quebec's Intergovernmental Affairs Minister Gil Rémillard to say, "Canada can survive without Newfoundland." Mulroney called the recision a "useless provocation," and Ontario Tory MP Don Blenkarn was moved to say, "I sometimes feel we would be better off if we towed [Newfoundland] out to sea and sank it."

After first declining their invitation, Wells appeared before a special travelling Commons committee on the Constitution chaired by Quebec MP Jean Charest in St. John's on May 1, and while his tone was conciliatory, his message wasn't. He said he was willing to look at McKenna's companion resolution to see if it could be changed to accommodate his concerns about the accord, but he held out little hope. He also repeated his attack on Bourassa's comments about Newfoundland's dependence upon Quebec's staying in Confederation. "What does that say to me? 'You people in Newfoundland are lesser-quality Canadians; you can't express your conscientiously held views and opinions on constitutional development because you're dependent on handouts from Ottawa'? That is unacceptable."

He urged the MPs to ask for a full constitutional convention when they reported back to the Commons on May 18, plus an extended deadline to find solutions to the Meech Lake deadlock. The fourteen-page report of the Commons committee did not accept Wells's advice, but it did recommend a companion accord. Even though Wells said the report's twenty-three recommendations "could point in a helpful direction," it was abandoned by Mulroney the minute Bourassa rejected it outright.

In an attempt to salvage the deal, Mulroney then announced he would meet each of the ten premiers separately over dinner at 24 Sussex Drive. On May 27, after a four-hour session with Mulroney, Wells said he couldn't support a Quebec veto on Senate reform and saw no solution to the impasse unless Bourassa would compromise. "The differences are substantial and serious, and resolution will not be easy. I find it difficult to believe that the concerns that Newfoundland has and Manitoba has can be addressed without Mr. Bourassa agreeing to a compromise that will allow those to be accommodated," he said. To which Bourassa responded, "It's not up to Quebec to make compromises."

About the only hopeful sign for Mulroney was McKenna's reaction to the objections of Filmon and Wells. During his private one-on-one with the prime minister, McKenna called them "radical and extreme." Outside the meeting, McKenna said he thought a deal could be struck on a companion resolution. "I believe, with respect to New Brunswick, that the bridge is not so difficult to cross that we cannot find some accommodation."

For Wells, however, the gap was more like the Grand Canyon than a bridgeable gorge. Federal officials still believed that Filmon would come around, and their main strategy had boiled down to isolating Wells, believing he would ultimately cave in if he was all alone in objecting to the accord. Two days later, still hoping to soften Wells's position, Murray and constitutional lawyer Roger Tasse flew to St. John's to brief Wells on the legal implications of the distinct society clause.

"I thought we were getting close to a meeting of the minds on the clause, on the effect of the clause on the Charter and on the division of powers by the time he and Tasse had this discussion in my presence," Murray recalled later. "He knew Tasse and respected Tasse as a legal scholar. They talked about different formulations which could be used and so on, but I think there was a complete meeting of the minds on the effect of the distinct society on the Charter, and while Wells would have preferred different wording, there was essentially agreement on the effect of the distinct society on the division of powers.

"I felt we were making headway on a legal point more than a political point at that meeting, and if that could be set aside, as I thought it could be, I thought, well, how can we deal with his other objections, which included especially the amending formula? He objected to the unanimity provision for Senate reform. He wanted the Triple-E Senate with a double majority for Quebec on matters of language and culture. This he thought would satisfy Quebec. I wasn't really looking at it in terms of whether I was optimistic or not. I felt we'd made progress, but there were some pretty important issues outstanding.

"I really don't think [Wells] has any appreciation of how difficult it is to govern this country. His idea of a Senate is really a formula for paralysis. He sees the Triple-E Senate as being an essential part of federalism. . . . For him, each of those Es is non-negotiable."

Following that meeting, Wells surprised observers by announcing he and the federal negotiators were close to an agreement on the distinct society question. That didn't impress Quebec Tory MP Denis Pronovost, assistant deputy speaker in the Commons. He called Wells a "mental case" over his objections to the accord. Pronovost, who later apologized and stepped down as assistant deputy speaker, had also told an open-line radio audience in Trois-Rivières that Newfoundlanders had a mentality that differed from that in the rest of Canada. He said most are unemployed and forty-four per cent have trouble reading and writing. His comments came a few days after Mulroney's chief Quebec lieutenant and close personal friend Lucien Bouchard had quit the Tory caucus and bolted to the Bloc Québécois, saying, "As the trials of the Meech Lake accord have shown, English Canada has not taken Quebec's minimum conditions seriously. Whoever starts to negotiate on his knees is very likely to end up flat on his face." Apparently many Quebecers agreed with him, since the daily Tory polling showed an immediate fallout of Bouchard's move when support for the accord plummeted twenty per cent in Quebec. In the rest of Canada, support was also dwindling.

At the same time, a leaked strategy paper prepared by one of David Peterson's senior aides exacerbated the already poisonous political atmosphere by suggesting several ways to discredit the three premiers who remained opposed to the accord, the main thrust of which was to use the CBC, which the pro-Meech forces saw as on-side, to plant doubts not only about the positions of the three premiers but about their personal stability. The paper suggested portraying Filmon as "politically erratic," Wells as suffering from "an overwhelming lack of trust," and McKenna as "part of the problem." Peterson personally telephoned Wells to apologize, after claiming publicly that the memo was rejected before he even saw it. A former senior Peterson aide, however, said, "The only thing he was apologizing for was that the paper was leaked. Listen, I sat in on meetings with Peterson in the room, and he was enjoying the Newfie jokes right along with everybody else. Given the high-stakes poker game we were playing, you're not going to get some civil servant going off on his own and drawing up provincial political strategy. Let's be serious here."

By the end of May Mulroney, desperate for an agreement and deliberately having set up the eleventh-hour, pressure cooker situation, announced he was inviting all the premiers to a private working dinner in Hull on June 3, the third anniversary of the accord's signing. If there was progress at the dinner, a full-fledged first ministers' conference would be held the next morning.

"While I do not underestimate the divergences on the remaining issues — and they are there and they are serious — in point of fact what is in dispute is modest, extremely modest, when compared with what is at stake," he told the Commons. "What is really at stake is Canada."

What Mulroney didn't tell the Commons, but what would become obvious during his infamous "roll the dice" interview a couple of weeks later in the *Globe and Mail*, was that he had deliberately prolonged the final meeting hoping to pressure the critics into surrendering their objections. As usual, he hadn't reckoned on Clyde Wells.

9

Dinner
à la Carte

A ND SO IT BEGAN. On the evening of Sunday, June 3, 1990, twelve men — the eleven leaders plus Lowell Murray — sat around a single long table in the fifth-floor curatorial wing of the spectacular Canadian Museum of Civilization in Hull for a meal of fresh artichokes, grilled shrimp, beef tenderloin, roast potatoes and fiddleheads, chocolate terrine, and two Ontario wines.

The multiwindowed room afforded an unimpeded view across the Ottawa River to the Ontario side, beyond the stately Parliament Buildings to the Langevin Block where, exactly three years earlier to the day, an all-night session had hammered out the accord, which, said Mulroney, "heralded a springtime of hope for our country."

But that was then, this was now. Three of the premiers who had signed that accord were gone — Peckford, Pawley, and Hatfield. Only one, Nova Scotia's John Buchanan, had been part of the 1981-82 constitutional deal and the entire Meech Lake dispute. None of the three new premiers — Filmon,

McKenna, and Wells favored the deal, although McKenna had pretty well been won over.

Wells had arrived in Ottawa genuinely expecting to bargain. Murray had raised this expectation deliberately, by sending a series of discussion papers to the holdout premiers, giving the clear impression that things were still on the table when, in fact, the seamless-web approach remained intact. Because Wells, relatively speaking, has an unusually high level of personal integrity for a politician, he assumed that others did, too. They didn't. In his meeting with Wells a couple of weeks before, Murray had even suggested a compromise wording to the distinct society clause, but the Quebec premier would not countenance it, making it a non-starter from the outset. Wells had given Murray his suggestions for the legal language on several issues, and Murray had done nothing to dissuade Wells from believing he was taking the suggestions seriously. The federal-provincial relations minister had also sent both Wells and Filmon documents entitled "State of Play" and "State of Play II," based loosely on the Charest report, which addressed some of their concerns and appeared to part of a process of looking for a solution to the impasse.

Deborah Coyne, Wells's chief constitutional adviser, urged him to walk out that first evening in Hull after it became apparent the federal government had no intention of dealing seriously with his or Filmon's objections. In a later interview, Wells said if he had to do it again he would have left the table.

After dinner, Mulroney spoke for forty-five minutes, but rather than dealing with the issues that divided them, he spent much of the time reading articles from the *Wall Street Journal* and *New York Times* concerning the serious economic consequences of separatism if Meech failed, singling out a recent thirty-year $150-million bond issue Newfoundland had floated on the New York market, which he said would cost the province an extra $20 million to $30 million more in interest because of uncertainty over Meech. Wells disputed that, saying the figure was closer to $10 million.

At one point, Mulroney even read from his book, *Where I Stand*, prompting Peterson to scribble a note to Buchanan, who was sitting next to him, saying, "This is stupid." Wells, in addition to his constitutional points, had been arguing that whatever meetings the leaders held should be open to the public, citing from Mulroney's book, which argued the same point. "The trouble is, Clyde, you read the wrong section of the book," Mulroney told him. "You should read this part," and he pointed to a reference he'd made in the book that the Churchill Falls deal with Quebec was unconscionable.

The premiers had been told by federal officials that Mulroney would canvass them at dinner to see if there was some sort of consensus, or even the hope of one, which would allow them to hold a full-bore constitutional meeting with a chance of reaching agreement. Instead, Mulroney offered what many premiers described later as a patronizing lecture. Still, because such issues as Senate reform, distinct society, the Charest report, and suggestions for alternative resolutions from New Brunswick, Manitoba, and Newfoundland didn't even get discussed, Mulroney and the premiers did agree to meet the next morning across the river in the Conference Centre.

As the men emerged from the five-hour Sunday dinner — in a portent of things to come, a short, violent thunderstorm struck at about the same time — Canadians watching the proceedings live on CBC Newsworld, which some of the premiers would later derisively dub Meechworld, had no reason to think a deal was near. All involved agreed it had been a civilized encounter, with none of the open anger displayed the previous November.

Shortly after 11 a.m. in the dreary, windowless fifth-floor boardroom of the Conference Centre, dubbed The Bunker by officials, Mulroney, Murray, and the premiers gathered around a large oval table to begin the process again. Across the hall, in a cafeteria-style room they called Camp Meech, an army of advisers, ministers, constitutional lawyers, bureaucrats, and assorted hangers-on had set up shop waiting for word from their commanders, passing the time by talking to each other on their cellular phones, drinking coffee, and watching television.

Monday morning was essentially a waste of time. They spent most of the ninety minutes debating what they should discuss first. Wells and Filmon were wary of Mulroney's strategy, suspecting him of wanting to get some of the simple items resolved first, thereby building a subtle pressure on them to agree to the major items. They weren't having any. When Mulroney called a lunch break, Filmon emerged to complain, "I can't believe that we're here after this much time has passed and they have nothing to propose on any of these things [Senate reform, gender equality, the supremacy of the Charter of Rights]."

That would change at four that afternoon, when Mulroney tabled a five-page blueprint for discussion. Wells, whom Coyne again had urged to walk out, was furious that the new document didn't even mention the distinct society issue. Filmon, having spent his extended lunch-hour meeting with Sharon Carstairs and Gary Doer, who had flown in from Winnipeg that morning, was equally annoyed that most of his complaints were no longer on the table for discussion, let alone resolution.

Mulroney's document divided the issues into two categories: those to be resolved immediately, in order to get the accord ratified by its June 23 deadline; and those to be discussed during a staged process later, such as Senate reform — he proposed a full-fledged conference September 17 for that issue — gender equality and the constitutional status of native people and ethnic minorities. The whole proposal, however, required the dissenting premiers' approval by June 23 before talks moved on to the other three stages.

Wells, his face flushed with anger, slammed his copies of

Murray's earlier proposals on the table and demanded to know what had happened to them. Bourassa, stunning both Wells and Filmon, said he'd never seen those documents and would not discuss anything to do with the distinct society clause.

Wells and Filmon were even less impressed when they discovered Mulroney and McKenna had planned a stage-managed public relations coup. Mulroney would release the document, making it appear as if he was being flexible and Filmon and Wells weren't, and McKenna, who had been criticized by many pro-Meechers for getting the whole deal off the rails in the first place, would make amends by rushing out to the television cameras — which he did — to announce he was suddenly on-side with the accord. Wells angrily tore a strip off McKenna, and even the other pro-Meech premiers were appalled at the New Brunswick premier's move.

McKenna's announcement, while giving waiting journalists a little something to chew on, barely made a ripple in the overall scheme of things. McKenna, who at one point had been seen as a future prime minister, looked sheepish and uncertain when he said that he and his advisers had made a spontaneous decision to help save the accord. Later he would say, "I felt terrible. It was the worst day of the whole week. It was a suicide mission, but we wanted to keep the whole thing going."

At the meeting's end, Getty set the tone for everybody else when he said, "I'm not the slightest bit optimistic after this meeting."

Going into dinner in his fourth-floor suite in the Chateau Laurier with the other premiers — McKenna, apparently feeling too ashamed, turned down the invitation — Wells told reporters, "I'm not entirely happy with what I've seen put forward. In fact, I'm quite unhappy with it. I'm certainly not satisfied with the matter as it stands now." Adding insult to injury, the federal proposals, which had been circulated at the meeting, were taken back before the premiers left the room. While a few premiers grumbled privately about that, it remains a mystery why they allowed themselves to be used that way by Mulroney.

British Columbia's Bill Vander Zalm was actually the one responsible for the dinner, although it ended up being something different from what he'd intended. Because Mulroney was not moving on Senate reform, Vander Zalm's original plan was to get Wells and the four western premiers together to forge a common front. "What we were hoping was to find some element of compromise, and we didn't think we could do that with Quebec and Ontario until the rest of us could find some agreement," he says. "Quebec and Ontario were pretty well dug in. So were Ghiz and Buchanan. We felt if we could find a little breakthrough with Clyde, we could sufficiently influence the meeting, and we thought at the end of the night we'd achieved something."

Vander Zalm says everybody knew that Wells had been receiving enormous support from across the country through mail, telegrams, faxes, word of mouth, "the sort of thing that tends to cement you in your position. . . . He had a tremendous wave of support, and there would have been immense disappointment if he changed his mind. You walk into his suite and you see the whole place packed with bouquets of flowers from supporters. . . . I was looking at some of them to see if they came from British Columbia. When you're on the other side and you see such an outpouring of support for Clyde, believe me, it makes you think. Conversely for him, it had to have an impact. He didn't want to let those people down."

As word got around, the other premiers, with the exception of McKenna, wandered in for dinner. Nobody was there from the federal government. To make sure nosy reporters couldn't listen at the door, they packed hotel bathroom towels around the base of it to prevent sound from leaking out into the corridor. Wells and Bourassa ended up sitting next to each other and had a long and deep discussion about many issues, including the distinct society.

Vander Zalm left about midnight, but the meeting went on for another two hours. "We had actually got somewhere," he says, "but somebody on the federal side, I think it was Norman Spector, was out there planting certain things in the media which caused a breakdown of what we were doing and really upset Clyde and a few others. What we didn't know was that the feds had their own game plan going, and the two collided the next morning."

The prime minister presented a completely revised agenda, treating all the contentious issues as a package to be agreed to in principle, with nothing to be finalized until each point had been resolved. The federal strategy was obvious. Mulroney wanted to keep any discussion of the distinct society off the table, knowing Bourassa would walk out of the meeting if he didn't; if the accord had to fail, he'd prefer it bog down over Senate reform which, although a life and death matter for many premiers, was hardly something your average Canadian cared much about.

After kicking around a host of suggestions for Senate reform, Ghiz finally offered an idea put to him by former federal cabinet minister Jack Pickersgill, which was a national commission on Senate reform. If no reform could be negotiated within three years, the four western provinces and Newfoundland would get four more seats in an expanded Senate, and Prince Edward Island would get one. (Actually, after Ghiz pleaded for a bonus, they all agreed to give him two.) What's more, no province would have a veto.

Sixteen hours after slipping into The Bunker, the premiers emerged in a much more buoyant mood. Getty, almost in tears, now told reporters, "I love my battered country." Even Wells was, if not optimistic, certainly less gloomy. "I would have to conclude that we've made a good deal of progress," he said. "If that's optimism, then okay, I share that."

Asked if he was sticking to his previous promise to put the deal to a provincial referendum, Wells said, "It's a definite possibility." A recent poll by Baseline Market Research found that sixty-seven per cent of Newfoundlanders favored a referendum on Meech. A solid majority still opposed the accord, but sixty-three per cent said they would support a compromise deal if Wells endorsed it.

While the *Ottawa Citizen*'s headline after Tuesday's apparent breakthrough proclaimed, "A Good Day," not so the Wednesday-morning headlines in the French-language newspapers, where Bourassa was attacked for "selling out" on Senate reform. Indeed, the night before, while the other premiers were expressing various levels of guarded optimism, Bourassa was virtually mobbed by angry Quebec reporters as he tried to enter his car, all of them demanding to know why he would agree to give up Quebec's veto.

Much is said in the English-language media about the propensity of Quebec journalists to be separatists, and this specific event is often used as an example to show that federalism isn't getting a fair shake in the Quebec media. It's true. Most Quebec journalists, especially those covering Parliament Hill, are separatists. It's equally true, however, that most English-language journalists, if not all, are federalists. While the Quebec journalists were furious at Bourassa's "selling out" Quebec's interests, English journalists were euphoric that a deal was near and federalism would be saved. Both sides consistently expressed a clear bias. CBC's Peter Mansbridge gave us a wonderful example. Shortly before the conference began, he was interviewing Wells and McKenna. At one point, seeming to forget he was a journalist eliciting information and acting as if he was a federal in the negotiations, he asked Wells, "What would it take?"

Vander Zalm says much of the hostility that pervaded the week-long meetings can be placed directly at the feet of Mulroney and his officials. "Sometimes we'd [have to] sit around a few hours before all the players showed up," he said. "It happened not only in the morning, but after the break at dinner or lunch. They'd announce a time to begin again and we'd all be there, but Mulroney and Spector wouldn't. So tempers would flare before the meeting even began. It wasn't a good way to set the tone. Now I'm not a negotiator . . . but they were doing a psychological thing, trying to wear us down a bit. I believe that was their thinking. But it tended to make the situation more tense than it needed to be."

Bourassa arrived for the Wednesday-morning session to say that the tentative Senate deal was off because "it could not work in any circumstance in Quebec." Quebec had twenty-four of the 104 seats — the same as Ontario — and under the proposal, Quebec's proportion of Senate seats would fall from twenty-three per cent to nineteen per cent, a concession Bourassa simply couldn't risk politically. He said if the West and Newfoundland got more seats, Quebec would also need more to keep its percentage intact.

The Senate agreement wasn't the only thing to go sour that day. Soon the premiers got tangled up in a legalistic battle over the so-called Canada clause, essentially a clause to entrench in the Constitution the fundamental characteristics of Canada. Federal and provincial officials were up all night working on at least five different versions of it. Filmon insisted the Canada clause replace Quebec's distinct society clause and that it recognize Canada as a federal state with three fundamental components: English- and French-speaking people, aboriginals, and multicultural communities. Bourassa appealed to the premiers to understand that he could not accept anything that would lessen the distinct society clause. Wells, having witnessed the beating Bourassa took in the French-language media, actually agreed at that point. Newfoundland proposed the Canada clause be inserted in the preamble, not in the main body of the Constitution.

One provincial official in Camp Meech recalls that, at one point on Wednesday afternoon, there were at least six draft proposals on the table at once. "It was chaos . . . no one could figure out which one came from which province. We were trying to recognize them by the typewriter face. It was nuts — we had no idea who was making changes to what draft even then. No one had the slightest idea which one the premiers were talking about."

Round and round they went, getting nowhere, sparking several shouting matches, mostly aimed at Filmon and/or Wells, until finally it was time to break so the politicians could make their nightly appearance on the television news. Filmon was prompted to say the progress after another full day of talks could be measured in "inches."

Wells sounded almost conciliatory. "I have great understanding for the difficult position Premier Bourassa finds himself in politically," he said. Adding that Bourassa's position is in "significant conflict" with his and Filmon's, he concluded, "We've got to find a way of adjusting and accommodating that conflict. And the only way to do that is for both parties to compromise or find some kind of middle ground that is acceptable to both."

The same day another meeting was taking place, involving four of Canada's major native groups with Newfoundland, Manitoba, and Quebec. While both Wells and Filmon had agreed to strengthen protection for aboriginal people under the Constitution, Quebec wouldn't agree to their demands to also be recognized as a distinct society. Murray had offered them a draft that would merely recognize native "rights" in the preamble to the Constitution, but that was something the Supreme Court had already recognized. Native groups wanted recognition for their communities in the body of the Constitution as a "fundamental characteristic" of Canada with "distinct society status." Murray had also proposed a constitutional meeting on aboriginal issues, but George Erasmus, then national chief of the Assembly of First Nations, said the proposal was a step backward from the Meech Lake accord because it would make the issue of native self-government dependent on the will of the province instead of the federal government. "Manitoba and Newfoundland have positions we can live with," he said. "But we couldn't get Quebec on board in recognizing [us] in the body of the Constitution. They said they would address it in later rounds after Meech Lake — so we're still pushing."

The fact that they had managed to get Wells on-side, however, was in large measure a tribute to the tireless behind-the-scenes efforts of Western Arctic Liberal MP Ethel Blondin, a Dene Indian. In early February 1990 Blondin had boarded a plane in Montreal to begin the tortuous journey to Yellowknife, and Wells happened to be on the same plane headed for Winnipeg, first stop on a six-day speaking tour in Regina, Edmonton, Calgary, and Vancouver, accompanied by Coyne, his press secretary Judy Foote, and his senior aide Robert Dornan. Seizing the opportunity, Blondin began to discuss native issues with Wells, and by the time they arrived in Winnipeg, Wells had invited her to join them at the head table where he was speaking — giving her a ride downtown in his limousine — and he and Dornan met later with her in his hotel room. "We talked about where we were going to go, about my specific concerns with the North and aboriginal issues," Blondin says. "I wasn't sure where he stood on land claims and self-government. He reassured me he would take a look at it. He said whatever position he took would be fair to everybody concerned."

From that beginning, Blondin began to keep in regular touch with Wells's office. "I always defended him on the basis of being a principled man. In the Atlantic provinces, your word is your bond. I felt he was cannibalized during Meech Lake by Mulroney and that whole bunch. He was severely traumatized."

In August 1991, just before the premiers' conference in Whistler, B.C., Wells visited Yellowknife and Fort Rae in Blondin's riding. "It was like watching a caterpillar turn into a butterfly," she says. "He had come so far in understanding our issues and in expressing that understanding, whereas before we had a blank wall. He obviously researches his subject, his location, his geography. The native people just loved him. I was flabbergasted at how well he did. We took him to a Dog Rib group, a Dene cultural camp. He had a real native meal, whitefish and dried meat, although we had a salad, too. I went out on a boat with him. It's funny what you learn about people in these situations. He absolutely loves eagles. He's fascinated. He was totally enthralled when we found an eagle's nest near Frank's Bay. They ended up giving him an eagle feather, which symbolizes truth. [Senator] Joyce Fairbairn was there, too. She said she wanted to give him two. One for him and one to give Mulroney, where it might be helpful.

"The elders chronologized the history of the native peoples. They brought in elders from all over the area. The thing that really got to Clyde was the connection of those people to the land. We are the land. When Mulroney had been at Fort Rae it was completely different. He was so annoyed [at having to sit] on the stage for hours of the initialling of the land-claims agreement, which ultimately fell through. You could tell, Mulroney just wanted to get it over with and get out of there. . . . With Clyde, it was different. He was genuinely interested in what they had to say."

During Meech week, Blondin, working out of the Chateau Laurier, was cornering premiers and officials at every opportunity. At the Wednesday meeting, Blondin recalled, Quebec's Intergovernmental Affairs Minister Gil Rémillard wouldn't even discuss Quebec's veto over NWT's becoming a province. "He said, 'If you want to talk about Quebec's veto, don't even talk to me.' He and Erasmus had a wild argument over that. We never had a veto over Quebec. Why do they want one over us?

"Peterson was always supportive rhetorically. 'We'll try to help. We'll do all we can.' But in the end, we knew he wasn't going to support us. I told him, 'If you take the lead people will follow.' He said, 'This is the Quebec round. We'll look after you the next round.' He had no idea how many times we'd been promised that and how many times the promises were broken.

"I met Clyde and Dornan when Clyde went to his room on that last day to hole up for a while," says Blondin. "He was under such pressure the response I got was he's going crazy, we've got to calm him down. He was being asked to soften his position. I was told to go to Clyde. People were saying to me, 'You know him. He likes you. Talk to him.' He was in a pressure cooker.

"I know a lot of people don't like him. I don't mix who I like with what politics they have. Some politicians, if your views are opposite to them, they personalize that. It's crippling. You have to separate the two. I was challenged time and time again. 'How can you support Clyde Wells? He's not open to aboriginal issues.' I said he understands facts and figures. If it can be proven to him there is a case and it can be done sensitively, he's open to that. You have to show him. Make your case.

"Maybe I feel as strongly about Clyde Wells as I do because he fought the good fight, and so did we. He stayed in there with his principles, and so did we. He was the underdog, and so are we."

Blondin believes there is little doubt that native people have more public support now, and that there are a lot of wise and prudent and brave native leaders. If the government, however, doesn't deal with their issues this time around, she doesn't even want to think where that could lead. "But I can tell you this," she declares, "after that Meech experience, we are not going to be taken for granted again. Never."

Newfoundland Liberal MP Brian Tobin says that one of the great ironies of the whole Meech Lake exercise was that Wells had always been totally opposed to Brian Peckford's confrontational style of fighting in Ottawa. Wells "talked a great deal about how easy it was to be in a confrontation mode with the national government. How easy it was for a Newfoundland premier to beat his breast and exhort his troops to rally behind him and be in a fight. But how counterproductive that kind of role was! And I think he felt as a citizen it was time to put aside some of the politics of passion, pride, and prejudice and begin a new era of constructive approaches to Ottawa. . . . I think that's what really drove him, so that it's somewhat ironic that the role the public best identifies Clyde with is the one of confrontation with Mulroney. . . . That is not a role he would have sought."

Shortly before 3 p.m. on Thursday, with a watered-down deal looking possible, the other premiers asked both Wells and Filmon to meet downstairs with Carstairs and Doer and present the case to them. There is still a dispute as to whether Wells and Filmon had already agreed to a new package at that time, as the other premiers and federal officials claim, or whether they simply agreed to test the reaction of the two Manitoba opposition leaders before finalizing anything, a more likely scenario given the circumstances.

In any event, Wells left The Bunker first, making his way to Camp Meech to update Deborah Coyne and then justice minister Paul Dicks. Coyne was furious and said so, believing the constant pressure of the closed-door sessions was finally beginning to cloud Wells's judgment. Wells conceded the Canada clause was still a problem, but said the others had agreed to placate his concerns about the distinct-society clause by producing a letter written by Roger Tasse and other legal experts saying it did not confer new legislative powers on Quebec.

Soon, the Newfoundland delegation joined Filmon, Carstairs, Doer, and three Manitoba legal officials, along with Tasse and constitutional lawyer Peter Hogg representing the federal position.

One official who was in the meeting described it as "totally convoluted . . . unbelievable. . . . Tasse was fronting for Quebec.

He had their approval. He'd orchestrated the thing and all we heard was how we had to accommodate Quebec."

At one point during the three-hour meeting, Bourassa came in alone and the unelected officials were sent out of the room. Bourassa told the four politicians that they must understand that he could not possibly agree to anything less and sell it to Quebecers.

He also reneged on an agreement he had made earlier in The Bunker to a Newfoundland suggestion for a phrase recognizing Canada as "a federal state with a unique national identity." Bourassa's officials had objected that the word "national" was too loaded politically, so the Quebec premier told Wells, Filmon, Carstairs, and Doer that it had to be expunged.

While Bourassa was inside the meeting, New Brunswick officials in Camp Meech were trying to convince their Newfoundland counterparts to come on-side and isolate Filmon. "It was incredible," recalls a Wells aide. "The whole thing was nothing more than a power play. Everyone started to dump on Manitoba. They were also trying to split up Wells and Carstairs because they were both Liberals. It was beginning to look then as if there was no chance for a deal, so the spin was to shift the blame."

Around six o'clock that night, Wells and Filmon returned to The Bunker. With Filmon remaining silent, Wells, still standing, said Carstairs and Doer were insisting on entrenchment of a Canada clause before June 23, and Wells himself wanted a clarification of spending powers, along with a political declaration from the first ministers on protecting the Charter from the distinct society clause. That was just too much for Bourassa.

The veteran Quebec premier, who rarely loses his cool, yelled, "If that's the way you feel, fuck you." Peterson was equally furious. He, too, screamed at Wells, asking at the end of his tirade, "Whose side are you on?"

According to Lowell Murray, Wells and Filmon had been sent

out with specific instructions to sell a deal to Carstairs and Doer. But "Wells wasn't able to sell, if he even tried to sell, and when he returned there was a good deal of frustration and bitterness in the room.

"Wells kept saying he didn't appreciate the pressure that was put on him. But hell, he's a big boy, you know. The pressure was peer pressure. Nobody was threatening him with anything."

In his book *A Deal Undone*, Andrew Cohen writes that at this point, Wells "was in tears. He was a proud man, overcome by strain." Wells hotly denies this, yet he is quoted by Cohen as saying, "I took the worst browbeating of the conference that day. [They said] that I was threatening the future of the nation by not agreeing to do what everyone else was doing, that I was holding up the nation. Emotional speeches were directed at me. I let myself get emotional, and I can't forgive myself for that, because I don't think that served any good. I lost my self-control and I regret that."

Indeed, McKenna told Cohen that Wells was "very strung out at that point." And a senior official from one of the Maritime provinces, reading from his notes of the period, told the author that Wells "cried several times . . . he was exhausted, completely fried . . . we were calling the whole process the 'hostage taking.' Clyde was dysfunctional and they were concerned he'd had a nervous breakdown. . . . New Brunswick thought he [Clyde] was psychologically unreliable. . . . He'd go into the room and appear to agree to a number of things, then go see his advisers and come back and be totally different. He'd even deny having agreed before. . . ." Vander Zalm makes the same complaint. "Sometimes when discussing things, you'd think we were getting somewhere. You'd end the day and feel a degree of camaraderie and the feeling you were getting things resolved, and suddenly you'd watch the TV news and you'd wonder, holy smokes, what happened [to Clyde] on his way to the microphone?"

Federal officials and those from Ontario and New Brunswick in particular were in a feeding frenzy to make sure the story of Wells's alleged unbalance got out through sympathizers into the mainstream media. A couple of days later, for example, in a long feature on the week, the CBC dutifully reported that Wells was "emotionally distraught" and a commentator added that Wells is "widely viewed as being an extremely inconsistent person." By whom, one might ask?

Throughout the piece, Wells and Filmon were constantly portrayed as the "holdouts." At one point, the CBC referred to Doer and Carstairs as potential "villains." With few exceptions, the national media were shamelessly shilling for the federal case. This nasty allegation against those resisting Meech Lake came essentially from two places: pro-Meech officials whispering to reporters in the corridors, and the nightly background briefings by Stanley Hartt and Norman Spector, where reporters who attended the sessions agreed not to identify these highly politicized officials by name.

There seems little doubt that, by the end of the week, Wells was on the edge. But he wasn't alone. Saskatchewan's Grant Devine was there with him. Apart from *Ottawa Citizen* columnist Roy MacGregor, few journalists east of Manitoba bothered even to mention Devine's babbling inanities about Benjamin Franklin and Winston Churchill, whom he said he had felt in the room with the premiers, or about how he believed Chairman Mao's spirit had been in touch with him on a trip to China.

The difference was, of course, that Devine was pro-Meech.

Shortly before Bourassa prepared to leave the meeting Thursday night, he turned to Wells and said, "Clyde, you will destroy any hope of national unity, you will destroy any hope of Senate reform, but you will keep your vanity." After a few seconds of silence, Wells replied, "There is no one more committed to bilingualism and francophones than Clyde Wells."

Joe Ghiz interjected with a passionate speech about how

Canada was a great country, where the son of a penniless Lebanese immigrant could end up as a premier. At one point in the proceedings he'd called Wells a "fucking prick," which he later denied. Three premiers privately confirm Ghiz did say it, and what's more, agree with it.

Constantly, from all around the table, the other leaders were hammering away at Wells, saying if he didn't agree to Meech Lake he was going to destroy Canada. In his book, Cohen quotes Wells as saying of that strategy, "That's the way it went. That's no way to build a Constitution. It came down to that ultimate threat. How can you say no to that? That's what's wrong with that godawful process, where people can get away with that in the secrecy of a room. In public they could never do it; they would be cut to pieces."

But Wells had his own fallback position. As one premier puts it, "I remember Clyde saying to me, 'Well, if I'm wrong, I'll resign.' I said, 'Clyde, you are immaterial to this whole thing. We all are. There is no one politician who is indispensable to this whole thing. If the deal fails, the country's gone, so who cares if you resign?' This is the kind of logic he was using.

"At the end of the day you'd say, 'Clyde, that just doesn't make any sense in law.' Some guys in that room understood as much about constitutional law as he did, who knew their brief, and a lot of other advisers did. And his response would be, 'Do you know how many letters I got today from Manitoba who agree with me?' He had it down to a daily [tally of] how many letters he got. And he loved to have 'The National' in there going through his file and saying here's how many letters Clyde Wells got and a poster saying Clyde Wells should be prime minister. . . . I remember one time he had a bunch of letters with him and he was waving them around. . . . We all get letters, big deal . . . but intellectually, that was his last refuge of every argument. 'Look at the support I've got.'

"It reminded me of Diefenbaker in his dying days. When everybody dumped on him, he'd go to his office and read letters from little old ladies in Prince Rupert or North Battleford or wherever, saying you're a great Canadian. And that's where he got his intellectual sustenance from. Clyde completely misread the thing . . . [and was] fuelled by vanity."

Another oddity about Wells emerged that day when, during a break in the action, he came downstairs briefly to meet with the small group of reporters, some from Newfoundland, who had been specifically assigned by their organizations to cover him. When Wells was asked how things were going, he said what bothered him most was that it had become so personal. Pressed for an example, it soon became apparent he wasn't speaking of the closed-door exchanges at all, but of some of the feature stories being written about him, specifically the constant references to his "steely-blue eyes"!

After Bourassa's heated refusal to even discuss the distinct society issue, a five-line communiqué was released, its timing neatly coinciding with the six-o'clock news. It stated Bourassa wouldn't even sit at the table if the discussions had anything to do with the distinct society, and Day Five came to a sudden and dramatic end. Wells, visibly angry, told waiting reporters, "Settlements are made of compromise and not capitulation. And if there's not to be compromise, then I can only say maybe there won't be a settlement."

Wells thought he had made what he called a "significant concession" to Quebec by dropping his demand that the clause giving Quebec special status be amended directly in the text of the accord rather than the preamble. He was "shocked" by Bourassa's news release, and also dismissed as "totally and completely false," Spector's and Murray's claims that he'd returned to the table after his meeting with Filmon, Carstairs, and Doer with tougher demands than he'd left with, even though it later became obvious he had done just that.

As he stormed into his hotel room that night, Wells vowed that Newfoundland would make no further concessions, saying the only way out of the impasse was for Bourassa to begin to negotiate the serious issues. But Bourassa repeated he would not accept anything that affected the distinct society clause.

By Friday, the Newfoundland troops were getting restless. Wells and Carstairs met for a 7:30 a.m. breakfast with three of Jean Chrétien's senior strategists — Eddie Goldenberg, John Rae, and Eric Maldoff — all of whom wanted Wells to make a deal. The Liberal leadership convention was just two weeks off, and Chrétien was trying his best to deflect criticism that he'd opposed Meech Lake. Bringing Wells around would certainly be a major feather in his cap. Coyne, of course, was furious that Wells was buckling under, and Eugene Forsey had resigned from the provincial delegation.

In the meeting in The Bunker afterwards, Wells told Mulroney he was going to hold a press conference to vent his concerns, but once again he held back when Mulroney asked him to wait. He later told Andrew Cohen, "I couldn't understand how I let myself get sucked into that and stayed for all that length of time. A kind of collegiality develops, even though there may be strong views expressed. No one wants to do things to make life difficult. So you keep going, you make concessions, you agree. A little bit more, a little bit more, a little bit more, and finally you are on that thing and there is no way off it."

For the first two hours, Bourassa didn't show up, underscoring his promise not to listen to any talk about changing the distinct society clause. By noon, Bourassa returned, and Wells had agreed to settle for a legal opinion on the distinct society clause prepared by a group of the country's top jurists. His major concern was that Quebec might use the collective rights of the clause to diminish individual rights in the province. The letter would be appended to whatever deal they reached, but none of the pro-Meech premiers would sign it. Progress, sort of.

At least, it was until they got onto Senate reform, at which point both Wells and Filmon, feeling somewhat compromised by their concessions on other issues, decided to get downright hawkish. Ghiz reintroduced his plan — which would give every province a five-year veto, after which, if they hadn't reached a better deal, seats would be redistributed. Wells wasn't happy with three more seats and Bourassa wouldn't hear of anything that reduced Quebec's percentage of Senate seats. Somehow the Ghiz proposal was taken off the table by Mulroney, and Wells, livid, threatened to walk. So did Filmon.

Mulroney was pleading with Wells to stay, but as long as the Senate plan was not on, Wells wasn't interested. At one point he gathered his papers and headed for the door, but Getty, the former quarterback, stood in front of him — no, he didn't tackle him as some of the more imaginative stories later reported. The delay, though, was enough to allow Peterson to rush in and play the hero. He offered to give up six of Ontario's twenty-four Senate seats and asked New Brunswick and Nova Scotia to give up two each, thus freeing up ten seats to be shared among Newfoundland and the four western provinces, while leaving Quebec's allotment intact. Peterson had found the idea earlier in a brainstorming session with his army of officials — Osgoode Hall law school professor James MacPherson had suggested it. Wells was impressed. He bought it and moments later, they had a deal.

Earlier in the day, at Mulroney's request, McKenna, Wells, and Tasse were asked to draft a provision to allow the first ministers to review the impact of the distinct society clause on the Charter of Rights and Freedoms after ten years. That seemed simple enough. It wasn't. It almost blew the deal. For one thing, Wells wanted the clause to give premiers the right to make amendments to the clause. McKenna knew Quebec would never buy that. Wells suggested they include it anyway. Tasse didn't object. And so the draft was sent off to be added to the text of the agreement.

All the premiers returned to The Bunker for dinner. Peterson and Wells wanted to pack it in for the night and hold the long-promised public session the next morning, but Mulroney wanted to wait for the complete text, so the bar was set up, the officials were called in, and it was party time. Not for Wells, however. He kept wondering where the five-line clause was that he, McKenna, and Tasse had written.

At 11:30 p.m., the five-page "final communiqué" was brought into the room for the premiers to initial. The clause was missing. Wells asked Mulroney about it, and the prime minister, after checking with Tasse, said it was left out because Quebec wouldn't accept it. Wells was furious again.

One Newfoundland official described the scene: "There was a celebration. Peterson was there with his sleeves rolled up and all that stuff. Wells was there, just really quiet . . . it was so sickening in a way. Then the missing clause came. There was no doubt about it. I'm sure that Wells did use that. He was looking for a way out . . . he knew how we felt about it. . . . Wells used that as a way to get out, and he got his momentum back."

Just past midnight, the media was told there was an agreement in principle but a few details to iron out. Bourassa said, "The mission is accomplished. It's a very great day for Canada." Federal officials claimed the missing clause was an innocent oversight. "It isn't a big deal," said one. It was to Wells. When asked by reporters if it was serious enough to block the deal, Wells snapped, "Absolutely. At the moment there's a problem. There is a roadblock and we'll deal with the details in the morning."

With that, he stormed off to his suite at the Chateau Laurier. But there wasn't much solace there. His wife, Eleanor, consistently at his side, had missed the entire week because she was ill, an absence those who know Wells say affected him considerably. In addition, his team of advisers were upset with him and felt betrayed that Wells had bent as far as he had.

At 1:30 a.m., Mulroney came downstairs and gave a brief statement: "We have a large measure of agreement on most of the important concepts. As you know, these arrangements are never really final until they're signed, sealed, and delivered."

On Saturday morning, on Mulroney's orders, Tasse telephoned Wells to apologize personally for the mix-up over the missing clause, even though it was not Tasse's fault. Norman Spector was the one who'd decided Quebec wouldn't buy it. But Wells was still unhappy, whatever faith he'd had in his colleagues shattered. Obviously, Mulroney knew this and was desperately trying to pacify the wounded premier. He even held a brief private meeting with Wells, during which Wells told him he wouldn't endorse the accord. The best he would offer was to take it back home for either a referendum or a vote in the House of Assembly.

Discussion over the missing clause went on for hours. Tasse and Wells met privately, with Wells returning to say it couldn't have been Tasse because "he is too fine a man."

The draft document had committed Wells, Filmon, and McKenna to seek "approval" of the accord, but Wells repeated what he's said to Mulroney — he'd put it to a free vote back home. He promised not to campaign against it — a promise he didn't keep — and said he would invite Mulroney and the premiers to speak in the House of Assembly. Even so, by the end of the day, the final communiqué committed him to submit the accord "for appropriate legislative or public consideration and use every possible effort to achieve decision prior to 23 June 1990."

Wells had several meetings with his officials. Coyne and Dicks were trying to talk him out of signing, but McKenna kept urging Clyde to sign. His officials told him to sign a separate piece of paper, but Wells dismissed the suggestion as a technicality, another decision he would regret. Eventually, he did sign, albeit with an asterisk. "I should have known better," he told Cohen much later. "But you try to agree. It was a compromise clause for all to sign. That was a gross error, but you get into that damn collegiality again. You lose your perspective. Collegiality destroys judgment."

Before that, however, the document went through at least

ten drafts during the day. By 6 p.m. the final draft was on the table. At 8:30 p.m. Mulroney's office told reporters that the first ministers would formally sign the twenty-nine-paragraph document at 10 p.m. in the main hall of the Conference Centre.

When they were all assembled for the television cameras, Spector carried the document from premier to premier for their signatures. When that was done, Mulroney asked Wells to speak first — he would normally speak last, since Newfoundland was the last to join Canada — to underscore the fact that Wells had signed and also to give the others a chance to rebut any criticisms he might make.

Wells was very specific about what he'd done. "I will take this proposal back — this is what I have committed to do and this is what my signature means, and it means only that," he said.

He called it "the most difficult decision I have ever had to make in my life. I found myself constantly being pressured to agree to do something under the fear and threat that failure to do it may do irreparable harm to the country. And I don't want any responsibility for doing irreparable harm to any part of this nation."

Later, as security guards rushed him through a large crowd of bystanders, Wells told reporters, "I'm not approving of this particular accord. I am submitting it to the Newfoundland people or the legislature. . . . I don't know how I could have allowed myself to be taken for a ride on this vortex. . . . I'm disappointed with the whole process from the beginning. . . . There is no question about where virtually all the compromise has been."

Asked about Mulroney's 1984 promise that Quebec would be brought into the Constitution with "honor and enthusiasm," Wells said, "I feel honor but very little enthusiasm."

10

Broken Promises

HE CRIED AGAIN. This time, tears of joy and exhaustion, not despair and defeat.

Returning home to a hero's welcome on the sunny Sunday afternoon of June 10, at the St. John's airport, he was met by about five hundred jubilant supporters chanting, "Clyde Wells. Clyde Wells." But his brother Alan and his son Mark, watching the arrival on TV, said they'd never before seen him cry. Not at his sister's funeral. Not at his father's funeral. Never.

Wells, tears streaming down his cheeks, called on Newfoundlanders to put their country first and their province second, the same advice he'd given to Robert Bourassa in his closing speech in Ottawa.

"I am going to ask you to give me support on one other point," he told the crowd. "I've been telling people all across this country wherever I've been speaking that I'm first and foremost a Canadian. That doesn't make me any less a proud Newfoundlander than anyone else in this room. I'm asking you tell the rest of the country that all of the other citizens of

Newfoundland and Labrador are first and foremost Canadians and we will put our country first."

As he moved through the crowd, people shook his hand, hugged him, and women kissed his cheeks. Signs saying YOU MAKE US PROUD were waved. "You did good Clyde, you did good! We love you, Clyde!" one man shouted. Many others cried, and smiled, and clapped, some began chanting, "Referendum, referendum." Soon people began to sing "Ode to Newfoundland" and then "O Canada."

It was, as they say, quite a sight.

His son David phoned home, where Eleanor was still ill, and said, "Mom, he's like a rock star."

From across the country, from the big cities and the small towns, from the farms to the penthouse suites, from Liberals and Tories and New Democrats, from the old and the young — but only a few from Quebec — the flowers continued to pour in, the telegrams, faxes, letters, and phone calls.

Clyde Wells, a man whose own emotions are so guarded, whose style is so professorial, whose interests are so technical, had struck a previously untapped reservoir of pent-up feelings over Meech Lake and unleashed a wellspring of emotion across the land. He had stood for something at a time when other politicians stood for everything and nothing. He had been beaten, battered, and bruised by an awesome array of political bullies, by the national media, by all three major parties, by an army of bureaucrats and constitutional lawyers, and he had somehow endured and walked away, head held high. He epitomized qualities the public was starved for in its leadership — dignity, integrity, honesty. And guts. He seemed as real as Peterson seemed plastic, as strong as McKenna appeared weak, as persuasive as Devine was ineffectual.

The public, of course, did not know the whole story. But what they knew, what they saw, turned them on to this man who, just a few months earlier not one in 100,000 Canadians had even heard of. Above all else, he is now seen by many

Canadians as a man of principle. But is he? Certainly more
so than Mulroney. Is he really more principled than, say, Joe
Ghiz, who supported the accord? Or for that matter, Grant
Devine or Don Getty who, had they wanted to take the easy
political route, could have won standing ovations in their
provinces by being seen to be sticking it to Quebec? Is it
principle, or is it simple bullheadedness? Or perhaps, as
former Newfoundland premier Frank Moores comments,
"I'm not sure it's a matter of real principle with Clyde. It's
more a matter of his believing himself to be absolutely
correct."

Wells did, after all, sign something he admits he didn't
believe in. And, in the end, whatever his protestations, he did
break his word.

But at that time, in that place, Clyde Wells was a true
Canadian hero, something in short supply. And for many, he
remains a hero today. Liberal MP Ethel Blondin says, "I was so
angry when I saw him cry. It was the epitome of what I hate
about politics. People hate you for what you believe. It was an
insult to Newfoundland to treat him that way. Here is a group
of people who are not nearly as principled . . . horse traders . . .
ready to sell out their principles in order to cut a deal."

By the next day Wells regained his old form, and the first
thing he did, after meeting with his cabinet and caucus, was
announce he would ask provincial legislatures across the country to extend the June 23 deadline for approval of the accord.
Freed from the pressure of Ottawa, regaining ironclad control
of his emotions, he challenged the other premiers to come to
Newfoundland and "publicly say what they said to me in the
secrecy of that room." He did not offer to publicly say what
he'd said to them, or to justify the major tradeoffs he'd made
of his cherished principles.

Wells had really wanted a provincial referendum, but he
knew there wasn't time. The beauty of the referendum route
was that it almost certainly would have backed up Wells's

desire to nix the accord — and thus have taken him off the hook.

Veteran Nova Scotia Tory senator Finlay MacDonald looked askance at the idea. "Can you imagine a referendum in New-foundland? And, I have to say it, among the semi-literate population? Clyde, an intelligent man, proposing to ask those people in a referendum whether they favor a distinct society for Quebec? He's got that Presbyterian-Calvinist fervor, like the missionaries going to Hawaii to stop the natives from copulating.

"He's the man who could have corrected the situation. I concede it was a fuck-up from the federal end, from Mulroney to Murray to Spector. All the games they played. But in the end, it's like a judge trying to decide the merits of the case. Even if it was presented badly, he still has the duty to make the decision.

"He was really the first person to capitalize on the general cynicism the public has about politicians. He was made for a comparison to Mulroney, and obviously in the public mind, it wasn't a favorable comparison for Mulroney, the consummate wheeler-dealer, against this 'man of great principle.' He took advantage of that and I dare say revelled in the adulation."

On Monday, Wells announced in the House of Assembly that a referendum was off, but a free vote on the accord was on. Saying it was unfortunate that certain other provincial legislatures — he was referring to Quebec and Nova Scotia — had shown, by refusing to extend the deadline, no consider-ation to the people of Newfoundland and Labrador, he repeated his pledge not to campaign against the accord, urging his MHAs to do what they thought was best for Canada and Newfound-land. Later he told reporters, "I'm sensitive to the fact that the vast majority of this province may well do whatever I ask them. The polls go further and indicate that what I do and what I say may well have an effect in other provinces as well, in Manitoba in particular. I don't want to abuse that trust by seeking to cause a particular result. I don't know with absolute certainly that I am absolutely right. I am not trying to cause a particular result, please understand that. Don't operate from the concept that I am carrying on a campaign to seek rejection of the Meech Lake accord. I am not."

Perhaps. But that didn't stop him from touring the province and freely expressing his personal opinions, advocating time and time again that the accord should be killed. He rationalized this by saying that people were asking him what his views were, and he had a duty to tell them. Anyway, he'd say, he was just one of fifty-two MHAs who had to vote.

Even in his detailed post-Meech format statement on June 24, responding to bitter attacks from both Mulroney and Bourassa, Wells insisted he had honored his commitment "to the letter, and I went further and not only did not campaign against [the accord's] acceptance — for which in some quarters I was criticized — but I invited the prime minister and the premiers to come to the legislature to give them the opportunity to persuade the members who opposed the accord to change their mind."

Liberal MP Brian Tobin says Wells took "a very altruistic type of approach. There's no question in my mind . . . that Clyde was campaigning for a 'no' vote. Whether he himself recognized he was running a campaign, I'm not sure."

Brian Mulroney, David Peterson, Frank McKenna, and Grant Devine all accepted Wells's invitation to fly to St. John's to speak to the house in support of the accord. One of those premiers later said privately, "I didn't want to go. I absolutely didn't want to. Why would I. I had lots of problems of my own. Clyde virtually insisted that I go down and speak to his legislature. . . . I went down only for Clyde because Clyde wanted me. If it was good for his ego to have a bunch of us parade in there and genuflect in front of him and have him pass judgment on us, so be it. I'd do anything to save Meech because the consequences were so grave. . . ."

The day after Wells had announced he would hold the free vote, Gary Filmon rose in the Manitoba legislature seeking unanimous consent to introduce the accord with the standard two days' notice. New Democrat Elijah Harper, a Cree Indian from the northern riding of Rupertsland, said in his low firm voice, "No," instantly catapulting himself (which was never his intention) and native issues (which were) into the national consciousness.

By the end of the week, with Harper still refusing consent and the tabling delayed until June 18, Filmon publicly warned that the accord might die in Manitoba rather than Newfoundland. Just as Wells had struck a chord with so many Canadians, Harper, too, became a symbol for natives and for those who believed his people were getting yet another raw deal.

As for New Brunswick, nobody had any doubts about what McKenna was doing. He had upset the pro-Meechers by being the first premier to question publicly the deal and call for changes, and he hadn't won any friends or any respect by slinking on-side late in the game under cover of his so-called companion resolution. As expected, his all-Liberal legislature approved the accord June 15, the same week he'd returned from Ottawa.

An Angus Reid poll conducted June 11, just two days after the deal had been struck, showed only eleven per cent of 1241 Canadians asked thought the deal was a good one, but fifty-five per cent — sixty-one in Quebec — wanted the Newfoundland legislature to ratify it anyway. Even more significant, asked if they approved or disapproved of the actions of the leaders during the negotiations, the three so-called "dissident" premiers headed the pack, with Wells getting the most support: sixty-eight per cent outside Quebec, seventy per cent in Atlantic Canada, but just twenty-five per cent inside Quebec. Filmon was a close second, with McKenna getting the nod from fifty-four per cent of non-Quebecers and forty-two per cent of Quebecers. By contrast, Mulroney scored fifty-eight per cent inside Quebec and just twenty-nine per cent outside, and Bourassa got sixty per cent in Quebec and thirty per cent in the rest of Canada.

Ironically, Peterson scored slightly higher in Quebec — fifty-nine percent — than in his own province of Ontario — fifty-seven — a message he should have heeded before his disastrous decision to call an unnecessary election that fall, which saw Ontarians elect an NDP government for the first time in their history. The perception that he had been too tight with Mulroney and Bourassa, and that he'd treated Ontario's Senate seats as if they belonged to him personally, offering to give some up without so much as a howdy-do, severely damaged Peterson's popularity.

On June 12 *Globe and Mail* readers were greeted with a front-page story on the prime minister. As a personal favor to *Globe* editor William Thorsell, one of his few unabashed admirers, Mulroney had agreed to help the newspaper make a splash of its brand-new design and so was interviewed by three journalists from the *Globe*'s Ottawa bureau: columnist Jeffrey Simpson, bureau chief Graham Fraser, and reporter Susan Delacourt. The story had an unforeseen significant revelation.

For weeks leading up to the Ottawa conference, several premiers and others had been calling for a meeting to get the issues resolved, but both Mulroney and Murray kept insisting that, while they were ready to meet, not all the premiers were. Asked why he had waited so late in the process before actually calling the premiers together, Mulroney recalled a May 1 meeting with his advisers. "I told them a month ago when we were going to start meeting. It's like an election campaign. You've got to work backward. You pick your dates and work backward. And I said, 'That's the day I'm going to roll all the dice.' It's the only way to handle it.'"

Delacourt, who picked up on the significance of this remark faster than her colleagues, asked Mulroney if that's what he had done — "rolled the dice." He said that's exactly what he'd done. Had it not been for Delacourt's dogged insistence, the comment wouldn't have even made the story to begin with. At first, Simpson and Fraser didn't see it as a big deal, but later, when senior *Globe* editors talked about not using the quote, the two men strongly argued it was an important development.

When Wells read it, he was furious. Mulroney telephoned him that morning to reassure him that the federal government didn't deliberately delay the meeting just to put more pressure on the holdouts. Mulroney told him, and later told the Commons, that his comments had been taken out of context to create a "false" impression of what he'd actually said. That weekend, senior *Globe* editors buckled under to heavy pressure from the prime minister's office and ran the entire transcript of the interview. At one point, Thorsell had agreed to insert a paragraph at the start, essentially saying that Mulroney had been quoted out of context. But when Fraser, Simpson, and others threatened to resign, the idea was dropped. It was now absolutely clear that Mulroney had deliberately created a false crisis situation during the negotiations.

Despite what he had been put through by Mulroney, Wells accepted the prime minister's initial explanation about the quote. Delacourt, a consummate professional who had spent months shuffling back and forth between Wells and McKenna covering the events leading up to this point, telephoned Wells to express her displeasure that he would trust Mulroney's word over her own.

"I was really pissed off at Wells," she says. "He said he had no choice but to accept Mulroney's word because he was the prime minister. Well, so what? He didn't exactly have the world's best record for veracity. I was quite insulted that Wells would believe him and, in essence, accuse me of lying. I lost considerable respect for him over that."

Wells, like Mulroney, was still trying to have it both ways. Despite saying publicly he had no choice but to accept Mulroney's explanation, he nevertheless used the opportunity

Mulroney had created to take another swipe at the process. Complaining he had been "violated" by Mulroney's manipulations, Wells said, "It's getting more and more difficult not to believe we've been manipulated when we tried to be openly honest and fair with Canadians," adding Mulroney's statements may have damaged the chances of getting the accord approved by the house. "It certainly won't help it. I hope we can undo any damage that may have been caused as a result of it."

One of the pro-Meech premiers said Mulroney's remarks were a serious mistake because "he ceded the moral high ground to Clyde. It happens in life when you're making an argument and you inadvertently make one bad example and the guy comes back and he seizes your example even though it's not that germane to your whole argument and it can kill you. But he ceded the moral high ground with the 'roll of the dice' thing, and Clyde just used it to shove it in his ear."

In the meantime, things were getting ugly in Winnipeg. A group of about fifty-five native people were denied access to the gallery of the legislature, told the seats were full. They angrily forced their way in and discovered there was room in the public gallery after all. Harper, cheered on by the natives, again blocked the debate, saying his move was planned "to symbolize the issues of the aboriginal people not being recognized. The first ministers should have dealt with aboriginal issues. It's not easy for me to make this decision, but who's going to speak out for us?"

Filmon was trying to introduce a resolution for a brief debate to set the stage for public hearings on the accord. These were to be followed by a vote before June 23, an impossible task even if Harper hadn't been holding up the process.

Sharon Carstairs, who had lost a lot of political credibility during the Meech week — complaining at one point she was so disturbed by the whole process she was thinking of quitting politics — later told writer Andrew Cohen that when the issue shifted to aboriginal concerns, "I had this incredible sense of calm, that it wasn't me anymore, it's somebody else." There seems little doubt that Filmon and Doer were also relieved. All three Manitoba leaders had agreed reluctantly to the deal, so if there was a way to scuttle it without their being blamed, so much the better.

Yet another Angus Reid poll published June 14 about whether the accord should be approved by Newfoundland indicated that, even though only thirty-eight per cent of Newfoundlanders who were asked approved of it (forty-seven per cent disapproved), forty-six per cent still wanted the house to pass it, while forty per cent said no. In Manitoba, public opposition was much stiffer. Only forty per cent said they wanted Newfoundland to pass it, while fifty-one per cent wanted it scrapped.

Wells, meanwhile, kept up the charade of his non-campaign against the accord in his own province. In a mid-week stop in Corner Brook, he said it was up to the Meech Lake supporters to prove to Newfoundlanders that rejection of the accord would harm Confederation. "I don't want to argue approval or disapproval by having an argument on the merits of the accord," he said. "What I and the people of Newfoundland want to hear now is whether there is any validity to the opinion that if we vote against the accord, there will be substantial political and economic harm done to Canada." At that point, Wells had scheduled a free vote in the house for Thursday, June 21. The nineteen Tories and two Independents favored the accord, but there was uncertainty over how many of the thirty-one Liberals did. For the accord to be approved, six Liberals had to vote for it and, in essence, against Wells.

In Manitoba, the situation looked even bleaker for the pro-Meech forces, when a dramatic procedural wrangle brought about by Harper forced Filmon to start the whole process all over again on Friday, June 15. Harper charged that there had been an error in the way MLAs were given notice of the constitutional resolution, making it impossible for public hearings to begin until Wednesday, June 20, just three days before the deadline. Speaker Denis Rocan, remaining in his office for ninety minutes to study the matter, ruled that Harper was right; proper notice had not been given.

Carstairs urged an extension of the deadline, but in Quebec City, Quebec Intergovernmental Affairs Minister Gil Rémillard said that after 12 p.m., June 23, Quebec time "it will be all over."

The next day, Wells gave an interview to *Globe* reporter André Picard in which he said that even if the process was derailed in Manitoba, Newfoundland would go ahead with its vote on the accord. "We've started the process, and I can't see us abandoning it unless there is some overwhelming evidence to do so." Nevertheless, one week later he adjourned the house without holding the vote, and the only "overwhelming evidence" he offered as an excuse was the fact that Meech was already dead in Manitoba. Even before that, Wells told a weekend conference with New England governors in the seaside resort town of Mystic, Connecticut, that his final decision on a vote would depend on what happened in Manitoba. "If Manitoba can't have a vote before June 23, then whether Newfoundland does or does not is academic. If it's an academic exercise, why do it?"

In Ottawa, Mulroney was getting worried. He spent Friday, June 15, huddled with his officials at 24 Sussex Drive searching for a compromise that would convince native leaders to abandon their procedural tactics in Manitoba. The day before, outgoing Liberal leader John Turner, in a rare appearance in the Commons, angrily lashed out at Mulroney. "Let no one put blame on Elijah Harper or on the aboriginal people of this country. The blame rests squarely on the shoulders of one man. The man who, in his own words, chose to roll the dice, and he chose the date when to roll the dice. The constitutional crisis is now his and his alone."

Federal Energy Minister Jake Epp, Manitoba's senior cabinet minister, had arrived in Winnipeg with a written proposal from Mulroney and the message that federal officials were ready to talk to the natives. In addition, lawyer Jack London, who was working with the Assembly of Manitoba Chiefs, was also talking with Ottawa officials. George Erasmus, head of the Assembly of First Nations, said he was willing to talk, but he wasn't impressed by warnings from Bourassa that the natives had better come on-side or Quebec would reject any future constitutional negotiations dealing with aboriginal issues. "The anglos are all on their knees trying to get Quebec in," said Erasmus. "But we are not going to exchange English suppressors for French suppressors."

Assembly of First Nations vice-chief Ovide Mercredi, a key strategist who later became chief of the assembly, had walked out of a meeting with federal officials two days earlier, saying Ottawa wasn't taking the issue seriously. "When I said we were open for talks and that they could call us later, [Justice Minister Kim] Campbell almost choked. I do not think they were dealing with reality."

The final week had begun. Wells, returning from his weekend conference, repeated his threat to cancel the vote if it remained stalled in Manitoba. In Winnipeg, it took Manitoba chiefs less than forty minutes to flatly reject the six-point federal proposal presented by Epp, Murray, and Spector designed to allay their concerns about the accord. Ottawa had offered a royal commission on native issues and a commitment to recognize native people as a fundamental characteristic of Canada.

Phil Fontaine, a lawyer and provincial leader of the Assembly of Manitoba Chiefs, dismissed the offer as "unacceptable. There was nothing there that we could consider." Fontaine said the accord is "an injustice to native people. Why would we condone an injustice to ourselves? We have been second-class citizens for far too long." Murray said he was "disappointed, but not entirely surprised, given that their objective, several times stated, has been to kill the Meech Lake accord and the companion resolution." Murray insisted, however, that Manitoba could still pass the accord if Filmon would just curtail the public hearings. "I do believe if the will is there on the part of the majority of members of the Manitoba legislature and their leaders, this can be debated and voted." All three party leaders said they had no intention of modifying the legislature's rules to ram Meech through. "We're going to respect our rules first and foremost," said Filmon. "It appears very definite that we do not have time to deal with the process."

Back in St. John's on Tuesday night, the eve of the historic debate on the accord, Wells said that if Quebecers want to separate, the accord "is not going to stop them. Nor is failure of the Meech Lake accord going to cause them to take that course."

On Wednesday, June 20, McKenna and Peterson displayed contrasting styles in the pro-Meech speeches they gave in the Newfoundland House of Assembly. McKenna, his voice filled with emotion, said a rejection of the accord would be interpreted by Quebecers as a rejection of them. It would lead to increased racism, higher unemployment, reduced investment from abroad, and international embarrassment for Canada. Pointing to the fact that several American news outlets were covering the debate, as well as a large contingent from across Canada, McKenna said, "They're not here for the great drama. They're here because, for the first time in the history of the world, they have the opportunity to see the destruction of a country without a shot being fired."

In contrast, Peterson's one-hour speech was essentially a low-key history lesson in which he attempted to dispel fears that Quebec would receive special powers under the distinct society clause, saying it would not affect the rights of anyone in Newfoundland or Ontario. Peterson said he didn't know what would happen if the accord was rejected, but he urged MHAs not to take the risk of finding out.

In his own speech to the MHAs on June 21, Mulroney raised the spectre of separation. Defending the Quebec premier, he said, "Don't believe the cheap shots. Robert Bourassa is a federalist. Meech Lake gives Mr. Bourassa the tools to fight any referendum and any election for a united Canada." He added that the accord "is hardly revolutionary. Rather, it is in the tradition of thirty years of constitutional discussions. Nobody invented anything at Meech Lake." Mulroney also warned that rejection of the accord "would send negative signals to international markets, because in their minds political stability is king, and money moves in quest of political stability."

Afterwards, Wells invited the prime minister to his house for dinner. Mulroney says that there, Wells again promised he would call a vote the next day, although he told Mulroney he was uncertain of the outcome but thought the accord would be rejected. Later, Wells would say he couldn't remember whether he promised to call the vote or not. Given his reputation as a stickler for detail, plus the significance of the event, it's unlikely Wells would have forgotten something like that. And if Mulroney's version was incorrect, Wells would certainly not have hesitated to say so.

Lowell Murray also insists that Wells promised he would hold the vote. "We left there that night having been told that. He told me, he told the PM, he told us both together, that he thought the PM's speech had made quite a difference in the Newfoundland legislature. . . . We came back on the plane together counting votes."

Meanwhile in Winnipeg, 5000 natives were gathered on the lawn in front of the legislature to celebrate Aboriginal Solidarity Day. To the beat of drums, chiefs from across the country, many of them wearing traditional deerhide costumes with full-feathered ceremonial headgear, came together to show their support for Harper. "What we want is more control over our land and over our lives," said Erasmus. "We have no other homeland." Fontaine said, "This country cannot rest on a lie. It must rest on the fact that the aboriginal people are also a distinct society." The next morning another smaller demonstration was staged on the front steps of the legislature.

One of the great lies fed to journalists by Ottawa officials was that Harper and his colleagues were being manipulated by a group of white lawyers, all part of the Grand Trudeau Conspiracy to kill the accord. Influential pro-Meech writers such as *Globe* columnist Jeffrey Simpson and the late *Ottawa Citizen* columnist Marjorie Nichols offered this scenario to their readers. So did Quebec journalist Michel Vastel who wrote in his book *Bourassa*: "In the crowd massed on the front steps of the Manitoba legislature on the morning of June 22, 1990, there were more whites than native people. Without being fully aware of it, the native people were being manipulated once more, by English Canada this time."

It wasn't true. London, one of the lawyers supposedly fronting for Trudeau in all this, calls the scenario "sheer nonsense." London, an early opponent of the accord, had attended the founding conference of Canadians Against Meech Lake in 1987. Deborah Coyne was also there. Jeffrey Simpson connected the two in a column. "He sort of flattered me by saying I had all this power over the country," says London. "But it was a defamatory piece. He should have been reading his own newspaper. A couple of days before I was hired by the Assembly of Manitoba Chiefs [June 12], I had admitted reluctantly to *Globe* reporter Geoffrey York that I felt the matter had gone as far as it could go, and that for the sake of national unity it should be ratified . . . and then I get accused of being part of the plot to destroy it."

London said he dropped out of the organization not long after that conference. "I had told Deborah I thought it was useless, because I didn't see any way Meech was going to be killed, so I dropped out. The next contact I had with Coyne was during the last two weeks in June. I called her twice on the Rock and spoke on the phone a total of three minutes. I've met Trudeau once at a conference in Montreal on Nuremburg. Meech wasn't even on then. I have no relationship with Trudeau."

He says that in the end Ottawa blamed Wells completely for Meech's collapse because "it was very difficult for a white government to acknowledge defeat at the hands of a bunch of Indians. It was easier, less ego-deflating, to blame it on a peer in another province. The truth is, I don't think Wells deserves either the credit or the blame. . . . The credit really belongs to the chiefs. If I had to pick a villain of the piece, it would be Bourassa. Had he shown any concern for native complaints at that time, I believe it would have produced an agreement. But Bourassa, for the crassest of reasons — to retain power for Quebec Liberals — not for any point of principle, but to maintain power, refused to consider anything."

London said the advisers in the Indian Affairs Department "should have known these guys were serious. And where was Jake Epp in all this? As far as I can recall, he played no part. [Unlike his Newfoundland counterpart, John Crosbie, who spent the final week trying to convince the MHAs to pass the accord.]

"My hypothesis [is that it is] essentially, I don't want to use the term 'racism,' it's not malevolent, it's often a very subtle racism in the form of not taking a person seriously. When you do that, you end up victimizing that group, but in this case they ended up victimizing themselves, which explains partly why they went after Wells."

Ottawa Citizen columnist Roy MacGregor was the only journalist who actually sat in on the native strategy sessions, and contrary to the Ottawa-fed rumors, he was also the only white face in the room. "This whole thing is absolutely incorrect," MacGregor says emphatically. "I was on the steps of that rally where Vastel says there were more whites than natives. Vastel wasn't. And I didn't see many white faces. The ratio would be a minimum ninety-five to five. I stayed in the hotel room the night before with Elijah Harper, and never once did I see a white lawyer.

"The only lawyers I saw were Mercredi, Phil Fontaine, and Bill Wilson, all natives. Jack London showed up outside the legislature one day, had a quick two-minute chat with Phil Fontaine, and that's the only time I saw him. But, of course, he became an excuse of convenience. Trudeau was manipulating the Indians through him, and manipulating Wells through Deborah Coyne, both of which are absolutely incorrect."

MacGregor says that "nothing really happened" at the lengthy native strategy session reported in the media. "Everybody was just sitting around drinking coffee, watching TV, reading, shooting the breeze. It was just to get Elijah away from the pressure . . . but there was never any sense they were waiting to have the pot sweetened. They were going to do it [kill the accord]. Mercredi said after they'd done it, 'It's what's morally right for the country.'"

Something else MacGregor noted was that, unlike Newfoundland, where Mulroney dispatched both John Crosbie and Tory MP Ross Reid in an attempt to persuade the politicians to pass the accord, the Tories didn't bother sending anybody to Winnipeg, not even Jake Epp, their Manitoba heavyweight. "I think they just thought it was the Indians, so it couldn't be all that serious."

Mulroney and Murray arrived back at the official residence about 11:30 p.m. the night of Thursday, June 21, to be met by Spector, chief of staff Stanley Hartt, and clerk of the Privy Council Paul Tellier. They met for several hours.

While they were plotting their final strategy, Wells finished his caucus meeting and then telephoned Filmon, and later Carstairs, for an update on Manitoba. Even though the debate had finally begun, the Manitoba legislature was slated to adjourn at 12:30 p.m. Friday and could not go beyond that without unanimous consent. Carstairs later told Andrew Cohen that "Wells thought we were going to hold a vote, which was nonsense. The prime minister was giving him the wrong information."

In any event, the crunch had come. Murray, who didn't get home from the meeting at 24 Sussex Drive until about 4 a.m., received a telephone call four hours later at his house from Wells in St. John's. Harper had earlier telephoned Wells to say he would continue his procedural battle, and Wells knew from both Filmon and Carstairs that there was no way a vote in Manitoba could be pulled together in time to beat the next day's deadline.

As Murray says, he told Wells during that phone conversation at 10:30 p.m. St. John's time about a last-ditch federal plan to refer the matter to the Supreme Court of Canada to seek an extension of the deadline for Manitoba, but only if the accord was approved by the Newfoundland house that day. So why, later that day, when Murray went on national television and announced the plan, did Newfoundland MHAs react with such surprised fury? And why did Wells, in his own emotional speech, after which the debate was adjourned without a vote, say of Murray's announcement, "I turned on the television and there he [Murray] was, rolling the dice again, trying to put more pressure back on Newfoundland. That's the final manipulation. We're not prepared to be manipulated any longer"?

Anyone hearing Wells's angry speech in the legislature would naturally assume that Wells found out about Murray's offer just like everybody else, by watching the senator's televised news conference. The importance of the discrepancy between Wells's and Murray's accounts cannot be overstated, and the question is, who was manipulating whom at that point?

The story Wells offered the nation was that Murray said he may have found a way to solve the problem and promised to call him back, but didn't. And just as Murray was leaving his office to go across Wellington Street to the National Press

Theatre, Wells telephoned Murray only to be told the senator had just left the office. The next thing Wells knew, there was Murray on national television announcing this last-minute deal.

But now Wells concedes that he and Murray discussed the plan in general terms in that telephone conversation. "In fact, I said to Murray at the time if you can get a decision out of the court in Manitoba, the only way you're ever going to get Meech through is to delay the vote in Newfoundland today, because if the vote is taken in Newfoundland today it will certainly be defeated. . . . I've got my own notes that were made at that time. I have a great sense of reliability on what I've said about this issue."

Wells also says he told his cabinet and caucus about the offer. "I didn't hide anything from the caucus. They knew whatever I knew."

In her book *Roll of the Dice*, Deborah Coyne writes that Wells told Murray during their telephone conversation that a reference to the Supreme Court would be useful only if Newfoundland adjourned its debate. Coyne claims that Wells discussed this potential deal-maker with his Liberal caucus after the 1 p.m. adjournment of the House of Assembly, well before Murray's controversial televised new conference.

But this version makes no sense in light of the Liberal MHAs furious reaction to Murray's televised announcement. If they already knew about it, why were they so upset?

Murray says Wells did not like the plan to extend Manitoba's deadline. "It had the effect of isolating Newfoundland. He said, 'Why can't there be more time for Newfoundland, too?' but time wasn't what Newfoundland needed. If given more time, he would have tried to renegotiate and reopen the accord again. He had given his written commitment that he would put the vote before June 23, and I'm willing to accept that was the only thing he committed himself to. But he did not honor his commitment. The others could not honor their commitments as it turned out. It did depend on Newfoundland voting and voting affirmatively. Now, I wasn't asking him for a guarantee that he could get an affirmative vote. All I was asking was that he do what he said he would do: put it before his legislature."

John Crosbie insists he discussed the plan with Wells that morning, three hours before Murray's televised news conference. "I don't know why Clyde hadn't explained [Murray's proposal] to his members. I've got notes about the fact Clyde talked to Murray. Yes, I was aware that Murray had told him. Clyde knew about that before the press conference. We discussed it . . . he wasn't for it. He thought this was just a concoction, it wasn't going to resolve anything, some attempt to manipulate him at the last minute, not a practical idea. He never gave it any thought really that this was something that could be tried.

"I think Clyde wanted the Meech Lake thing defeated and he saw that as a way where it might have all dissolved. He didn't want any more time given to Manitoba," says Crosbie. "Clyde was trying to give the impression of very high-mindedness; it was going to be left up to the Newfoundland house. But I'm damn sure he didn't want the Newfoundland house approving the accord, so this might have been a way of avoiding that possibility."

Newfoundland Liberal MP Roger Simmons sees the failure of Meech Lake as entirely Mulroney's fault. "He didn't understand what this country is all about. He didn't understand that you have these ten units called provinces and that you don't measure the weight of a province by how many people are in it. That's a bargaining chip that he brought from labor. And it worked in labor relations . . . but now he's into a whole new set of parameters where the Fathers of Confederation said we have ten provinces, not two provinces and eight quasi-provinces, or three and seven, or whatever. Had Mulroney been prepared to deal with Wells, just as he dealt with Peterson or

Bourassa, he would have been a lot better off and the country would have been a lot better served. . . .

"Clyde Wells and a lot of us in Newfoundland saw Meech Lake as locking us into a second-class relationship. And don't forget, we were a separate dominion until 1949. And when our people, my mom and dad and other people, voted to go from being a little nation to a province, that was fair ball, but our bargain didn't include going from a small nation to being one-quarter of a province, or a second-class province. We saw ourselves as having, while not as many people as Ontario, of having equality in terms of provincehood. And we were granted that status in terms of national programs, in terms of transfer payments, in terms of access to citizenship."

Ottawa Citizen reporter Paul Gessell, who spent that final Meech week in Newfoundland, said one of the more interesting byplays of the week was the fact that the French-speaking journalists were "completely hostile to Wells. A lot of the anglophone ones, of course, were cheering him on. You could see this split happening, and there we were all crowded into this tiny press room which had just enough room for four desks squeezed together with a little space to walk around, and all of a sudden there's thirty out-of-town reporters there trying to fit in. So we spent the week literally shoulder to shoulder. . . . It was so crowded I sat on top of the fridge one day and typed my story."

There is no doubt that, had Wells called a vote after the kafuffle created by Murray's announcement, the Meech Lake accord would have been dead. There is, however, considerable doubt, about the outcome had Murray stayed out of it altogether or if Wells had disclosed the offer to his members earlier in the day. Everybody has their own scenario. Wells says it would have been defeated, that only three of his caucus would have approved it. Most Tories say the accord would have been approved.

Several journalists who interviewed Liberal MHAs coming

back from their break for the afternoon session after Murray's televised announcement say the politicians had not had advance warning of the senator's proposal. *Ottawa Citizen* reporter Gessell says that most of the MHAs "hadn't been aware of Murray's offer. . . . They were being told about it by reporters. They were just screaming, they were so annoyed. They were saying it was some great act of manipulation." All day a group of prominent Newfoundland businessmen, led by Canadian Helicopters Corporation owner Craig Dobbin and lawyer and former Peckford aide Cabot Martin were milling about the lobby buttonholing MHAs and warning them of the economic consequences for Newfoundland should Meech fail.

Few Newfoundlanders, if any, are more plugged in to the current administration than Mose Morgan, the man Wells still reveres as both his mentor and father figure. Morgan is convinced that without the Murray matter, the accord would have been approved in a free vote that day. Although he had serious reservations about the accord himself, Morgan had decided by the end of the process that it would have been best to approve it and avoid the serious consequences of failure. That was essentially the message Morgan gave all the MHAs in a letter that final week.

Wells had always insisted that at most three of his Liberal caucus members would have voted for the accord, but Morgan sees it differently.

"I had also phoned several members the night before [six cabinet ministers are former students]," Morgan says, "and we concluded that there were at least eight Liberals the next day who would have voted for Meech Lake if things had been allowed to go their own way. Now I was in the house that afternoon and one of the cabinet ministers, a friend of mine, who was voting for Meech Lake, came up to me, and he was quite furious. He said, 'There is no way that I'm going to vote for that this afternoon.' They had been listening to Murray on the air. If Murray had kept quiet, Meech Lake would have passed in that legislature that afternoon. But . . . Clyde didn't want it defeated in the house, so he adjourned the debate.

"Now he's accused of breaking his word. Well, he brought it before the house. To me, it was an act of statesmanship what he did. Because if he had gone and had the vote, it would have been defeated, and that would have ended the whole matter. Instead of that, he adjourned the debate. . . . So why couldn't they [Ottawa] have gone ahead to the court and asked for the extension? The vote in Newfoundland is still pending."

Murray's response to that question is that the court may have granted the extension in Manitoba's case because it was simply a straightforward matter of the province's needing more time. Nobody had any doubt that the Manitoba legislature wanted to approve the accord, so the question before the court would be strictly technical. But Newfoundland was a different case. The issue there was not a procedural matter, nor a requirement for more time, but strictly political.

Wells buttresses his argument that the accord would have failed by telling about a meeting in the Speaker's chamber off the legislature where Tories Len Simms and Tom Rideout told Crosbie point-blank that a vote then would lose.

"I sat in the office with him [Crosbie], Len Simms, Winston Baker, and Tom Rideout. We told him that if a vote is taken it would fail, Meech Lake would be rejected. And Len Simms and Tom Rideout confirmed it for him. . . . Manitoba is stopping it, so the only way your reference to the Supreme Court would do any good is to adjourn the reference in Newfoundland and have it [the vote] taken afterwards. Besides, if you can delay it for Manitoba, why can't you delay it for Newfoundland to have its referendum? How am I going to justify to the people of Newfoundland that they can't have a referendum that I wanted to have, because of time, but you can have a delay for Manitoba? That's what I said to Murray at the time."

The key point, which Wells is conveniently overlooking, is the impact of Murray's televised statement. The meeting with the Newfoundland opposition leaders and Crosbie took place after Murray's televised statement. By that time, the mood of the legislature had changed dramatically. Some Liberals who had told Morgan they would vote for Meech had abruptly changed their minds because of what they perceived as Murray's blatant manipulation.

There is no doubt that after Murray's announcement the vote would have failed. That was when, after meeting with Wells, Crosbie telephone Mulroney — and the legislature resumed its debate briefly — to pass along Wells's offer to adjourn the debate if he could have Mulroney's approval to apply to the Supreme Court for an extended deadline. Wells says he told Crosbie he didn't really think it would work, but the only way it could work was "if Newfoundland adjourned the motion and maybe it might at a later time pass." Now, it would certainly fail, and nothing would be achieved except that Newfoundland would be blamed as the one who stopped the accord. "So that's why Murray tried to put pressure on me at the last moment and go on television and say it all depends on Newfoundland," he says. "If Newfoundland approves it we can succeed. If Newfoundland rejects it will be dead. They put the whole blame on Newfoundland because they couldn't justify blaming the aboriginal people, Elijah Harper. They wanted a scapegoat. And they wanted to put me in the position and Newfoundland in the position that they would have a scapegoat."

Wells had called an impromptu cabinet meeting on the floor of the legislature right after the break to announce the details of Murray's proposal. After another break, when he discussed the situation with Crosbie, Simms, and Rideout, the debate reopened while Crosbie telephoned Mulroney. Again, Wells announced a break in the debate and was told by Crosbie that Mulroney had agreed to give Newfoundland more time if Wells personally announced he'd support Meech Lake. "There's no way in the world I would ever sell what I believe in that way," declared Wells.

Crosbie doesn't deny Mulroney offered Wells an extension in exchange for his support, but says Wells had promised to hold a vote and didn't. "It was a pretty scurvy piece of work."

Halifax *Chronicle Herald* reporter Jim Meek says Crosbie was so angry during a scrum afterwards that "if he was ever going to blow a gasket, this was the time. He was furious, yelling and screaming, so obviously pissed off that Wells had lied. And the thing is, Clyde did lie. To me, he's the guy who fucked up big. I have some sympathy for Crosbie's views on that. [Wells] is a wonderful theoretician and constitutional lawyer and can make angels dance on the head of a pin. But basically he's a guy who lied to the nation. I still kind of like him in a weird way, but he's got the God syndrome real bad."

Gessell says that at this news conference in a tiny room above the legislative chamber, the francophone journalists saw Wells as the villain, "not Murray or Elijah Harper. They saw him as anti-Quebec, and there certainly was an anti-Quebec tone to the debate. . . . [Justice Minister Paul] Dicks, for example, compared giving in to Quebec to Neville Chamberlain's trying to appease the enemy. I'm not sure it was anti-Quebec in the racial sense, however. But it's just the little guy against the big guy. It wasn't English versus French, it was small versus big.

Murray certainly wasn't at peace. He stormed back onto live television, pointing to Wells's signature on the June 9 agreement, saying, "The decision taken by Premier Wells not to respect his commitment and not to have a vote . . . has killed the last hope of the success of Meech Lake."

Mulroney said later that, by refusing to hold a vote, Wells had "cancelled the most fundamental and noble dimension of a democracy. The real reason Clyde Wells cancelled the vote is that he was afraid to take a chance on Meech passing."

Senator Michael Kirby, a Meech opponent himself and Trudeau's chief strategist in the 1981-82 constitutional talks, says he, too, was surprised that Wells didn't hold the vote, "but what I've never understood is the complete blame Brian Mul-

roney tries to put on Clyde Wells for the failure of Meech. . . .
Quite apart from Mulroney's own responsibility in mishandling
the issue. . . . Is it just you can't attack native organizations
but you can attack white politicians? All the attacks on Clyde
Wells and not on Elijah Harper and the natives. I think that's
unfair.

"Why should Clyde have changed his mind? It's hard to
make an argument that the Quebec government changed its
mind on anything. Why can only the Quebec government take
a position on an issue of principle? If any anglophone takes a
position of principle, he's pigheaded. If the Quebec premier
does it, it's a matter of principle.

"None of this would have been an issue in the first place if
Mulroney hadn't raised it in 1985," Kirby says. "It was only
Mulroney's revisionist history, adopting the nationalist argument that Quebec had been hurt in 1981, that's the biggest
problem. If you're going to point a finger, point it at Mulroney
for raising the issue."

As for Mulroney, he made his feelings about Wells clear
when, in a meeting with Ghiz, McKenna, and various officials
shortly after Meech failed, he quipped, "The next time I go to
St. John's to see Clyde, I think I'll bring a gun."

In the end, there can be no disputing the fact that Wells had
promised his "best efforts" to hold the vote by June 23. Unlike
Filmon, who had no control over events in Manitoba, Wells
exercised complete control over his situation, yet he deliberately decided to renege on his promise, using Murray's televised address as the tool to justify it.

At the Liberal leadership convention in Calgary on June 23,
Wells insisted a vote on the accord would almost certainly have
been rejected. "I don't think Newfoundland bears any particular responsibility, except for exercising the democratic right
to express its opinions on the basis of a conscientious judgment
as to what . . . is best for the country and best for the province.
And nobody, surely, can be condemned for that."

But he did not allow the legislature to exercise its democratic right to express its opinions. He pulled the plug and adjourned without allowing the vote he'd promised time and time again. There also seems little doubt he withheld key information about Murray's offer from his own caucus, a tactic that had a major impact on events.

Certainly many cheered his actions. People at the convention were circulating buttons that read ALL'S WELL THAT ENDS WITH WELLS, and CLYDE NEXT TIME, along with CLYDE WELLS FOR PRIME MINISTER T-shirts. His entrance into the Calgary Saddledome was greeted by an overwhelming roar of approval from the assembled Liberals. But not surprisingly, there were boos from the Quebec delegation, particularly from the Paul Martin camp, as Wells worked his way through the crowd. Jean Chrétien, who had been shamelessly hedging on his position on the accord, hurt himself irreparably in Quebec by embracing Wells and thanking him for his help. Clearly, Chrétien hadn't meant his help in killing Meech, but the Quebec media, already painting Wells as the anti-Christ, portrayed his remark in that context.

When Wells reached his destination at the convention, the private box of former prime minister Pierre Trudeau, the two men greeted each other warmly, shook hands, patted each other on the shoulder, then sat down together to watch events unfold.

And, no doubt, to savor their victory.

11

Fiscally Frugal

BELL ISLAND IS a **striking** reddish rock poking defiantly out of Conception Bay, a comfortable drive and ferry ride west of St. John's. In 1894 the island began to prosper, its people living off the valuable iron ore deposits. By 1923 it had become the second-largest town in Newfoundland, and by 1966 the bustling mining community had grown to about 13,500 people. Then disaster struck. Technological change, combined with the poor quality of the ore, forced the mine to close in 1966, and about 6000 Bell Islanders, part of a massive federal employment initiative program, were relocated to Cambridge, Ontario, to work in newly constructed factories.

Within a couple of years, the population had shrunk to 4200 people, and unemployment had risen to seventy per cent. Since then, numerous make-work projects have been tried, one of the most imaginative a mushroom-growing scheme by former Liberal MHA Steve Neary, which worked on a small scale but failed to attract a large enough company to the island to make it worthwhile. In November 1991 the first of a planned thirty giant murals painted by local artists was unveiled by the town. Planned for walls on most public buildings, the murals depict scenes of people and places of the island's long mining history in the hopes of drawing tourists to the island. Also offered are guided tours of the old mines, which by 1966 extended about three miles under the floor of Conception Bay, but apart from a few farmers and fishermen, most Bell Islanders who do have jobs either work for the government or commute to St. John's.

In late October 1991, twenty-five years after the mine closed, Clyde Wells came to the island with Tory MP Ross Reid to speak at a fund-raising dinner for the local Boys and Girls Club. He did not come as a politician bearing gifts, however. Wells delivered a deadly serious polemic. He began by telling the people how tight money was in Newfoundland and therefore how difficult it was for the provincial government to pass money along to communities such as Bell Island. And the reason the province is so short of money, he said, was that the federal government had cut back in its transfer payments and job-creation programs.

"At that point," says Reid, "I was thinking to myself, 'Oh God, here we go. He's going to bash the feds and I'm going to have to sit up here and listen politely.' Instead, he went on to say that he couldn't fault the federal government, and for the next ten minutes he talked about how critical it was for Ottawa to make the tough decisions on the deficit, to take action on the deficit, and he said he thought it was the right thing to do."

Reid sees Wells as brutally honest but sometimes "too analytical and a bit too cold. I don't say he doesn't have personal feelings, but he doesn't show them." Reid admits that it's not fair to make extravagant promises about jobs, but "people need a little bit of hope. . . . There's got to be some encouragement to keep going."

There isn't a more fiscally conservative political leader in the nation than Clyde Wells, including Preston Manning, head of the right-wing Reform Party. Few might expect the premier of Canada's poorest province, the one most dependent on Ottawa's largesse, to speak publicly in support of federal cutbacks and possible changes to the nation's universal social programs. After all, Newfoundland has had chronic unemployment in the twenty per cent range, a small and unstable tax base, the lowest personal incomes in Canada (almost thirty per cent below the national average in 1989), the lowest credit rating of any province, and federal transfer payments alone make up nearly half the provincial budget.

Wells believes that whether it's in government or his private business, every penny counts. Literally. His former private secretary, who among other duties was responsible for depositing the weekly receipts from Wells's law firm, tells the story of being short by one cent one week. Knowing what a stickler for detail Wells is, she went over and over the books but still couldn't find the missing penny. In the end, exasperated, she simply took a penny out of her own purse, threw it in the sack, and deposited it in the bank.

On Monday morning, Wells called her into the office, looked straight at her with those piercing blue eyes of his, and said simply, "My dear, two wrongs don't make a right. You should have told me about the penny." He spent the weekend poring over the books himself.

In March 1990 the federal government discovered in an audit of its equalization payments that Newfoundland had received $37 million more than it should have for 1988-89 and an extra $34 million for 1989-90, a total of $71 million that it had to repay to Ottawa. This happens periodically because the system of equalization is based on estimates. It takes two years before the actual fiscal data become available, after which the previous payments are recalculated.

All of this money had already been spent, much of it by the previous Peckford government, but Wells, through a recovery formula that set a top limit of $60 per capita for repayment, agreed to refund the money over the years 1990-91 and 1991-92.

Shortly after Newfoundland was informed of the overpayment, Liberal MP George Baker ran into Wells in the terminal of the St. John's airport. "I said, 'Mr. Premier, I noticed that Newfoundland has to pay back an incredible amount of money under equalization. I got a letter back from the minister of finance verifying this. You people are paying back an astronomical figure. Not only that, but there's also been a drop in the amount of equalization, so you fellows are losing about $50 million a year from the Peckford administration. Maybe we should start kicking up a stink over this. We've got serious economic problems in Newfoundland and that's a lot of money. Not only that, they're blaming it on you when it wasn't your fault.'

"Clyde looked me straight in the eyes and he said, 'George, look, if kicking up a stink would change anything, we'd kick up a stink. But that's the way equalization works. We owe the money, so we pay it back. Why even mention it? If Newfoundland owes the money, Newfoundland is going to pay it back.'"

Most other premiers would have negotiated a deal for reduced payments, but not Clyde Wells. The province's current-account deficit was already $90 million and growing when he took over, and from the outset he made no secret that he planned to attack the deficit by slashing the number of cabinet ministers, the number of departments, the size of the civil service, and by eliminating several provincial programs, all of which he did. In his brutal March 1991 budget, for example, he bludgeoned the deficit, which by then was almost $200 million, down to $53.8 million, hacking off $37 million in programs, wiping out anywhere from 2100 to 3500 civil service jobs, depending on whose numbers you use — the lower government number or the higher civil service union number. But such reductions came at a cost, particularly in a small province hard hit by Ottawa's decision to freeze established program funding (EPF) at current levels until at least 1995.

For example, Wells had not only promised that he wouldn't close hospital beds but that he would reopen some that had already been closed. Instead, according to the hospital unions, he's closed more than 600 acute-care beds and either shut or downgraded cottage hospitals in several rural communities under the guise of centralizing services in larger hospitals. In a city such as Toronto, which has six or seven major hospitals within a short distance of each other, it may make sense to centralize some services, but St. John's or Gander or Corner Brook are not Toronto. Certain inefficiencies are endemic to the province, simply because of the remoteness of so much of the rural populace. A feature story in the October/November 1991 issue of the left-leaning *This* magazine by St. John's freelancer Gavin Will, for instance, pointed out that, since 1952, pregnant women living on Little Bay Island in Notre Dame Bay in the central region of the province faced a forty-minute ferry ride to Springdale to deliver their babies. "Not anymore," Will wrote. "Thanks to budget cuts in March, they have another ninety-minute drive ahead of them before reaching Grand Falls. And that's in good weather."

Tory Leader Len Simms, who took over the provincial party in August 1991, says you have to live in Newfoundland and watch Wells at work to realize just how conservative he is. "Clyde loves the national stage and the national limelight. The criticism you'll find here is he spends too much time on the national scene, particularly on the Constitution, and neglects the issues of Newfoundland. . . . He has all these conservative fiscal theories, but he doesn't seem to relate to what actually happens to people when the theory is put into practice.

"He's not comfortable talking about social issues," Simms says. "He seems uncomfortable in the assembly when he's asked about welfare. It's easy to irritate him over that. He gets red in the face and up on his haunches. He's forgotten his own roots. He's not comfortable on grassroots issues. But if you talk to him about the Constitution, he'll go on forever until the Speaker stops him."

Wells unilaterally rolled back wage settlements that had been negotiated with public service unions, touching off a bitter, province-wide war that saw many of the post-Meech CLYDE WELLS FOR PRIME MINISTER T-shirts replaced by shirts reading CLYDE LIED, the official slogan of the energetic union campaign.

The showpiece of Wells's economic development strategy has been the Economic Recovery Commission and its operating arm, Enterprise Newfoundland and Labrador, which he established in June 1989 to build up a small-business sector in rural Newfoundland in response to high unemployment levels among young workers and record levels of UI recipients. But despite the millions spent on a host of projects, the commission's real success stories have been rare — unlike its failures. It has been criticized for funding projects such as golf courses and fishing resorts, which, while nice for well-heeled tourists, don't put much food on the table for the economically deprived locals. One critic of the ERC has charged that it spent $6 million over two years and created only sixty-five jobs.

From the outset, Wells has not been happy with the federally sponsored Atlantic Canada Opportunities Agency, which he regards as merely a vote-buying device funded by taxpayers. Not only does ACOA fail in its stated purpose of diminishing regional disparity, he complains, it might even accentuate it, because after the agency was established, similar agencies began popping up all over the country to do the same things for the other regions.

In August 1990 on the eve of a meeting in St. John's with John Crosbie, who was then international trade minister, Wells again complained about what he saw as a lack of fairness in federal funding for Newfoundland, prompting Crosbie to accuse him of "deliberate, uncaring, negligent, scurvy policies and tactics, and false propaganda." Crosbie says Wells's attitude was "destroying the spirit of co-operation and shared enterprise," particularly in such cases as federal-provincial co-operation agreements, ACOA, the fishery, Hibernia, and financial relations between the two governments. Arguing that with the exception of the Economic Recovery Commission, all the major efforts to improve Newfoundland's economy are "initiatives of the federal government, not of the provincial government," Crosbie cited such federal funding as the $1.4 billion in transfer payments, $2.7 billion in direct grants and loans for the Hibernia project, and a $584 million adjustment program to deal with the crisis in the fishery.

Wells's expressed contempt for ACOA did not dissuade him from signing a four-year $7.1 million ACOA/Enterprise Network Co-operation Agreement with Crosbie in April 1991, which his deputy premier, Winston Baker, heralded as "among the most important economic development agreements ever signed by the federal and provincial governments." The aim was to develop a computerized information network to help develop small and medium-sized enterprises in the province, including setting up electronic "telecentres" to provide communities with access to computing and communications facilities, business planning services, teleconferencing, and consulting services.

Unlike his predecessors, who actively avoided becoming part of co-operative political and economic efforts with the three Maritime provinces, Wells has also shown considerable interest in the notion of a scheme to drop interprovincial barriers and in the elimination of the practice of local job preferences between the four provinces. Policies that have not been universally applauded by business and labor groups in Newfoundland, they remain, at this point, more exploratory than real.

For all his promises, Wells has not been able to make a dent in the historically high unemployment numbers in Newfoundland — current estimates have it hovering around twenty per cent, four points higher than when he took over. Contrary to his election campaign pledge, the boys have not been brought home. Although the current uncertainty over Hibernia, the crisis in the cod fishery, and the federal freeze on funding programs are not Wells's doing, as a politician he must accept responsibility for the bad, just as he would take credit for the good.

From the outset, Wells argued he would achieve more economic benefits for islanders by using his cold logic than the feisty Peckford did with his fiery lip. While Peckford was deliberately belligerent and combative, Wells attempts to be low-key and, to his mind, logical. Where Peckford provoked hostility by yelling and threatening, Wells generates a like response by his combination of stubbornness and condescension. Peckford, the provincialist, argued that Newfoundland had to stand on its own economically rather than depend upon Ottawa to solve its problems. Wells, the federalist, believes the province must strengthen its links, and its dependence, on the federal government. As a side issue during the original Meech Lake talks, Peckford forged an agreement that, during the second round of talks, Ottawa would pursue the notion of giving the province far more control over the fishery — all it could do was license fish plants — but that was one of the first things Wells discarded when he took over, believing instead the province's main industry would be better served by a stronger federal presence.

"I don't think there's any question, at least on the financial and economic side, he is far more conservative than I was or am, and more so than Moores and Smallwood," says Peckford. "We have right now a person who is far more conservative than any of the conservative premiers. But [the Liberals] haven't been as aggressive on the offshore as we were. It's one thing to negotiate a deal; it's another to follow up on that deal to make sure what you signed is what you're getting. . . . Even in the exploration days, before Hibernia started, we were monitoring everything on a weekly basis to make sure that, if there was a qualified Newfoundlander, they had first crack at the job. The same thing on the fishery. I don't think most Newfoundlanders get the impression that the [Wells] government is as strong as it should be on the fishery. [It's] been lucky in the sense that because Crosbie is the [fisheries] minister, that's taken the heat off a bit. If there was anybody else from outside Newfoundland, that would put more pressure on the provincial government to be more aggressive in that field."

Peckford sees Wells's hands-off approach as dangerous because it tends to weaken the influence the province will have in future over fisheries policy. "The biggest mistake we made in Terms of Union was to give up control of the fishery, hand it over to the feds," he says. "I've always taken the view that I want a constitutional change to realign fisheries responsibilities, to make it more equal, if you will, concurrent, jurisdiction with the federal government, where we would be consulted on a wide range of fishing issues."

Wells has been criticized by some for keeping the entire operation — indeed, the entire government — under his thumb. Many Newfoundlanders say he runs a one-man show, but Wells argues that in order for his long-term economic strategy to work, it has to be co-ordinated by him. "Now if you've got fifteen ministries and another twenty or thirty different agencies, all separate and autonomous enclaves fighting for their own turf, there's never any co-ordination of planning, and you'll find that one group is working against the other half the time. You've got to co-ordinate, say, environmental control with development, and forestry and agriculture. You've got to find the right balance."

For all his planning, however, Wells freely acknowledges that Newfoundland's economy isn't exactly buoyant, although he says it's not his fault. "The one thing any intelligent, plus fair-minded, objective person would say, there's nothing any government in Newfoundland can do to shield Newfoundland from the consequences of a national economic recession. There's nothing we can do to shield Newfoundland from a reduction in the total allowable catch (TAC) in the fisheries, a reduction from 266,000 tonnes in 1988 to 120,000 tonnes this year [1992] . . . even though people know only a fraction of that will be caught.

"The number of jobs lost in the fisheries alone exceeds 10,000. Just imagine what our unemployment numbers would look like with those 10,000 jobs, and the spinoff effect of those 10,000 jobs, in place. We didn't cause this. There was absolutely nothing the provincial government could do to stop it. . . . We couldn't make the fish grow in the sea if they weren't spawned. So it's true, unemployment is up, [but] it's not up proportionately as high as it is in Ontario. . . . Economically we're in more difficult shape now. But so's the whole world, or much of the world at least. Canada in particular has suffered. No government of Newfoundland can shield the province from that circumstance."

Things were about to get drastically worse.

Guy Hackett is a big man, over six feet tall, husky, ruddy-complexioned. On a bitterly cold Friday in mid-March 1992 in Ottawa, his huge gloveless hands were wrapped around a sign that called on the European Community to stop its fleets from overfishing off the Grand Banks of Newfoundland.

Dressed in a shocking-orange jumpsuit, the forty-two-year-old Hackett stood outside the European High Commission and Spanish Embassy building in Ottawa, not far from where Fishermen, Food and Allied Workers union president Richard Cashin was blasting the EC for its hypocrisy in continuing to fish the Grand Banks after having virtually shut down the Newfoundland seal hunt.

Hackett has been going to sea since he was fifteen. Now, there are no fish to fish, or at least no northern cod, which in Newfoundland is what they mean when they say "fish" and is what he catches on a deep-sea trawler for National Sea Products (NatSea) out of St. John's. Now, for the first time in his life, the father of four has had to go on unemployment insurance. In 1991, he earned $42,000. This year, he'll be lucky to get $14,000, including UI. "I know people think we're all on UI, but we're not," he said. "I always knew about it, but I was proud of never having to go on it. Now, well, when you get people used to working all their lives, it's hard. I'm at my wit's end. It's a hard life fishing. Not much for the workers' families sometimes, away for days, home for forty-eight hours, then back out to sea again. But it's been my life, and was my father's life before me. This is how we live."

It has been how Newfoundlanders have lived for five hundred years. More than anything else, the sea has sustained them. Cod has been as important to Newfoundland as cars are to Ontario, timber to British Columbia, oil to Alberta, wheat to Saskatchewan. In late 1991 and early 1992 some 5000 Newfoundlanders lost their jobs in the fishery, with more to come.

Cashin was talking openly about this impending disaster in the industry back in 1989 when he told reporters he hoped the newly elected premier would change the government's line of thinking. "What first has to happen is that they have to be generally seized by the importance of the problem, and they aren't. I still think there's a belief there that this [disaster] isn't going to happen." Cashin, a former Liberal MP who went to Dalhousie University in the 1960s with both Wells and Mulroney, said the crucial questions for him included extension of fishing jurisdiction, increased spending on biological research, the seal question, and the use of appropriate technology in harvesting sea stocks.

In 1977 Canada extended its territorial waters from one hundred to two hundred miles, grabbing control of ninety-five per cent of the fish-rich Grand Banks in the hope of eliminating fishing by overseas fleets within the new boundary. In 1986, to discourage foreign overfishing even more, Canada closed its ports to European Community fishing vessels. The problem is the five per cent of the Grand Banks not under Canadian jurisdiction — the so-called nose and tail of the Grand Banks, to where the fish migrate at certain times of the year and are scooped up by the foreigners. Which meant in 1991, for example, that despite an internationally negotiated quota of 27,000 tonnes of cod, EC trawlers, mainly Portuguese and Spanish, took 42,000 tonnes. That, combined with overfishing by Canadian fishermen as well as the voracious appetites of the exploding seal population since European pressure essentially ended that industry twenty years ago, has led to the worst fishing crisis in Canadian history.

At his first premiers' conference in August 1989 in Quebec City, Wells put the subject of the fishery on the agenda. Downward revisions by federal scientists of northern-cod stocks had already led to lower quotas and substantial fish-plant layoffs. After the conference, Wells and his Fisheries Minister Walter Carter met Joe Clark in Ottawa. Clark was chairman of a special federal cabinet committee set up to deal with foreign overfishing and the northern-cod crisis. In October 1989 Wells said the federal and provincial governments must plan a more orderly economic development so that Newfoundland could become less dependent upon fishing, although he offered few specifics on how.

Wells's first major challenge came at the end of the year when both Fishery Products International (FPI) and NatSea announced they were shutting down some of their plants. Then fisheries minister Tom Siddon slashed the northern-cod quotas to 197,000 tonnes, down from 235,000 tonnes in 1989 and 266,000 the year before that. In January, blaming Ottawa for having mismanaged the resource and setting aside his free-enterprise philosophy, Wells rushed in with a $14 million rescue package for FPI to stop the St. John's-based company from closing three Newfoundland fish plants and eliminating more than 1300 jobs.

A week later, Wells, who had rejected a company proposal for the province to buy its St. John's plant, offered NatSea $3 million to abandon its plan to close the plant and wipe out five hundred jobs. Wells noted Ottawa's recent $1 billion bailout for Prairie grain farmers struck by drought, saying the justification for the federal government's accepting responsibility for the fish crisis was even greater. "This is not a problem that can be attributable to God. This is a problem that's attributable to the federal mismanagement of the fish stocks," he said. In May Ottawa responded with a five-year, $584-million Atlantic Fisheries Adjustment Program, about $150 million of it for Newfoundland, which Wells dismissed as "woefully inadequate."

At the August 1991 premiers' conference in Whistler, B.C., Wells managed to get the provincial leaders to agree to push the issue of foreign overfishing as a national problem, thus pressuring Ottawa to give it a higher priority and even "strengthen the federal government's position in dealing with the European Community by telling them just how strongly the nation as a whole feels about this."

In October Crosbie announced a $39 million emergency aid package to help about 10,000 Atlantic fishermen and plant workers devastated by the industry's collapse, about 6600 of them Newfoundlanders. Most of the money was for make-work projects, such as upgrading fish plants and building docks, to help workers qualify for unemployment insurance and prepare for the next fishing season. Ottawa had already provided $18 million to about 9000 Newfoundland fishermen and three hundred in Quebec to compensate for ice conditions throughout the summer. Some industry officials were saying that poor landings were an indication that declining stocks were in danger of collapsing completely if they weren't allowed to rejuvenate, but Crosbie said scientific studies showed stocks were improving and there was no need to cut back quotas more severely — a prediction he'd have to reverse dramatically a few months later.

In the meantime, the mood of the fishermen was turning ugly. In Port aux Basques demonstrating fishermen had gone on a rampage and ransacked a federal fisheries office, destroying furniture, smashing windows, and tossing computers and file cabinets from second-storey windows. In October 1991 furious fishermen in St. John's, convinced their own union officials weren't doing anything to stop the fishery from collapsing, kicked in a window and a wall in their union offices, threw a phone across the room, and shouted obscenities, demanding that the union get tough with fisheries officers who were seizing their vessels, as well as fish alleged to have been caught in a restricted zone on the Grand Banks. Union president Cashin said he understood their anger. "There's a deeper frustration in the fishery today than at any time since the 30s. We're going to change that."

If nothing else, the provincial government certainly began to make more noise after the demonstration. Carter said the sealing industry "has the potential to make a worthwhile contribution to our provincial economy, and certainly from an ecological point of view it's absolutely necessary." The TAC of seals was 186,000 animals, but the sealing industry, with European markets having banned the pelts, was harvesting less than thirty per cent of that quota.

Later that fall of 1991, Wells blasted foreign overfishing as "a form of international piracy" and "a crime against mankind," and demanded that Canada and other fishing nations form a high-seas police force to stop overfishing in international waters on the Grand Banks. He said if other countries wouldn't help, Canada should act on its own, a suggestion immediately dismissed by External Affairs Minister Barbara McDougall as not realistic. A couple of weeks later Wells himself conceded, "It was not my brilliant idea. It came out of a question in a news scrum."

Newfoundland's major complaint is that the Northwest Atlantic Fisheries Organization has agreed that Canada would set allocations for northern cod around the nose and tail of the Grand Banks, but the EC, notably Spain and Portugal, who are among the eleven member states of NAFO, has disregarded NAFO quotas, setting its own "independent, unilateral quotas." And despite warnings about the depleting stocks, Wells claims the EC vessels continue not only to exceed NAFO allocations, but their own EC-set quotas. In the meantime, quotas for Canadian (largely Newfoundland) fishermen continue to be slashed because of declining stocks, and while our fishermen are unemployed, European fishermen continue casting their nets unabated just outside the two-hundred-mile limit.

To make matters worse, while the Canadian fishing industry has just one factory-freezer trawler, the federal government has licensed about a hundred of these mammoth, four-hundred-foot floating fish factories from countries such as Japan, Russia, Cuba, and South Korea to fish inside the two-hundred-mile zone. (Canadian fishermen cannot go to any other country in the world and fish.) Barbara McDougall said those countries support fisheries conservation, respect NAFO quotas, and aren't fishing for northern cod, but Gander–Grand Falls Liberal MP George Baker, who represents 13,000 licensed cod fishermen in his riding alone, argued that in fact these "Star Wars" equipped ships are catching fish the northern cod feed on.

In December, Wells released details of the Canada-Newfoundland Fisheries management board, saying that "joint management is the only way to comprehensively manage the fishery in the future for the benefit of Canada in general, and Newfoundland and Labrador in particular." The idea was for an equal number of federal and provincial appointees to sit on the board, under a jointly appointed chairperson, to make recommendations concerning the TAC for different species of fish within the Newfoundland zone and decide on the creation and transfer of licences. While Wells liked the idea, Quebec and Nova Scotia didn't, and Crosbie said the proposal won't work unless there is agreement from all the provinces affected. He had proposed a joint board with all the provinces, but Walter Carter said Newfoundland wasn't interested in being "only one voice in five" when it came to fisheries.

The union didn't like either plan. FFAW secretary-treasurer Earle McCurdy likened it to asking an opponent of capital punishment if he prefers the noose or the electric chair. "We're quite concerned about the implications that would have for fishermen and for the people in the industry, because a public utilities board type of undertaking, we believe, would be more in the interest of the rich and powerful and not of the individual fishermen in the system."

In the midst of all this, Crosbie told a conference on international boundaries in London that from 1986 to 1990 EC fleets had caught more than five times the quotas of cod, flounder, and redfish allocated to them by NAFO on the nose and tail of the Grand Banks, and if all else fails, Canada could be forced to take unilateral action, such as extending the two-hundred-mile zone.

In mid-February 1992 the Canadian Atlantic Fisheries Scientific Advisory Committee recommended a 25,000-tonne reduction of the Canadian catch for the first half of the year, a cut equal to half of the catch during the same period for 1991, sparking an emergency debate in the Commons, and charges and counter-charges between Crosbie and Newfoundland Liberal MPs, each side blaming the other for the bleak prospects of another potential 3500 layoffs on trawlers and fish plants on top of the 1000 temporary layoffs already announced by FPI the week before, a devastating prospect for an industry that accounts for about one-quarter of all jobs in the province.

Crosbie acknowledged the problems were serious, but chided those predicting an end to the Newfoundland fishery. He said that in addition to federal diplomatic efforts to deal with the problem, since 1990 the Atlantic Canada Opportunities Agency had approved 485 projects in Newfoundland worth

1356 jobs. He acknowledged, however, the problems of uncertain scientific estimates of fish stocks, foreign overfishing, and the impact of the growth of the seal population on the fishery. After a high-profile campaign led by Brigitte Bardot and other stars, none of whom had to scrape a meagre living off the ice floes, the Europeans have boycotted seals since 1983, decimating the $12-million-a-year business to about $1 million a year. Current estimates are 3.5 million seals, up from two million in 1983. The average seal eats 1.5 tonnes of fish a year, which means the amount of fish eaten by seals has increased by 1.8 million tonnes a year, or 3.6 billion pounds of fish.

Just the mere mention of a seal hunt is enough to stir up the activists who capitalized on gory pictures of sealers clubbing helpless baby seals to death on the ice. In March 1992 Crosbie called it "abysmal" and a "terrible commentary on the state of intelligence of the average British member of Parliament" that the International Fund for Animal Welfare claimed that 115 British MPs had put forward a motion warning of a boycott of all Canadian fish products if more seals are killed. The IFAW launched a $100,000 newspaper advertising campaign in Newfoundland and Nova Scotia attempting to refute Crosbie's claim that seals are partly responsible for the declining cod stocks, and actress Loretta Swit was featured on several television newscasts frolicking with seal pups on the ice floes.

George Baker said that for the first time in eighteen years he had to arrange for welfare to bring back the men, women, and children who migrate to communities such as Punch Bowl on the Labrador coast to spend their entire summers there fishing. There were no fish and so they couldn't afford to pay their way back.

"And for the first time in eighteen years, I went down to a meeting in a place called Crow Head. It was in the month of December. Sixty-seven long linermen, crews, sixty-seven vessels, and they did not have enough [work weeks to qualify] for unemployment insurance. They had to arrange to go out and pick up rocks and garbage under the snow to get their stamps, their unemployment insurance stamps. . . . The greatest fishermen in the world were picking up rocks and garbage to get enough for their unemployment insurance to feed their families. It never, ever happened before in our history."

While the fishermen continued to haul in empty nets, the politicians argued back and forth over who was at fault. There is no doubt federal officials must accept some of the blame. In his 1989 report, former Memorial University president Dr. Leslie Harris (a Wells university contemporary) warned there would be problems because the numbers of spawning fish had seriously declined, but in 1990 then fisheries minister Bernard Valcourt — whom Wells demanded be fired for incompetence — disregarded Harris's advice to cut quotas to 100,000 tonnes, setting them instead at 190,000 tonnes.

On February 24, 1992, Crosbie announced cuts of 65,000 tonnes, or thirty-five per cent from the 1992 quota, and even offered his tacit approval to threats from angry Newfoundland fishermen that they'd sail into international waters and cut the nets of European fishing vessels who were plundering the cod. "I can't approve their tactics ahead of time," said Crosbie. "But there's nothing that says we have to sit back and do nothing. . . . It's difficult to get the attention of humanity on this issue."

John Efford, head of the United Fishermen of Newfoundland and Labrador, was calling for a massive kill of seals, and he invited Icelandic officials to Newfoundland to explain how their militant actions in 1975, led by the country's coast guard, resulted in chopping the nets off British trawlers to solve their overfishing problem. FFAW boss Richard Cashin was demanding action from Ottawa and announcing plans for a fishermen's flotilla — supported by the major fish companies — to confront the Spanish and Portuguese fishermen just outside the two-hundred-mile limit.

Through much of this feverish activity, Wells remained

silent. Indeed, he spent most of that dramatic week skiing at Marble Mountain in Corner Brook. But then, on March 2, at a news conference of the four Atlantic premiers, Wells and Nova Scotia's Don Cameron said Ottawa should send in the Canadian Navy to stop foreign overfishing. "It may take the forceful efforts of the Canadian Forces to do it, and if so why not?" said Wells. "Canada cannot stand by and see the economic interests of two of its provinces devastated in this way. Nor can it stand by and do nothing while irresponsible nations devastate a food supply for the world."

Two years earlier, when Liberal MPs George Baker and Brian Tobin had suggested using the navy to discourage overfishing, Wells had attacked them for being irresponsible. "They were calling me 'Tugboat Tobin' at the time," complains Tobin. Wells argued then that diplomacy, not force, was the right and proper way for civilized nations to deal with these issues. A week after his Corner Brook pronouncement, after he'd met with Mulroney in Ottawa and been told the feds weren't interested in "gunboat diplomacy," Wells claimed on CBC radio's "Cross-Country Checkup" that the media had misconstrued his comments. They hadn't.

The declining fisheries are "more than an economic problem in Newfoundland," says Wells. They're "a social and cultural problem. The fishery is so significantly a part of our economy, in the past particularly, that it's become part of our way of life. You can't separate the two. . . . Just suppose the northern cod, once so prolific that Cabot discovered by dropping the basket over the side [he could bring] it up full of fish, so prolific that a number of years ago, the total quantity taken out of here was 800,000 tonnes in one year. So devastated that now the total biomass is estimated at less than 800,000 tonnes. The total quantity left in the sea. That's what's happened to the stock in the last few years."

Wells says even though the offending Spanish and Portuguese are fishing just outside Canada's limit, if the stocks disappear, the world will hold Canada responsible, not Europe. "What's the world going to say when they look at this? It's Canada's continental shelf. Canada had control. How could Canada ever let that happen?"

For all the controversy, however, Crosbie has consistently rejected Opposition MPs' demands to assume management of the disputed waters off the nose and tail of the Grand Banks. He refuses to set a time limit on how soon Canada should press for extended jurisdiction, but has said it won't be in 1992, preferring instead to pursue diplomatic channels to achieve an end to the problem. There has been some progress. In April Panama agreed to take sanctions against Panamanian-flagged vessels engaged in overfishing, including fines and cancellation of their registry in Panama, a move that could affect two dozen vessels active in the northwest Atlantic. But so far, the EC countries have resisted all pressures to amend their fishing practices.

In late April 1992 Mulroney held a three-hour meeting with EC president Jacques Delors and Portuguese prime minister Anibal Cavaco Silva. The best Delors would say is he "understands the Canadian problem," but the EC would take no action until results of a NAFO scientific study were known in the summer. Two days earlier, Crosbie, who had been blasting the EC call for further studies, flipflopped and agreed to yet another study, saying, "We are willing to go the extra mile on this issue because it is so important for the future of the resource."

In late March union boss Richard Cashin led a flotilla of seven fishing trawlers out to confront the Spanish and Portuguese trawlers, trying to embarrass them into cutting back — for their part, the Europeans dismissed Canadian claims out of hand. Crosbie then said he and Mulroney would take the issue to the United Nations. FPI boss Vic Young and Wells flew to New York with an emotional plea to stop overfishing. Wells called the Europeans "international pirates" and even compared them to Iraqi dictator Saddam Hussein.

By late spring, after Wells carried his battle about overfishing directly to several European capitals and as Crosbie continued his diplomatic efforts, the recalcitrant European Community finally responded, announcing a temporary moratorium on northern-cod stocks. While the news was greeted in Canada with cautious optimism, Newfoundland fishermen's union official Earle McCurdy said the move was likely more commercially than environmentally motivated "because the [EC] catch rates haven't been very good and there's an obvious reason for that — the fish are scarce."

Just how scarce was reinforced a few days later when a study by the scientific council of NAFO found that cod stocks were close to their lowest recorded level. John Crosbie responded by saying he was prepared to close Newfoundland's main cod fishery for several years to allow badly depleted stocks to rebuild.

Wells, stating the obvious, said, "Nothing much worse could have happened in this province. . ."

On July 2, something worse did happen. In a devastating blow to Newfoundland's already battered economy, Crosbie formally shut down the $700 million northern-cod fishery for two years, essentially putting about 20,000 fishermen and plant workers on the dole, and striking a blow to the island's unique sea-centred lifestyle from which it may never recover.

Fishermen who had been earning up to $50,000 a year were suddenly reduced to an interim ten-week compensation package of $225 a week — even top unemployment benefits reach only about $400 a week — sparking angry vows by Cashin that they'd ignore the moratorium until Ottawa sweetens the offer. Wells called the package "inadequate."

FPI's Vic Young predicted his company would lose $55 million in 1992 sales because of the moratorium, while NatSea president Henry Demone said they'd lose $10 million.

Worse still, Wells said the province could be hit with $110 million in obligations to the Fisheries Loans Board because many boat owners and fish plant owners have their loans guaranteed by the province. He said the drastic drop in provincial revenues "greatly reduces the province's ability to deal with these issues."

Five days before his announcement, Crosbie and Wells had traded friendly barbs while signing a series of federal-provincial economic agreements worth $39 million designed to kick-start investment and economic development in the province.

Shortly before that, Wells unveiled his own $388 million plan to salvage the sinking economy, dropping taxes from ten per cent to five per cent for small businesses, from seventeen to sixteen per cent for corporations, and harmonizing Newfoundland's twelve per cent retail sales tax with the federal GST.

But any enthusiasm for these measures was quickly smothered under the blanket of doom that settled on the troubled island like an early-morning fog.

Most Newfoundlanders, Wells included, begrudgingly supported the moratorium, or at least understood it, as the only realistic way to revive the depleted cod stocks. But there was widespread anger and dismay over the paltry interim compensation payments.

There were also strong indications in Ottawa that the compensation package was designed more to punish Wells for his constitutional steadfastness than to help Newfoundlanders keep food on the tables and pay interest charges on their boats and equipment. Even the timing was cruel, coming just after most fishermen had spent several thousand dollars gearing up for July. And Wells had not been asked for his advice, finding out details of the plan just a few hours before Crosbie's announcement.

Shortly after the announcement, one federal cabinet minister conceded privately that "sure, Crosbie pushed for more [money]. What would you expect? It's his province, too, not just Clyde's. But how do you think some of the Quebec ministers felt about it? I'll tell you how they felt. It wasn't always this overt, but basically their attitude was 'screw them. They've got that little bastard [Wells]. They can learn to suffer with him.'"

Crosbie himself, a few days after his announcement, said in St. John's he was considering resigning if he couldn't talk his federal colleagues into a package that is "supportable."

About two weeks after introducing the initial emergency package, Crosbie, saying "perhaps we undercalculated the shock effect this would have," almost doubled the total pot from the original $500 million to about $800 million. The 9000 fishermen and 10,000 plant workers affected by the shutdown began receiving between $225 and $406 a week in August, an average weekly taxable payment of $385. To get more than the minimum, fishermen had to decide by December 1 to either take early retirement, sell their licences back to the government, take retraining outside the fishery, upgrade fishery skills or work elsewhere in the industry on projects such as conservation.

True to form, Wells insisted the federal package contain a clawback provision where fishery workers must deduct any money earned from other work from their compensation payments, prompting Cashin to say, "This is the most righteous and moralistic government you can imagine. This is a state of mind to the right of southern Alberta." But Newfoundland Fishery Minister Walter Carter said if a fisherman is receiving compensation, "it would be very unfair for him to compete for a job with a guy who is unemployed and isn't receiving anything."

Even more depressing, many experts feel two years is not a realistic timetable for replenishing the northern-cod stock, and the moratorium is more likely to last three to five years before a fisherman can return to the only way of life most of them have ever known.

The economic impact by itself will be horrendous. "Ask

yourself what would be the effect in Ontario if 400,000 people involved in the auto industry were suddenly told, 'You can't for the next two years earn your living the way you have in the past,'" Wells said.

More than that, however, is the impact on what Wells called "the human dignity of the people involved." The cultural after-shocks to thousands of people scattered around hundreds of remote outports are unprecedented in this country. Life has always been tough on the Rock, but it was always said that no matter how bad things got, you could always fish. Not anymore.

Some began predicting a mass exodus of people on the scale of the Depression-era flight of Prairie farmers. Leslie Harris, who recommended drastic cuts to cod quotas in 1990, which Ottawa basically ignored, said even the moratorium doesn't guarantee the stocks will recover. "If they don't, the East Coast is dead as a place to live."

In Wells's first three years as premier, not only is unemployment up dramatically, but real gross domestic product is down, as is retail trade, housing starts, and overall employment. Current prospects look even worse.

In his first budget, June 6, 1989, Finance Minister Hubert Kitchen complained that despite a 3.8 per cent after-inflation growth in gross domestic product, the Tories had not been able to balance their budgets, and out-migration had created a net loss of about 4000 people every year during the 1980s. He also complained federal cutbacks would take $80 million out of the Newfoundland economy, but predicted a surplus on current account of $5.3 million, a sharp turnaround from Peckford's $90 million deficit, resulting in a host of tax increases to raise $31.5 million in 1989-90 and $43.4 million the next fiscal year. Commodities hit by these tax increases included fine-cut tobacco products, some children's clothing, gasoline, driver's licenses and vehicle registration fees, liquor and wine taxes, and both corporate and personal income tax (up two percentage points). The budget also included $14 million to honor commitments Peckford made to the failed Sprung cucumber-growing project, despite Wells's election campaign promises that his government would not honor all those bills.

In March 1990, during his second budget, Kitchen boasted the unemployment rate fell to 15.8 per cent, the lowest in eight years. The current-account surplus, projected at $5.3 million, was $37.8 million, but the total provincial debt was $5.2 billion, more than $9000 for every man, woman, and child in Newfoundland, one of the highest per-capita debts in the country. Among other things, Kitchen announced a major reduction in the number of government vehicles and a dismantling of the $236,000 ombudsman's office, no longer apparently the "vital link" Wells had hailed it in 1966.

But if people thought the 1990 budget was tough, they hadn't seen anything yet. In January 1991 Wells told the house he had decided to delay implementation of a restraint program pending receipt of available federal funding for the year. He had earlier projected a $120-million deficit on current account and said if nothing was done it could reach $200 million in 1991-92 and up to "several hundred million in 1995-96." In late April, Wells told the house that before his government could bring the province to the top of the ladder "we've got first to build a secure ladder, which is what we've been doing for the last nearly two years."

Two days before the March 7 budget, Wells had warned that current federal budgetary measures, such as the three-year cap on Established Program funds, could signal the end for the medicare system. The real crunch came when Kitchen announced in the March 1991 budget the province was laying off 1300 permanent employees, seven hundred part-time and seasonal employees, and eliminating five hundred vacant positions. In addition, executive and management positions were reduced by ten per cent. For those who kept their jobs, the Liberals imposed a one-year wage freeze throughout the entire public sector, wiping out previously negotiated wage increases for the 1991-92 fiscal year.

Despite all the gloomy news, Kitchen was happy to say that Hibernia, the $8.5 billion megaproject, was rolling ahead. Contracts worth $1.8 billion had already been awarded, work had begun on detailed engineering and preparation of the construction site at Bull Arm, where the workforce would grow to more than a thousand people by the end of 1991.

On February 10, 1985, Brian Mulroney and Brian Peckford had signed the sixty-eight-point Atlantic Accord during a news conference at the Hotel Newfoundland in St. John's, ending eighteen years of negotiations and disputes between Ottawa and Newfoundland over control of the offshore. The agreement, which both men heralded as the beginning of a new era of prosperity — John Crosbie said it meant that Newfoundlanders were "no longer going to be the comic figures of Confederation" — established a $300 million Canada-Newfoundland Development Fund ($225 million from Ottawa, $75 million from the province) to finance major projects. Under the accord, offshore oil and gas resources were to be managed by a joint agency called the Canada-Newfoundland Offshore Petroleum Board, with each government appointing three board members, and the chairman being jointly appointed. Optimism was running so high that the agreement contained a complex formula based on Newfoundland's evolving from a "have not" into a "have" province from the offshore development revenues.

In a February 1989 interview with the *Calgary Herald*, Wells said that "Newfoundland desperately needs that kind of economic input. If Hibernia doesn't go ahead, we're almost looking at a nothing future." For a time, it looked as if Hibernia wouldn't go ahead, as the complex on-again off-again negotiations between the governments and the four oil companies — Mobil, Petro-Canada, Gulf, and Chevron — dragged on through the spring and summer of 1989. In an October 1989 *Financial*

Post interview, Wells was openly sceptical about the whole thing. "We've lost perspective. The former [Peckford] government painted [Hibernia] as a savior. It isn't." He said the number of permanent jobs generated would be only 1600, about the size of two fish plants, and construction would bring only $2.6 billion to Canada, of which Quebec would get $1.5 billion and Newfoundland $770 million. Even with higher oil prices, royalties would only produce $8 million a year for Newfoundland.

Former Newfoundland Liberal leader Bill Rowe, who now operates a popular radio call-in show in St. John's, says Wells "was against Hibernia on my show. I asked him the question about $2.6 billion in federal funds in terms of loans and loan guarantees, if he agreed with it. He said no. I said, 'Would you have done it?' He said, 'No, I wouldn't have done that. I found myself in a situation that was take it or leave it. I didn't negotiate it. I wasn't in a situation where I could say no to $2.6 billion on principle [but] yes, we will take it. But if I had my choice, I wouldn't have spent it that way. There are better ways to spend it.' That was the day after he signed it."

Even so, progress appeared to be being made early in 1990, but then Wells got involved in his well-publicized war with Ottawa over the Meech Lake accord. Following the accord's death in June 1990, Quebec Tory MPs publicly announced they would block approval of the Hibernia deal, Bill C-44, to punish Wells unless they could be convinced it had considerable economic benefits for Quebec. Finally, on September 14, 1990, with Mulroney pointedly absent from the ceremony, Wells, Crosbie, federal Energy Minister Jake Epp, and the chief executive officers from the four oil companies signed the deal to begin development of the oilfield located on the Grand Banks, 315 kilometres south-southeast of St. John's, predicting they'd be pumping 100,000 barrels of oil a day by 1996. Ottawa provided grants of $1 billion and loan guarantees of $1.7 billion for the project. Mobil Oil Canada Ltd. had a 28.125 per cent interest, Gulf Canada Resources Ltd. and Petro-Canada Inc. 25 per cent each, and Chevron Canada Resources Ltd 21.875 per cent. The project was expected to cost $5.2 billion prior to production and another $3.3 billion on capital expenditures. Operating costs over the eighteen-year production phase were estimated at $10 billion. Even before the Hibernia deal was signed, Newfoundland Energy Minister Rex Gibbons announced that Petro-Canada was developing new plans for its 406-million-barrel Terra Nova field 40 kilometres south of Hibernia.

Under the pact, the province agreed not to charge sales tax on its thirty per cent share of total capital spending of $8.5 billion and the tax would be cut by two-thirds, to four per cent, on operating expenditures of $10 billion during the eighteen-year production phase. Newfoundland would earn $2.3 billion in royalties if oil prices during production average $25 U.S. a barrel in 1989 dollars. Ottawa would get $1.9 billion under the same conditions. But for every dollar the province received in oil royalties, the federal government would reduce its equalization payments to Newfoundland by ninety-seven or ninety-eight cents. A study by Memorial University professor Wade Locke concluded that meant the province's net take from Hibernia revenues would be only about $100 million, or roughly $4 million a year. "Newfoundland has made one hell of a lot of concessions," says Wells, adding that without the 1988 agreement Peckford signed forcing him to, he is doubtful he would have agreed to the final terms.

The problem from the outset was that the project depended upon escalating oil prices. Unlike about seventy-five per cent of the world's oil, which can be produced for $4 a barrel, Hibernia's production costs were between $17 and $20 a barrel. Still, in a province where 42,000 people were unemployed, the prospect of 2000 jobs a year over six years plus 1100 full-time jobs during the production phase was welcome. In addition, the government saw Hibernia as what Energy

Minister Rex Gibbons, a geologist by trade, described as "the beginning of an offshore [development] that's going to include Hibernia, Terra Nova, Whiterose, and other fields." With any luck, the Rock was slated to become an East Coast Alberta. But that seemed a little less likely in February 1991, when a federal geological survey concluded there was only about half as much oil off the Grand Banks as predicted in the early 1980s, setting the estimates for Hibernia at between 525 and 650 million barrels, a far cry from an earlier forecast of more than one billion barrels.

Even so, construction moved ahead. At Bull Arm, a ninety-minute drive from St. John's, a seven-kilometre road had been built into the isolated Great Mosquito Cove, where the giant concrete base for the offshore development would be built, and a townsite for a community of 2600 people was well under way. Hibernia officials had even cut a compensation package for local fishermen, worried about the impact of the project on their livelihood. Things were going so well that at the November inaugural convention of Women in Trades and Technology (WITT) Bill Gaulton of the Oil Development Council said his group would recruit, train, and place women for work with Hibernia. "We're going to remove barriers," he said. "We're paving the way with the workforce with regard to workplace attitudes."

A week later, after months of negotiations, Epp and the Canadian Imperial Bank of Commerce announced a deal wherein the bank agreed to head a syndicate that would offer loans up to $415 million, or twenty-five per cent of the total $1.66 billion guaranteed by Ottawa, but only after Hibernia begins production in 1996, thus reducing the federal government's risk and bringing more private-sector involvement into the deal.

Everybody was happy. Or so it appeared.

On February 4, 1992, Chuck Shultz, president and chief executive officer of Gulf Canada Resources Limited, announced in Calgary that Gulf was dropping its twenty-five per cent interest in the deal. "This is a difficult decision, but since there is no mechanism for partial withdrawal, we had no choice but to file our notice of complete withdrawal," he said, explaining, "Our business environment has become very onerous."

Wells, who was expecting Newfoundland to lead Atlantic Canada with four per cent growth in 1992, largely because of Hibernia, said he was disappointed but there was no reason to panic. "I don't see any immediate cause for concern. It will take some time to resolve it. If I develop a worry in a month or two months or six months, I'll let you know, but I'm not worried at the moment."

Everybody else was. Gulf had been trying to sell its interest for two years but could find no takers. Calgary oil analyst Ian Doig, a critic of Hibernia, said there was "a good chance" the project would collapse. Epp, acknowledging the pullout hurt, nonetheless said, "The Hibernia project will go ahead."

The next day, Imperial Oil announced it was cutting 1700 jobs as soon as possible and shutting down 1000 service stations over the next two years. Within a week, Epp was saying the Gulf decision might force a delay in the project. "It cannot be ruled out." And a few days later, Petro-Canada president Norman McIntyre, chairman of the Hibernia executive committee, after meeting with Epp and Wells, told a news conference in St. John's that work on the project would be slowed dramatically and spending cut by half, and no new work would be started while the search for a new investor continued. Almost immediately, four hundred workers were laid off at the Bull Arm site, and the prospects for other workers looked dim. In March, Epp said the partners have less than a year to find another investor. Asked what would happen to the megaproject if they didn't, Epp said, "I can't speculate." But the message was obvious.

Petro-Canada chairman Bill Hopper had already said Hibernia was dead unless a new partner could be found within sixty days. Wells says Hopper may have just been trying to put pressure on Ottawa. "These are difficult times — everybody understands that. I can't imagine that these kinds of comments from Mr. Hopper could be helpful. . . . It harkens back to a plaque my mother gave me many years ago. It said, 'Be sure your brain is engaged before you put your mouth in gear.'"

Engaged or not, Gibbons was saying essentially the same thing as Hopper in the house — that if no new investor was found by June, "things would be getting very serious. . . . The best I can say on that is we have a few months" — prompting Tory Leader Len Simms to charge that the Liberals misled the public in February when they said the consortium had until the fall to find a replacement for Gulf's $1 billion share. The next day, March 11, after a private scolding from Wells, Gibbons told the legislature that June was not the deadline, adding, "Maybe I was speculating too much."

When Hubert Kitchen stood in the house March 26 to deliver the 1992-93 Newfoundland budget, there was little mention of Hibernia and certainly nothing new. Kitchen noted the provision for funding of $63.2 million provided under the Offshore Development Fund for two major Hibernia-related projects, plus money already allocated for construction of a dry dock and fabrication facility at Bull Arm and the $11.2 million to be spent in 1992 on the $40 million oil rig facility at Cow Head, but the only thing new in his budget concerning Hibernia was a $1.1 million program to fund Hibernia-related training through the Department of Education.

Kitchen insisted the three remaining partners remain committed to the projects, but he said, because of the crisis in the fishery and the slowdown in Hibernia, the Wells government predicted a net decline in the province's gross domestic product of .5 per cent, matching the final figure for the current year. What's more, unemployment would jump to 20.4 per cent from the current 18.4 per cent, and with the abolition of Newfoundland's school tax balanced against increases in income and tobacco tax, the overall impact of his budget would be to increase the burden on individual taxpayers by $8 million while decreasing taxes on businesses by $2 million.

Still, Wells continued his fixation with the deficit, predicting a current-account deficit of $28.9 million, a little less than half the $59.5 million shortfall they'd predicted for the fiscal year just ending. (In fact, they ended the fiscal year $95 million short.) Interest payments as a percentage of revenue had declined from a peak of 17.5 per cent in 1986 to the current 12.8 per cent.

For a province the size of Newfoundland there are few options. It could borrow more, but that's a catch-22 situation. It's already heavily in debt — although much of that is long-term debt, with interest rates already set — and has the country's lowest credit rating, which means that if it does borrow it must pay more for the privilege than the other provinces. It can also continue to tax people more, but with the highest unemployment and lowest per-capita incomes in Canada, that isn't exactly attractive either. Wells has tried to cut government costs, and while he's had some success in fiscal terms, he's managed to exact a high cost in human terms.

To make matters worse, John Manuel, general manager of Corner Brook Pulp and Paper Ltd., told the St. John's Board of Trade in a January 17, 1992, speech at the Hotel Newfoundland that the prospects looked "bleak" for the newsprint industry. Worldwide production capacity outstrips consumption by about two million tonnes, he said, and with the tremendous growth in the southern U.S. of modern, non-unionized, efficient newsprint plants, aided by fast-growing indigenous fibre and proximity to the markets, the Americans can deliver newsprint at $100 a tonne cheaper than the average Canadian mill.

This has meant the Corner Brook mill has had to abandon its modernization program, on which from 1985 to 1989 it had already spent $245 million, "because we are not generating enough cash right now to continue, and we need to spend at least that amount again in the next five to six years if we are to remain competitive." He also noted a worldwide trend toward declining newspaper readership.

As is the case with Newfoundland's fish and offshore oil industries, the factors conspiring against the pulp and paper industry are dictated by international conditions more than by domestic provincial policies or actions, although in April Bob Collez, resident general manager of the Abitibi-Price paper company, told the Grand Falls–Windsor Rotary Club that the provincial government's decision to apply a one per cent payroll tax in its recent budget to companies in the resource sector would cost the company $300,000 for 1992 alone and, combined with the recession, would act as an incentive for companies to cut the size of their workforces.

Public funding became so tight in 1992 that the Public Libraries Board was forced to announce it was closing the province's 107 libraries for two weeks to save money, prompting the St. John's *Evening Telegram* to chide the government's "professed commitment to stamping out illiteracy" while at the same time closing libraries.

In May another fiscal rocket hit the island with the news that Lundrigans Ltd. of Corner Brook, one of Newfoundland's largest home-grown industries, with interests in construction, gypsum, car rentals and sales, and concrete and building supplies, owed the Bank of Montreal $24 million and was headed for receivership, threatening the jobs of three hundred employees and the spinoff jobs of hundreds more.

Wells, true to his small "c" conservative fiscal approach, told Lundrigans officials that he'd help find another buyer for their Atlantic Gypsum plant, the only one in the province, but that it wouldn't be fair to Lundrigans' competitors to offer government assistance to their other holdings.

The only positive side to all this is that Newfoundlanders are used to hard times. Unlike affluent Ontarians, who are having great difficulties adjusting to the current recession, Newfoundlanders are more philosophical about tough economic conditions. With the exception of the relatively small but powerful merchant class, that's all most of them have ever known.

Which perhaps helps to explain one startling economic statistic that speaks volumes about the Newfoundland character. Even though they're least able to afford it, no other Canadians give more money to charity than they do. According to Statistics Canada, their 1991 median donation was $220, nearly double the $120 median for Canada as a whole.

This generosity of spirit, which clearly flows from a tradition of helping one's fellow human beings, is just one character trait that most Newfoundlanders would proudly point out in their belief that they, too, are — dare we say it? — a distinct society.

12

The Autocrat

ROUTE 440 ACROSS the Humber Arm above Corner Brook snakes through some of the most spectacular landscapes and breathtaking vistas to be found anywhere as the visitor travels through such colorful communities as Irishtown, Hughes Brook, Summerside, Meadows, and Gillams, all nestled comfortably in the naturally sheltered arms of the Bay of Islands.

At McIver's, the road suddenly leads north, slashing its way through rock and trees, winding left and right, up and down, until about forty kilometres in from the Trans-Canada Highway at the crest of Cox's Cove Hill where the town of Cox's Cove huddles snugly in the valley, its tiny houses clinging precariously to the rocks. The cove is surrounded by the water of Middle Arm, Penguin Arm, and Goose Arm, and framed by the caribou country along the snow-capped Southern Mountains.

Cox's Cove, a town of about 1000 people, was originally settled in 1840 by Thomas O'Grady and George, John, and William Cox, all herring and lobster fishermen. By 1911 it had a school, a store, and a herring-processing plant; in the 1930s the Island Timber Company set up a mill there employing 250 men, although that was eventually phased out. For many years, there was no major employer until the provincial government established a fish plant there in 1970, five years after the community became the first town to welcome families from Penguin Arm and Brakes Cove under Smallwood's federal-provincial resettlement plan, and one year after the town was officially incorporated.

In the March 1985 provincial election, Tory Ted Blanchard won the Bay of Islands seat, which includes Cox's Cove, by fifteen votes and was immediately named Peckford's minister of labor. But in Wells's April 1989 provincial election, even though about eighty per cent of Cox's Cove voters supported the new Tory candidate — their former deputy mayor, Leonard Gillingham — he still lost the seat to first-time Liberal candidate Ed Joyce. But Joyce quickly resigned his seat so that Wells, who had lost next door to his old nemesis, Tory Lynn Verge, could take over the riding. Wells, of course, was acclaimed in May 1989, while Joyce became his special assistant in charge of the premier's office in the Sir Richard Squires Building in Corner Brook.

About a year later, a problem arose between Wells and the elected but unpaid town council led by Mayor Tony Oxford, a Tory, principal of the only school in town. The dispute revolved around a $300,000 provincial program to compensate ten private recreational-cabin (cottage) owners at Frenchman's Cove, just outside of town, where a new water system was to be built.

The town council refused to go along with the government's plan for council to borrow the money on the basis of a government-guaranteed loan to compensate the cabin owners, all but two of them from outside town, for cabins that had been built illegally on Crown land around the pond (anywhere else in the country it would be called a lake) that was to become the community's new water supply. "If I'm going to spend

$300,000, it will be for the people of the community," said Oxford. "We still have people with no water and sewer, and they want us to spend $300,000 on outsiders. It's ridiculous." Even though the province itself would repay the loan, council feared, with some justification, that the forced imposition of such a large, long-term debt on the town's books would make it impossible for it to borrow for future projects. The last thing they wanted to do was limit their options for a group of relatively well-to-do cabin owners from outside town.

Inspiring natural beauty notwithstanding, somewhere between thirty and forty of the 350 families in the community have no water and sewer services, and many of the steep roads in the community are more suited to mountain goats than automobiles. So, the seven-member town council decided to go ahead without provincial approval and divert about $26,000 of the federal-provincial allocation for the capital-works project on what council felt was much-needed road work. The province responded by stopping payment on the cheques, saying money for that project should come from the council's budget.

Wells met with the council in February 1991 hoping to sort out what he called "a difficult situation," telling them not to expect provincial funding if they proceeded with the road work. Oxford, however, said that by the time they got a firm answer from Wells, the work had already been done. And so the argument continued through the summer and into the fall. According to Oxford, and Wells has never denied it, the premier promised to appoint an adjudicator to conduct a full independent investigation to straighten out the matter.

"That was fine with us," says Oxford, "but it never happened."

What did happen was that Wells, without warning, fired Oxford and his entire council. He also enforced a provision in the Municipalities Act barring them from seeking elected office for two years, and appointed a hand-picked three-member commission to run the town — and do his bidding — until a new election was held in March.

At the same time, a news release from Wells was delivered to every mail box in Cox's Cove. "They didn't have the decency to talk to people," says Daniel Baldwin, chairman of a concerned citizens committee, formed to protest the firing. The people of the town were outraged, and there were large turnouts at various public meetings to protest the premier's move. Oxford called the move "a total disgrace. If you go out and commit a felony you get an independent hearing. Yet we were a voluntary council trying to do the best we could, and they treat us this way. He's the guy who's been going across the country preaching truth and justice and calling for a full public airing on the Constitution. Well, maybe he should practise that at home rather than just promote himself by talking about it on the mainland."

Verge accused the provincial government of being arbitrary and running "roughshod" over the elected council. She also accused one of the three commissioners Wells appointed to temporarily run the town of being in a "serious" conflict of interest because his brother was one of the cabin owners. "In addition, two sisters-in-law of another commissioner are among the ten cabin owners whom the government has directed the council to compensate. That leaves a majority of the commissioners clearly in a conflict-of-interest situation," Verge said. Municipal Affairs Minister Eric Gullage said they weren't in conflict because they wouldn't be required to vote on that matter since the decision had already been made by the government to compensate the cabin owners. In other words, being rubber stamps doesn't contravene Section 415 of the Municipalities Act, which states that a councillor shall not vote on or speak to a matter where a relative of the councillor has an interest in the matter.

Kathy Dunderdale, president of the provincial branch of the Federation of Municipalities, called the council's firing "regrettable" and called for the appointment of an independent adjudicator. Nearly the whole town turned out for a mock funeral to bury democracy.

Tory leader Len Simms says the atmosphere in the community has been "poisoned" by the province's "heavy-handed" approach. He argues that Wells is sending out this message to people who volunteer to govern municipalities across the province: do our bidding or we'll hire people who will. He also called for an adjudicator, adding that the $26,000 in "misdirected funds" Wells referred to was not significant enough to warrant firing the entire council. "Surely recovering this amount from future municipal grants would have been sufficient reprimand."

Not for Wells. For him, that money was "illegally" diverted, council was given every opportunity to rectify the situation, but didn't, and "accordingly, the government was left with no alternative but to dismiss the council and ensure the funding was properly managed."

In exercising his authority that way, Wells joined another well-known Newfoundland autocrat, Joey Smallwood, who did essentially the same thing to Corner Brook in 1963.

Dr. Noel Murphy, whom Wells defeated in the 1966 election, represented Corner Brook at the time, along with lawyer Bill Smith. He'd been complaining to Smallwood about the council's continual fighting, and one morning Murphy and Smith received telegrams from St. John's telling them to go to the capital immediately because they were opening the House of Assembly that afternoon.

"So we went down to the station and got on the train. It was due to leave at three o'clock," says Murphy. "But about thirty seconds before that, somebody came running along the platform shouting, 'Dr. Murphy! Mr. Smith! Get off the train!' So we got off and he said he had a message for us — the house is adjourned and they've dissolved the municipal government in Corner Brook and appointed a commission."

Cox's Cove is only one example of Clyde Wells's autocratic style. The same day Simms criticized Wells for his "heavy-handed" approach at Cox's Cove, at a news conference in the Opposition caucus room, he said the government had also promised to compensate the town of Mount Pearl for its fire station from provincial revenues — under Bill 50, the amalgamation law, the town's fire services were taken over by St. John's — but then reneged on the promise. After weeks of bickering between the province and the mayors of St. John's and Mount Pearl, Gullage decided the province would pay only $638,000 of the $2.6 million, and all the municipalities served by the St. John's Regional Firefighting Service Board would pay $2 million.

Indeed, throughout much of 1991, amalgamation became the major domestic issue in Newfoundland, apart from the economic problems of the fishery. Wells's whole approach to amalgamation, as you'd expect, mirrors his constitutional theology on the benefits of centralization.

In May 1969, Wells, supporting Smallwood's plan to dramatically reduce the number of outport communities, said, "It does not take a financial genius . . . to come to the conclusion that we in the province cannot afford to maintain a thousand communities and provide for them the health services, the municipal services, the educational services, and all the other services that government is expected to provide for its people. We cannot do it. There is only one answer to it, and that is centralization . . ."

In July 1989, shortly after becoming premier, Wells decided centralization was still the answer to much of Newfoundland's problems, and he issued a list of 115 communities that were ripe for amalgamation, solemnly promising, however, that any community that didn't wish to be amalgamated didn't have to be. Three of the biggest battles were in the St. John's suburban communities of Mount Pearl, Wedgewood Park, and Goulds, all part of the government's plan to make what the media dubbed a "supercity" out of St. John's. In all cases, the residents opposed amalgamation. In all cases, it didn't matter.

In May 1991 Wells stated in the legislature, "Our preference is to persuade municipalities to agree voluntarily to amalgamate where it makes good sense for them to amalgamate. . . . I understand self-interest; I am not critical of people saying — take Wedgewood Park, for example — it is better for us to protect our own little municipality, totally surrounded by St. John's, because we are better off and we have lower taxes and so on. I understand their wanting to protect what is essentially a kind of privileged or special position. But the government must govern in the overall best interest of the people of the province as a whole. Now in some cases, where we are unable to persuade municipalities that the right thing for the overall [good] is to amalgamate, then it may well be that we may have to ask this legislature to act."

Which is exactly what he did do, despite petitions showing that ninety-nine per cent of Wedgewood Park residents opposed amalgamation. Mount Pearl Mayor Harvey Hodder at one point openly accused Wells of being "arrogant and dictatorial," and both communities felt so strongly about the matter they took it to court — and lost — in an effort to maintain their independence.

In late fall 1991 Gullage introduced Bill 50, which annexed Wedgewood Park and Goulds to St. John's. The immediate impact of the move were estimates that the tax rates of both communities would nearly double, with no increase in benefits, because the homes would all be reassessed using St. John's standards. Goulds Mayor Peter Murphy said, "If Clyde Wells thinks this is fair, then he doesn't know what he's talking about. The government hasn't been able to show us one area where amalgamation will benefit the people."

At the same time he was refusing calls for a plebiscite or public hearings near St. John's, Wells announced that the people of the municipalities of Massey Drive and Mount

Moriah, which is in his riding, could decide for themselves whether they wished to amalgamate with Corner Brook. In November, after Verge said residents of the three municipalities opposed the plan and Simms tabled a petition signed by 277 Mount Moriah residents who opposed amalgamation, Wells told the house, "If they don't want it, the government is not going to foist it on them."

Even so, Wells rejected Verge's demand he hold a plebiscite in the area because it was already obvious that an "overwhelming majority" of Corner Brook residents favored the plan. "You only need to conduct a plebiscite if you're not satisfied that the preponderance of support is one way or another," he said. Verge accused Wells of "being guided solely by his backroom discussions with the council of Corner Brook and, more precisely, the mayor of Corner Brook [Ray Pollett]."

In a February 1992 cabinet shuffle, Gullage, who'd become known as "Eric the Amalgamator," paid the price for carrying the ball on this unpopular policy by being shifted out of the municipal affairs portfolio, trading places with former social services minister Bill Hogan. Gullage insisted that the controversy over amalgamation had nothing to do with the transfer, but two weeks later Hogan announced that thirty-three municipalities — including Stephenville Crossing — had been dropped for the old amalgamation list. Forty-four communities had already been amalgamated, and another fifty-seven — including those surrounding Corner Brook — were still under consideration.

Amalgamation wasn't the only defensible idea Wells has put forward that was criticized more for the way he did it than what he did. The Newfoundland school tax issue was another major case in point.

The first school tax authority was set up in Corner Brook in 1954, but the province-wide school tax system didn't really get going until the early 1960s, when twenty-one School Tax Authorities were set up around the province. These authorities are composed of representatives from the local government and the school boards, and in many areas, because of either lack of interest or church influence, some tax authority members were appointed by the church, which had a direct interest in keeping the historic, but inefficient, denominational system going (which Wells is also about to dismantle). In 1991 these authorities collected about $35 million. In reality a poll tax, not based on property or ability to pay, it covered about ten per cent of the total cost of education, the provincial government paying the rest. The problem was that it set up serious disparities because of the different economic realities around the province. To an average classroom of thirty students in the Avalon area, which includes St. John's, the tax provides $11,280. But to a similar classroom in the Vinland/Strait of Bell Isle School Board district, it would provide just $4890. Put another way, the school tax raises about $400 a student in Avalon schools, but only $98 a student in rural schools, making it impossible for them to provide even close to the same level of education as the relatively wealthy urban schools.

Few people argued that the system wasn't unfair. During the 1989 election, in fact, Wells talked about either reforming or possibly abolishing the system. But that's the sort of major move one would expect to come only after it was discussed with those directly involved. The trustees, for example, had suggested a series of reforms in the past, mainly reducing the number of school tax authorities and making them more equitable across the province. They argued that keeping the tax in another form, perhaps on property taxes, at least allows school boards to have some autonomy over the education in their districts.

On November 19, 1991, Kevin Breen, president of the School Trustees Association, was among the luncheon crowd at the St. John's Board of Trade where Wells was guest speaker. Wells not only launched into a tirade about the unfairness of the school tax system, he announced, point-blank, he was abolishing the school tax authorities and giving the province sole responsibility for education funding. Breen, caught off guard, said later, "I was a little shocked by the way I heard it, but I wasn't surprised. I'm a little disappointed I had to come to a Board of Trade function to find out." And Jack Parsons, president of the province's Association of School Tax Authorities, which hadn't been consulted either, complained, "This is not the proper way to announce this kind of thing." He said Wells was being "dictatorial" for political reasons, and could put the more than a hundred school tax employees out of work across the province.

Wells's old schoolmate Myrle Vokey, an official with the Newfoundland and Labrador School Trustees Association, says Breen and other officials met with Wells later that day to express their concern. "People's lives, people's employment, and so on were affected by that," says Vokey, "and he had announced it right out of the blue. I wasn't at the meeting, but I'm told he . . . said he was sorry, he shouldn't have done it that way. So he's not beyond recognizing his mistakes when he makes them. But in his opinion, he doesn't make very many. One of the things that causes Newfoundlanders to smile was that Clyde left Joey because Joe was too dictatorial, too autocratic. That causes some laughter in Newfoundland circles today."

Despite a petition signed by almost 10,000 people in St. John's to retain the school tax, Finance Minister Hubert Kitchen announced less than three weeks later that the tax and the authorities would be abolished as of June 30, 1992. He said the revenues to the schools would be made up in other ways, but school officials, recognizing the serious financial constraints facing the government, remained sceptical.

One area where governments everywhere traditionally reward their loyal friends is in the lucrative tourism advertising field. In Ontario, for example, both Norman Atkins and Hugh Segal prospered, at least in part, from Bill Davis's legendary Big

Blue Machine in the 1970s and then from Brian Mulroney in the 1980s, thanks to cushy government contracts with their advertising firm. Atkins, of course, is now an influential Tory senator, and Segal is Mulroney's current chief of staff.

In April 1990 news came from Development Minister Chuck Furey that the government had pared down the candidates for its $2.3 million tourism advertising contract to two firms. Both of them — APPA Communications Inc. and Total Communications Ltd. — had close ties to the Liberal party. Furey said he was not concerned about any appearance of political favoritism. "No matter what you do in this industry, you're going to be cursed. If I give it to company X, people are going to be unhappy. If I give it to company Y, people are going to be unhappy."

Apparently somebody was unhappy with Furey, because the next day he announced he had invited two more firms to make proposals — Marbury Atlantic and M-5 Advertising — only one of them, Marbury, with obvious Liberal connections. Furey said he'd reopened the bids at the request of his five-member team of senior bureaucrats, instead of the traditional two, appointed to review the proposals. Another change from the previous year, he said, is that Wells's chief of staff Edsel Bonnell, and press secretary Judy Foote would not take part in questioning the firm about their proposals, although Furey himself would be involved.

So who did get the contract in May? APPA Communications Inc., a fledgling company formed less than eight months earlier by three partners: Rick Pardy, who had headed Research Associates Ltd., the provincial Liberals' polling agency; Gary Anstey, who was executive assistant to Liberal MP Bill Rompkey during the Trudeau years; and Jeannette Pelley, formerly with Saga Communications, a Tory-connected firm that had the contract for several years during the Peckford regime. A year earlier, Saga had billed the Tory government for $819,268, but had decided not to bid on the three-year, $2.3

million Liberal contract. However, Total Communications was a joint venture between Saga and members of C.C. Keats Advertising Ltd. Ches Keats, whose firm had done advertising work for the Liberal election campaign, described the new firm as an honest effort to "provide a non-political approach."

Marbury, an affiliate of Toronto-based Marbury Advertising Communications Ltd., which had worked for David Peterson's Liberals in Ontario, had co-ordinated the Liberal election campaign advertising in Newfoundland. It, too, was new to St. John's, setting up a one-person office there less than a year earlier. Even before bidding began, one local firm complained about the possibility of political interference. "I simply wrote them back and said they had no grounds for concern," said Furey. They didn't make the short list.

When APPA was awarded the contract in late May, Furey said the action was very fair. But Ches Keats didn't agree. "Everybody knows there's something wrong. You can smell a rat; you don't have to see it, you can smell it," he said. "I know we lost this because of political alliances and friendships, both maybe in a bureaucratic sense and in the political sense more definitely."

In the house, the Tories had also accused Furey of political porkbarrelling, and in June Keats asked the province to reopen the contract for an evaluation by professional advertising executives unconnected with the current government, which he believed "would help to eliminate the political stigma that is attached to this account once and for all." Keats said most people in the local industry were "appalled" by the government's move. "It's unheard of in the industry to give a close to eight million dollar contract to a company without a track record. . . . It should not matter what your political stripe is; what should count is your ability to perform."

Naturally, Furey disagreed. He insisted the contract was based on a fair evaluation.

In September Tory development critic Neil Windsor issued a press release accusing the premier's political staff, Bonnell and Foote, of being involved in the deal, charging "political interference from the highest levels of the provincial government in the award of the tourism advertising contract," and repeating earlier Opposition calls for a public inquiry into the awarding of the contract. Furey dismissed the charges as "way off base . . . the product of a sick mind." He said Foote and Bonnell did not sit in on the review, although they had the year before, because, according to Bonnell, "we were both public relations professionals, who knew something about the business." Wells, of course, refused to budge on the contract, and the controversy eventually died down.

Besides the shift of Gullage out of municipal affairs in February 1992, the most intriguing part of the cabinet minishuffle was the official elevation of former Liberal leader Ed Roberts, a senior law partner with the major St. John's firm of Halley, Hunt, Barristers and Solicitors, to justice minister and attorney general. His new position announced by Wells before Christmas 1991, Roberts was seen by many as a replacement for Wells should the premier decide to exercise his federal ambitions.

Just as Smallwood had reached outside his elected caucus in 1966 to bring in Wells, Crosbie, and Hickman, Wells told the house on November 12, 1991, he had asked the unelected Roberts to accept the job, shortly after the resignation of then justice minister Paul Dicks, one of five ministers who has either resigned or been fired since Wells became premier. (In the case of Dicks, it is still uncertain which category he falls into, although for public consumption he resigned for "personal" reasons.)

Bonavista South MHA Aubrey Gover, a rookie who won the 1989 election by just twenty votes, was named acting justice minister while Roberts cleared up his private legal business. In February, Gover was sworn in as minister of works, services, and transportation the day Roberts, still without a seat in the house, was formally elevated to cabinet.

The fifty-one-year-old Roberts, one of the group of Young Turks, including Wells, recruited by Smallwood in the 1966 election, served in cabinet from 1968 to 1972, then took over the party after Smallwood was defeated by Tory Frank Moores. A St. John's native, he attended St. Andrew's College, a private school in Aurora, north of Toronto, where Moores also was a student. Roberts took law at the University of Toronto and for a time was associate private secretary to Jack Pickersgill and then Smallwood's executive assistant. Roberts kept the leadership until 1977, when he lost it to Bill Rowe, but he remained an MHA until 1985, then didn't seek re-election.

One of the problems Wells was having was that nobody in cabinet held the same convictions as he did, not to mention his obsession with constitutional issues. Roberts, however, does, which is why Wells immediately named him as chairman of the provincial committee on the Constitution, saying, "There is no other lawyer in the province who has his capabilities in constitutional issues," although Wells refused a request from Simms to table Roberts's constitutional credentials. Wells had set up a committee to hold public hearings around the province only after consistent hounding from the Opposition, who argued, quite reasonably, that Wells had complained about the lack of public consultation during Meech Lake, but was refusing to allow the process in his own province in dealing with the post-Meech Lake proposals. Part of the problem was that Paul Dicks, who had been with Wells through the Meech Lake fight, did not share all of the premier's views on the matter and believed that other issues were being neglected as a result of the emphasis on the Constitution.

Asked about the widespread speculation he'd been picked as the heir apparent should Wells move to the federal scene, Roberts denies it. He says the two men have never discussed it, and even if Wells did leave, he doesn't know if he'll seek the leadership. Besides, he doesn't want Wells to leave Newfoundland. "I think the job he is doing at present is so important and I think he's doing it so well that he shouldn't leave. I have a very deep and growing admiration for Clyde Wells, his values, policies, approaches, and attitude, and what he is doing as premier and what the whole cabinet is doing."

Roberts easily won a June 25 byelection in the Labrador district of Naskaupi, defeating Tory businessman Bill Flowers 1919 to 1410. That same day, however, Tory Loyola Sullivan beat Liberal Tom Best by 125 votes in the southern-shore district of Ferryland, the first byelection loss for the Liberals since Wells became premier. NDP leader Cle Newhook failed, for the fifth time, finishing a dismal third in Ferryland.

The Naskaupi seat had become vacant for Roberts because of the resignation of former cabinet minister Jim Kelland.

Kelland was the first Wells minister to fall, resigning his environment portfolio in June 1991 for personal reasons. On March 9, 1992, Verge charged that a police investigation of sexual assault allegations against Kelland had been stalled by "political interference." She told the house that the woman who'd made the complaint against Kelland first took the matter to the Royal Newfoundland Constabulary in August 1990. When she heard nothing from the police for more than a year, she inquired about the status of the case in October 1991 and was told the police file had been "accidentally shelved." At that point, Verge said, the woman concluded that "this was not a case of RNC incompetence, but that there had been political tampering to delay the investigation to allow the member to qualify for his severance pay and depart."

Wells went through the roof. For all his emphasis on civility and his criticism of Peckford's combative nature, it is not difficult to ignite what has come to be known in Newfoundland as "Clyde's Irk." (Veteran Newfoundland satirist Ray Guy, about the only journalist in the province during Smallwood's halcyon years in the 1960s with the courage to criticize him, wrote the satirical play *Review '89*, about King Clyde and the Knights of the Brown Table. Directed by Rising Tide artistic director Donna Butt, the review had actor Rick Boland portraying the character "Clyde's Irk," a clever and colorful reference to his sudden, scarlet-faced outbursts of moral indignation.)

Nobody on earth, it seems, can spark "Clyde's Irk" better than Verge, who, it should be said, often seems to be carrying the entire official Opposition. Wells, absolutely livid, shot back that in all his years in politics he had "never seen that kind of low level of behavior," sparking cries of "Shame! Shame!" from the Liberal benches while Wells hotly denied that any member of his government had interfered in the investigation, adding that for Verge to publicly raise an unproven allegation when Kelland was not there to defend himself was "nothing short of despicable."

Verge responded that there was obviously something "drastically wrong" for a police file on a cabinet minister to have been lost for more than a year, and she demanded that Wells initiate a judicial inquiry into the matter, a demand Wells dismissed out of hand. He also accused her of "pressuring" a public servant by taking her complaint to Colin Flynn, the director of public prosecutions, instead of discussing it with Roberts. Later, outside the house, Verge said she didn't take it to Roberts because of media reports he was considering running in Kelland's riding and therefore might be "in a conflict-of-interest situation in this matter."

Wells went even further and demanded that Speaker Tom Lush formally censure Verge for her actions on the grounds she breached parliamentary privilege. Kelland later asked for the same thing, but Lush reserved judgment on whether he would permit a debate on the motion.

The next day, New Democrat MHA Jack Harris waded in to question why it took Wells so long to learn about the woman's sexual assault complaint against Kelland. Wells said he first heard of it in early March after receiving a letter from NDP leader Cle Newhook, but Harris said it was reported in January by the CBC. "We don't keep track of, or have anything whatsoever to do with, prosecutions or police investigations. That's for the police," Wells said. "We have no knowledge of it whatsoever, nor should we."

And so it went for several days, accusations and acrimony flying back and forth. Verge escaped formal censure even after refusing the Speaker's request to withdraw her statements by pointing out her accusations did not cast aspersions on any particular member of the legislature. "I am not pointing a finger at anyone in particular," she said. She and Harris kept demanding a judicial inquiry or at the very least a full explanation for the delay in the case, but Government House leader Winston Baker said the matter is under investigation and "we cannot prejudge a police investigation."

For all the moral outrage from Wells, he never did explain the delay of more than a year. Asked about the Kelland affair now, Wells says, "Somehow, for some reason or other — I don't know whether it was at the insistence of the lady who'd made the complaint — Mrs. Verge now concocts it into political interference. Now there's as much truth to that as an allegation that you're responsible for the loss of the Challenger space craft that blew up over Cape Canaveral a few years ago. That's how unsound it is. . . . Now it may well be, I don't know, the police were somehow lax, or they failed in their duty, or they lost the file, or whatever they did. I don't know. But what I don't want is any interference at this stage that will prevent the laying of a charge if one is justified, and the carrying out of a successful prosecution, if it's justified, or that will in any way cause it to be laid if it shouldn't be laid."

Kelland eventually announced he would take a brief leave of absence from the house rather than step down, seemingly cutting off the hopes that Roberts had to find a seat for himself. In May 1992 police announced there were insufficient grounds to lay any charges against him, and Kelland finally said he was leaving politics altogether.

In the heat of the debate over the Kelland affair, Verge reminded Wells of another matter he'd just as soon forget. In April 1991 Wells had set up a judicial inquiry to investigate Opposition allegations that an aide to former social services minister John Efford had attempted to interfere in a public service job competition, a much less serious matter than Kelland's alleged misconduct. "Why is the premier trying to avoid having a judicial inquiry into a much more serious allegation?" Verge asked.

Wells said he wasn't trying to avoid an inquiry, but the government could not take action that might "prejudice the proper administration of justice."

Possibly, but he certainly didn't hesitate to dump Efford from cabinet October 30, 1989, when Arthur Petten of the Eastern Shipbuilders Ltd., in a letter to Wells, claimed the Fisheries Loan Board was treating him unfairly because Efford had been involved in a court action taken by his brother Harold Efford against Petten's company. John Efford, it turned out, had attended meetings with various officials involved in a dispute with the loan board, which Petten claimed gave his brother Harold an advantage in the dispute.

"This morning [Efford] assured me that any actions he has taken in the matter have been totally innocent and were not intended to, and in fact did not, result in his brother's receiving preferential treatment by reason of being the minister's brother," Wells told his legislature. "Nevertheless the minister was concerned that this entire matter be reviewed and cleared without his influence being felt in any way. Accordingly he has asked that I relieve him of responsibility as minister . . . until the allegations have been thoroughly examined and a determination made as to whether or not there was any impropriety by the minister."

Then Wells announced he had asked for a judicial inquiry

"to do an independent assessment of all facts relating to the matter and advise the government as to whether or not there was any impropriety on the part of the minister." Subsequently, Newfoundland Supreme Court Justice John Mahoney was named to conduct the inquiry.

On December 5 Wells reinstated Efford to his cabinet post after Mahoney's report concluded that "it may have been ill-advised or imprudent" for Efford to have helped his brother in a legal matter after receiving advice from the justice department, but he found "no evidence of any attempt by John Efford to obtain preferential treatment for his brother in this matter . . . [and] nothing John Efford said or did, as a minister of the Crown, throughout this affair constituted an impropriety."

In an odd twist of logic, Wells added, "However, he and all other ministers are fairly warned that such actions on behalf of any constituent, related or otherwise, in the matter of a claim of a constituent against the Crown or any agency of the Crown is totally unacceptable and in future will result in a request for an immediate resignation."

That prompted then Tory leader Tom Rideout to ask why, if Effort's actions are totally unacceptable, "which I am sure most people would agree with, the premier then goes on to do nothing more than to slap the minister on the fingers, give him fair warning, and say that if you ever participate in this kind of action again, then you are gone? So, is it one chance, five chances, ten chances?"

Efford's last chance came in April 1991 when he was accused of patronage in appointing former Liberal MHA Beaton Tulk to his department, helping two of his campaign workers — Ambrose Stoyles and William Nosworthy — gain positions on the Social Services Appeal Board. In June 1991 Wells conceded to a question from Rideout that, indeed, he did know about a memo Efford had sent to all Liberal caucus members asking for recommendations for appointments to boards under the minister's jurisdiction. Wells said he ordered its "immediate recall and recision to a proper standard and instructed every other minister accordingly." Rideout was asking the question in the wake of Wells's appointment of two defeated Liberal candidates to the Workers' Compensation Tribunal. Wells's response was that "a great many of the most capable people in this province are Liberals," adding a Liberal "will never be precluded from being appointed to any board or office where his or her merit overrides any political considerations, and that is precisely what happened here."

Even though Efford himself had dismissed as "frivolous" allegations surrounding the circumstances of a public service job competition in late 1990 for twelve positions of Facilities Operations Manager at the Whitbourne Boys Home, Wells called a public inquiry into the matter under Mr. Justice Geoffrey Steele.

Nosworthy, former chairman of the Social Services Appeal Board, an appointment made at Efford's recommendation, alleged his fellow board member, Stoyles, received a list of questions for the job competition interview from Efford's executive assistant Roland Butler, before the interview itself. Stoyles, who subsequently flunked the interview, denied having seen the questions in advance. Efford, it seems, was fired for not taking the complaints seriously. He said Nosworthy was angry because, at the time, a reclassification process for the Social Services Appeal Board, which would have meant more money for Nosworthy, was not yet completed.

"I never dreamed I'd lose my position due to allegations that someone had been given preferential treatment, received questions he failed for a job he didn't get," Efford said. "All I can say is the man [Stoyles] must be some stunned to have had the questions and fail. I believe I should still be social services minister. . . . I had to resign for an error in judgment for not reporting allegations that I considered frivolous," something he complained cost him not only his position, but more than $80,000 a year in salary and pension benefits. In June

1992 Justice Steele said that Efford was "in breach of duty" for not reporting serious allegations about the job competition, but concluded there was no evidence that the former minister was involved in giving the interview questions to Stoyles.

Wells had been premier for only about six weeks when in June 1989 he was beset by a string of three cabinet ministers whom the Opposition accused of not living up to the strict conflict-of-interest rules. As Opposition leader himself a year earlier, Wells had launched a strong attack against Peckford's finance minister, Dr. John Collins, who owned about twenty-five per cent of a company that rented and negotiated leases, sometimes to provincial government clients, in a downtown St. John's building. Provincial rules prohibit ministers, or for that matter members, from doing business with the government. Wells insisted that Collins should either get out of the company or get out of cabinet. At the time, Wells said he did not blame the minister, but "I blame the premier [Peckford]. If the premier says that it is okay, then what I complain about is that the standard is unacceptable."

That being the case, then, Rideout demanded to know why it was now acceptable for Wells as premier that his forestry minister, Graham Flight, still owned property in Buchans that was rented to the provincial Board of Liquor Control. Flight, of course, was the backbencher who stepped aside in 1987 to create a vacancy when Wells won the leadership. He was re-elected by 171 votes in 1989 and was named to Wells's first cabinet. In an argument that carried on in the legislature for several days, Wells said the situation was okay because Flight had told him of his interest in the building and promised either to try to sell it within three months or, if not, get out of a lease that had eighteen months remaining on it.

During the third day of heated exchanges over the issue, Wells also admitted that his justice minister, Paul Dicks, owned substantial shares in a company that owned a property in Corner Brook leased to the Board of Liquor Control. Once again the Opposition attacked Wells, with some justification, for having a double standard. Dicks, unlike Flight, had not informed Wells of the potential conflict when he was named to cabinet, a breach Wells conveniently dismissed as an "oversight." That situation set off several more days of acrimony, of charges and counter-charges, until once again, nine days after the original controversy, Rideout attacked Health Minister Chris Decker for holding a $75,000 mortgage in Caudelle Manor, a licensed nursing home that receives regular grants from his own department.

Decker had owned Caudelle Manor but had subsequently sold it, and through a company called Roddickton House Company Limited, which is ninety-eight per cent owned by Decker, he took back the mortgage as part of the deal. Rideout argued that because the health department pays $12,640 a month in subsidies to the home, Decker's $75,000 "financial interest has been repaid partly out of taxpayers' money."

Wells, apparently ignoring the spirit of the law and sticking fast to the precise letter, argued that Decker did not have a financial interest in the home. "His financial interest is in the company, Roddickton House." When Wells had gone after Collins, he'd dismissed the Tory's technical argument that somebody else in the firm, not Collins, had negotiated the leases with the government clients. But when his own ministers were under attack, Wells took the narrowest of possible definitions of conflict and scolded the Opposition for "trying to smear people unfairly."

Dicks was back in the news again in November 1991 when he quit cabinet, ostensibly to spend more time with his family. At the time, Employment and Labor Relations Minister Patricia Cowan was on an extended leave of absence — she later returned — for health reasons after she was diagnosed with a thyroid problem. Once again, in November 1991 Wells was playing word games with the Opposition. Tory House Leader Bill Matthews said he could "live" with the fact that Ms. Cowan was receiving full ministerial pay and perqs, since she had been temporarily relieved of her duties for health reasons, but he objected to Services and Transport Minister Dave Gilbert receiving the same thing. Wells "relieved" Gilbert of his ministerial duties, but not his cabinet pay, following an RCMP investigation into complaints about the sale of his Beothuk Ford car dealership in Grand Falls the year before. Since then, Dennis Jackman, the new owner, had filed a civil lawsuit in the Newfoundland Supreme Court against Gilbert, seeking more than $500,000 in damages, plus court costs.

(Apart from basic MHA salaries and tax-free allowances of $57,044.43, ministers are paid an additional $39,834, plus an $8000 car allowance and travel and district expenses).

"I think it's wrong," Matthews said of the Gilbert situation. "I don't think a person in the legislature who's not carrying out ministerial responsibilities and duties should be paid ministerial salaries and benefits." Wells said that while Gilbert had been relieved of his duties, "that's no reason to cut off his pay as a minister."

Four days later, the Tories again attempted to clarify Gilbert's status. Wells said that while Gilbert had been "relieved" of his duties, he had not been "dismissed," even though he no longer sat in cabinet meetings and conducted any cabinet duties.

In February 1990, after the RCMP announced it had laid fraud-related charges against Gilbert, his wife Anne Marie, and son Scott, Gilbert formally resigned his portfolio.

Jackman's statement of claim against Gilbert alleged that the former minister failed to disclose outstanding income taxes for 1987 and 1988 totalling $112,940 and that over a number of years he improperly charged more than $319,000 in expenses to the car dealership. The money was allegedly spent on constructing a house for Scott Gilbert and on salaries paid to family members, who did not actually work at the business.

Wells said he accepted Gilbert's resignation with regret. "His letter assured me of his innocence, and he was going to take steps to ensure it was established." Gilbert circulated a prepared statement saying, "I am innocent of all charges and simply can't believe that the police have laid such charges against me and my family."

Later that month, Gilbert, his wife, and son elected trial by judge and jury on charges of fraud and theft when they appeared in provincial court in Grand Falls–Windsor. A preliminary hearing was set for June and later postponed till fall, and a ban placed on publication of any information coming out of the preliminary hearing. Gilbert was charged with six counts of fraud and five counts of falsifying books and documents. His wife was charged with four counts of fraud, four counts of falsifying books and documents, and one count of theft. His son was charged with two counts of fraud and one count of falsifying books and documents. Gilbert, maintaining his innocence, said he still plans to remain an MHA and run in the next provincial election.

In April 1991 the Tories were again raising the spectre of Liberal patronage, this time involving the prominent St. John's law firm of Halley, Hunt, headed by former Liberal leader Ed Roberts. The first accusation hit particularly close to home for Wells. Rideout said the fact that Wells's daughter, Heidi, was hired as a part-time summer student by the firm contradicts the government's conflict-of-interest laws, which also apply to family members. Wells told reporters that his daughter, then twenty-four and in her second year at the University of Moncton law school, had applied on her own and been accepted as a summer employee. He said his daughter, like every other law student, has to apply to article with a local law firm, and just about every local company of any size does some sort of business with the government.

But Rideout argued that Halley, Hunt wasn't just your average local law firm. A contract worth between $700,000 and $800,000 was taken from the firm of Stirling, Ryan, which has no known political connections, and given to the Liberal-connected firm within days of the premier's daughter being hired. "This may be the most innocent transaction in the world," said Rideout. "But you'd have to be awfully naive not to have questions come to your mind."

Asked about the contract in the house, Wells countered by accusing the former Tory regime of having given all the legal business to "two or three select firms," mostly Tory-connected, "and our policy that we put in place was to spread the work around and rotate the work."

More serious accusations of political patronage exploded in November 1991 when Len Simms attacked Wells for awarding a $24 million contract to Trans City Holdings Limited, with construction to be undertaken by Marco Ltd., for new health-care facilities in Burgeo, Port Saunders, and St. Lawrence, even though the company, owned by Wells supporter Tom Hickman, had not submitted the lowest bid. Simms said none of the three contracts was awarded to the low bidder, saying the total of the low bids for the three buildings was $18 million, $6 million less that the contract awarded. In addition, Simms said there was "tampering with the bids . . . changes made to the tendering process in such a way as to, in the end, make it fit a very specific bid by a specific company in the business, which is a friend of the Liberals."

Deputy premier Winston Baker denied that, saying there were about eighteen proposals as a result of the tender call, but during the analysis process it was decided that the cheaper proposals, which called for wood construction, were not suitable. Nor was a proposed tin structure, which left the brick-and-steel proposals to be examined in more detail.

Simms also said he had information from "usually reliable sources" that Wells met with Marco's president Tom Hickman, a Liberal bagman, before the tender was awarded. Baker said, "I have no knowledge of that." He said different bids were based on different materials because the government had called for "wide open" proposals. "We were simply trying to get a little bit of inventiveness and innovation in terms of the proposal."

The next day, Wells indignantly dismissed Opposition charges as "totally without foundation. There is no merit whatsoever in it. It was done through the normal processes, through the department of public works." In fact, the tenders *were* different, deliberately vague by their own admission, something Baker said the government wouldn't repeat. Even Wells conceded they may have avoided some of the problems if the tenders had specified brick-and-steel structures, which the government later decided were the best options, instead of leaving it wide open.

Wells also denied meeting with Hickman or anybody else connected with the project to discuss it.

But according to John Crosbie, "They called these proposals in a peculiar way. They asked for proposals for the financing and building of these, and you had to suggest what the design would be like and so on. And lo and behold, the winning proposal, the one they selected from among those who put in proposals, were firms controlled by Hickman and [Trans City Holdings president Bill] Case . . . another long-time Liberal supporter. . . . There were lower bids, but they were able to finagle around because they can say, well, your design wasn't what we wanted, or the financing is better under this proposal, or whatever. The other developers involved were suing the government . . . asking for an injunction. The Opposition [is] protesting this as massive patronage.

"Now Clyde, of course, is on record as doing away with all patronage. There has been evidence in this case that the deputy minister of public works didn't recommend this proposal, that they recommended others that were better. But they were directed by the cabinet to give it to Hickman and Case. It's convincing evidence that patronage is still the name of the game in Newfoundland

"Hickman was in Florida. I was down there at the time when

the debate in government was going on about those proposals, and I think they were thinking of giving one of them to one of the other firms. So he [Hickman] went back from Florida the night before to see Wells to make sure they got all three of them. I don't think there's any doubt that they got them because of their support for Clyde. It's the same old game," says Crosbie.

"This is going to be dangerous for Clyde . . . portraying himself as Mr. Morality. . . . You know, you can't do away with patronage. I mean, I'm not an advocate that you can. I don't know how political parties are going to operate if they're not going to reward their friends. What they need to do is be a little more honest about it and say it. It's all a question of degree. You can overdo it, as Trudeau was doing in his last few years. Or you can be sensible about it."

Six companies that bid unsuccessfully on the contract hired lawyer Barrie Heywood and demanded the government either award the contracts to the low bidders or re-tender them. Four of the unsuccessful bidders even claimed the contracts should be awarded to N.D. Dobbin Ltd., which submitted the lowest original bid for two of the centres, and Health Care Developers Inc., the lowest bidder on the other one.

By December, work had already begun on the projects even though five companies launched a Supreme Court lawsuit and also held a hearing regarding an injunction application over what they said was a violation of the Public Tendering Act. Dermot Dobbin, president of N.D. Dobbin Ltd., said a committee of representatives from the department of works, health, and finance, established to review all bids for the contract, as well as the Halifax consulting firm of Hanscomb and Associates brought in to do a cost analysis, recommended to cabinet that Health Care Developers Inc. build all three centres, but cabinet decided to go with Trans City.

Simms said he is "convinced there was skulduggery" in the awarding of the contracts, but Baker insisted the winning bid will save the province millions of dollars in the long run because of better financing arrangements.

For his part, Wells calls the allegations of patronage in these contracts "utterly false. It's a total fabrication. . . . The simple fact is that they didn't design the tenders properly. . . . They should have had more specifics instead of leaving it to whatever the individuals wanted to propose."

He insists the government is saving a half million dollars a year in interest alone because of the financing terms of the Trans City bid, which he says contained a downward adjustment keyed to interest rates.

On January 10, 1992, Newfoundland Supreme Court Justice David Riche denied the application for an injunction to halt construction on the three health centres.

The deal may ultimately turn out in the taxpayer's favor, but legitimate questions in this case, and several others, remain unanswered. Wells's approach to such controversies also demonstrates that whatever his personal integrity — and nobody questions that — his government has managed to plunge itself into some questionable dealings and fumbled several of its most important domestic initiatives.

His autocratic style is often compared in an unflattering way to that of Oliver Cromwell and Joey Smallwood. Wells exhibits what author M. Scott Peck calls "excessive scrupulosity." He has the courage to draw a line in the sand, but often lacks the wisdom to straddle that line in the interest of satisfying the legitimate concerns of others who don't agree with him. That honest, straight-arrow style may have led to his election in the first place, but it could ultimately spark his political undoing. Wells's re-election, while still likely, is by no means a sure bet.

13

"Clyde Lied"

THE KING WAS not amused. King Clyde, that is. It was the third week of April 1991, and Wells was still fuming over a confrontation three days earlier by a hundred union activists who had staged an angry protest in Corner Brook.

Meeting with Corner Brook Mayor Ray Pollett, Wells was harassed by members of the Corner Brook District Labor Council as he left his office in the Sir Richard Squires Building. When he refused to talk to them, they blocked his car, forcing him to walk down the street until an aide could get through to pick him up. Visibly upset, Wells shouted at some of them when they accused him of not listening to their concerns. (An aide later denied Wells had exchanged angry words with the demonstrators, even though reporters present saw the exchange and reported on it.)

Now, walking into the Radisson Plaza Hotel in St. John's for a Rotary Club luncheon, Wells was again confronted by a dozen protesters carrying "Clyde Lied" signs to protest his government's controversial March budget, which featured not only a public service wage freeze and huge cutbacks, but unilateral rollbacks of recently negotiated settlements.

Having attempted for a time to ignore the dogged labor protesters, who appeared everywhere he and his senior cabinet ministers went, Wells conceded that day he was becoming annoyed and upset over what he called the "dishonest representation" by the public service unions, particularly the Newfoundland Association of Public Employees (NAPE).

Despite his campaign promise to "create an atmosphere of rational co-operation in developing labor legislation and in dealing with the public service," the very unions that had helped elect him were now dedicating themselves to making Wells a one-term premier. He and the unions were at war, and not for the first time.

(Newfoundland is by far Canada's most unionized province. While 34.1 per cent of all Canadian workers are unionized, in Newfoundland, 52 per cent are. Compare that to Quebec, which is second at 40.2 per cent, Ontario, 31.1 per cent, down to Alberta, at 25.8 per cent, the least unionized workforce in the country.)

The first two bills Wells ever introduced, in 1967, forced some 125 striking non-professional employees of the Central Newfoundland Hospital in Grand Falls back to work, made hospital strikes unlawful, and contained provisions for decertification and heavy fines. In February 1969, after Wells had left Smallwood's cabinet and taken up residence across the aisle as an Independent Liberal, Wells endorsed a comment by Smallwood that the unions at Churchill Falls are not doing enough to make sure more Newfoundlanders were hired for the giant hydro project, under construction at the time.

Wells said that when the contracts were signed with the unions during his tenure as labor minister "all of us were worried that entering into such an agreement might lure the unions into just sitting back and reaping the harvest of union dues that are docked off every month from anywhere to three to seven thousand workers and not having to do too much for it.

"Now, I do not have any solid evidence that this is the way the unions are reacting [but] this appears to be the situation. This is what is happening. There is a lack of union representatives on the job. Those that are there appear not to be too greatly concerned about protecting the rights of the workers, and I feel that it might be well to give as much public attention to it as possible — that the unions who are signatory to that agreement have no right whatsoever to stay there for the full term of that agreement, and the mere fact that they have signed it does not give them that right."

In his professional life, Wells consistently represented corporate clients — the bosses, not the workers — so his sympathies were well established long before he became premier. Even so, while the union leaders did not consider Wells pro-union, they did think at least he was a reasonable man, willing to listen to valid arguments. This contrasted sharply with their view of Peckford, who, during his first two terms of office, flatly refused to meet with fishermen's union boss Richard Cashin.

When Wells won the election, Cashin was optimistic that he and Wells could work together to improve problems in the fisheries. Similarly, Keith Coombs, president of the Newfoundland Teachers Association (NTA), said his organization would ask Wells to convene a meeting of all major agencies involved in education to study serious problems in the system. And Frank Taylor, secretary-treasurer of the Newfoundland and Labrador Federation of Labor said their group would be gunning for quick repeal of Peckford's Bill 59, which sharply curtailed civil servants' right to strike.

Fraser March, president of the 18,000-strong Newfoundland Association of Public Employees (NAPE), began on relatively good terms with Wells. Indeed, Wells tried to recruit him as a Liberal candidate in the election. The two men had several meetings after the election, and March described their relationship as "fairly friendly." On June 23, 1990, the night the Meech Lake accord died, March and Wells had a three-hour post-midnight meeting about the strike of essential employees at Hoyles (nursing) Home. March, who now calls Wells "the Preston Manning of the East," says that was the last productive meeting he and the premier had.

Dave Curtis, head of the Newfoundland Federation of Labor, said the unions were cautiously optimistic that Wells would be more sympathetic than Peckford, but they soon learned he wasn't. "He has a remarkable view of workers," says Curtis. "A classic master-servant view. He's the personification of the American dream. Because he's done well, everybody else who hasn't is personally at fault — 'They've chosen not to succeed. People choose to be poor. I've risen from humble beginnings. All these other people are either lazy layabouts or intellectually inferior.'

"There is a pragmatic side to him that people outside Newfoundland often fail to see. He is so unctuous and sanctimonious it is unbelievable. He has this unshakable faith in his own view and the correctness of his actions, irrespective of the impact on ordinary people."

Curtis tells the story of two Corner Brook social workers who were fired by the government after one was accused of sexual abuse, the other of physical abuse. "The case went to court and they were completely exonerated, but he still wouldn't take them back. So we went to arbitration and again they won, but he still wouldn't reinstate them. He won't let them go back to work because in his opinion they're guilty. I'm concerned what this attitude of his means for the future of collective bargaining in this province. How do you bargain with somebody who already knows the solution before bargaining starts?"

Wells's brutal March 1991 budget set off a chain of explosions in the labor field, which could ultimately lead to his political demise. In addition to cuts in services and jobs, Kitchen imposed, effective April 1, a one-year wage freeze throughout the provincial public sector, which applied to all unionized employees, managers, executives, cabinet ministers, and MHAs. He also cancelled retroactive payments required under the pay-equity agreement in the health sector and said pay equity would be phased in over a maximum of five years.

The unions were apoplectic. A wage freeze was one thing, but what the budget actually meant was that Wells was trampling on the collective bargaining process by unilaterally cancelling the provisions of agreements they had negotiated with his government, some of which, they claimed, were negotiated even after Wells had already decided he was going to impose the wage freeze.

Hence the "Clyde Lied" campaign, a phrase coined by the media but enthusiastically endorsed by the unions. They say a three-year deal giving group-home workers, members of CUPE, a 22.9 per cent increase, was signed by Treasury Board Chairman Winston Baker the day the budget was being printed, and March insists CUPE "was guaranteed the money was all safe, no problems." After the budget, Wells quickly introduced the dreaded Bill 16, the Public Sector Restraint Act, which authorized the budget freeze and cancelled any previously negotiated increases scheduled for the fiscal year, along with the provincial plans to make pay equity retroactive to 1988.

The previous June, the government had negotiated a three-year 22.9 per cent increase for the nurses. Perhaps reflecting on the fact that his wife, Eleanor, is a trained nurse, or responding to a large public relations campaign put on by the nurses themselves, Wells explained the high award by saying that nurses are "special," but he didn't expect all the unions to get that sort of increase. The unions, of course, had other ideas. Two mainland arbitrators, brought in to resolve a hospital strike, ended up using the nurses' deal to award lab and X-ray workers the same increase, which was not what Wells had intended. Their actions had a snowball effect on all sub-sequent union negotiations.

"They took the 22.9 per cent and gave it without question to every bargaining unit in the public service," said March. "The labor movement couldn't believe it. They were cracked, throwing money around like drunken sailors, some said. The government knew from June 1990 that their strategy was to give it to everyone, knowing they were going to take it back. Either that, or they were just stupid and incompetent."

Wells says the union accusations are "utterly false." He admits Baker signed contracts at the last minute, but said before he did that, Baker "went to Fraser March and said, 'Look, these agreements have been completed. You know from our private discussions that the government is going to be bringing in legislation.' He told that to Fraser March before he signed. But Fraser March said to him, 'No, no. We've got them completed. We might as well sign them.' So Winston signed them. Winston told me about it afterwards. And that's the basis on which they built the [Clyde Lied] campaign.

"It's hard to have even a modicum of respect for people who will stand in front of you and say one thing, and then, for their own political position, turn around and go say something diametrically the opposite," says Wells. "It's hard to have any respect for that lack of integrity, that lack of intellectual integrity that's inherent in that."

March says Wells's version is simply not true. "Baker said no such thing to me a couple of days before the budget." Wells had all the major union leaders in his office shortly before that, "but he wasn't specific then. He said there may be layoffs coming, pay equity may be in trouble, and the government may have to take other steps. He asked the unions for suggestions, but said he couldn't get into detail because it would be leaking the budget."

At this point, the government had signed about thirty-five agreements since 1990, all of them featuring the 22.9 per cent increase over three years. "We thought the wage increase was safe," said March. "Maybe we would have to suggest to government they'd trade layoffs for a percentage, but no one thought government would take away the whole increase with legislation. When the budget came down, the unions discovered they had nothing left to negotiate."

On April 20, 1991, March announced that a coalition of labor unions representing ten unions, forty bargaining units, and 35,000 workers, was going to spend at least $100,000 taking the province to court to fight the cutbacks and overturn Bill 16. "Surely, somewhere, sometime, some judge or some politician or some leader is going to say, when the provincial government of this province signs a deal it must mean something," said March. "We're going to ask the question everywhere it can be asked: 'Legally, when is a deal a deal with Clyde Wells?'"

But before beginning their legal fight, the unions announced they would "proceed through the arbitration process and then take whatever legal action is necessary afterwards . . . right up to the Supreme Court of Canada," if need be.

It wasn't long before the unions had distributed more than 40,000 posters and buttons with a cartoon picture of Wells with his fingers crossed, and the words "Clyde Lied" prominently displayed. They also had T-shirts and hats with the same slogan and even began talking about a province-wide strike against the government.

On May 9 Tory Bob Aylward wore a "Clyde Lied" button into the House of Assembly, tapping it with a ballpoint pen to distract Wells when he was speaking. When the Liberals complained, Speaker Tom Lush ruled the button couldn't be worn in the house because it is unparliamentary to accuse another MHA of having lied, and therefore just as unparliamentary to make the accusation on a button. Lush called the button "offensive and disrespectful of another member."

On May 22 nine members of the coalition, each wearing a

white sweater with one red letter in the centre, stood up in the public gallery while Baker was being questioned by Tory labor critic Norman Doyle about the wage freeze, spelling the words "Clyde Lied" and resulting in deputy Speaker Lloyd Snow ordering the public galleries be cleared. Baker later accused Doyle of having planned the demonstration to get "press coverage."

The campaign slowed down in the summer, but a June public opinion poll of 415 Newfoundlanders by Omnifacts Research Ltd. indicated Wells may have been hurt. The overall results showed Wells ahead of Tory leader Len Simms, but just thirty-five per cent to thirty per cent — down from his stratospheric mid-eighties ratings a year earlier just after Meech — with the NDP at ten per cent. More significantly, however, it showed that the labor vote, which had gone mostly to the Liberals in 1989 because of Peckford's perceived anti-union stance, was crossing to the Tories. The poll results among union members showed thirty-five per cent supporting the Tories, twenty-nine per cent Liberal, ten per cent NDP, with twenty-six per cent undecided.

St. John's native Nancy Riche, now national NDP president and a vice-president of the Canadian Labor Congress, says the idea of the "Clyde Lied" campaign was to "show people in other parts of Canada who love this guy that he's not as honest as they think he is. This is a guy who wouldn't even do the leadership without getting all those big bucks. . . . Everybody always says he's serious, but he's not too fucking serious. We assume he has some fun on his boat. . . . He's a guy who came into politics at his own time and demanded the big bucks to keep him in the style he's become accustomed to. It's the moral mercenary guy who wants to have power and needs money to do it."

(It is worth noting that, back in 1966 when Wells was first elected, he continued to operate his law practice, although by necessity on a more limited basis, something he banned others from doing when he became premier twenty years later. This primary concern he showed then for the maintenance of his lifestyle over the notion of public service emerged again in 1987 when he agreed to become Newfoundland Liberal leader only if his income could be supplemented.)

In late October 1991 about 2000 protesters formed a human chain from behind Confederation Building in St. John's and around onto the front steps calling for an end to both federal and provincial government cuts, part of a nationwide Day of Action, "Enough is Enough" campaign organized by labor and community groups.

CUPE official Bob Matthews charged that Wells had alternatives to his budget cuts but didn't exercise them. Pointing to a piece of paper being swept along by the high wind, he said, "There goes Clyde Wells's promises now."

Cashin said Wells's March 1991 budget made the Ottawa Tories seem left wing. "Newfoundland is the only place that can make Brian Mulroney look good because we have it so bad here," he said.

Wells, attempting to include the unions this time in pre-budget discussions, held a private meeting with about a dozen major labor officials to discuss the financial outlook for the province, after which Matthews accused the government of "trying to balance the budget on the backs of workers." Baker had told the *Evening Telegram* that the deficit for 1992-93 could reach $100 million. He said that figure "may change in the next three or four months," but if it didn't, it could result in further government cutbacks.

By November, the coalition of unions had hired veteran Toronto labor relations lawyer Jeffrey Sack to act as its nominee on the series of grievances the unions had launched as their first step in a legal challenge to Bill 16, all of which had proceeded to the arbitration stage. They accused Wells of trying to delay the process by at first refusing to appoint a provincial nominee to the arbitration board and then deliberately delaying appointment of a chairperson.

That same month, the government introduced two pieces of legislation, one the unions liked and one they didn't. Labor Minister Roger Grimes pleased the unions by announcing the government would outlaw "double-breasting," a practice some employers had used in the past to set up new companies with the same ownership and control to avoid adhering to collective agreements negotiated with unions at the original firm. But they were angered by proposed changes to the Election Act, which would limit campaign contributions to $2500 from individuals and $10,000 from corporations and trade unions, because they would effectively exclude the Newfoundland and Labrador Federation of Labor and district labor councils from active participation in an election.

The problem, according to federation president Dave Curtis, is that the 60,000-member group doesn't meet the Bill 55 definition of a union because it is not a bargaining agent, but rather a lobbying group and political arm of organized labor. "We want the right to contribute to a political party, the same way as an individual . . . the same right as a corporation," said Curtis.

On January 11 Wells said the government couldn't deal with its budget deficit without some combination of layoffs and wage freezes. He argued that if nothing was done, the deficit for 1992-93 would hit $114 million. He said between $28 million and $30 million could be cut from government programs, which would still leave a shortfall of about $85 million. "We felt we could logically plan for a budget deficit of something under $30 million," he said. "So that leaves $55 million to cut."

Fraser March said the coalition of unions rejected the wage freeze option and wanted current contracts respected. "Clyde Wells is prepared to sign collective agreements, and then go to the legislature and change them."

Wells said he was disappointed the coalition rejected his request they put forward suggestions on how to deal with the deficit. They didn't, really; they just rejected his suggestions. The unions made public a letter they sent to Wells asking for a meeting on January 23, saying they would compile their own alternative options. Wells had already said he expected a budget around the end of February.

"I greatly regret that they seem to be somehow just sort of playing games with this," said Wells. "This is very serious. We must make the decisions on budgetary matters very soon, and I would hope to have a response for them sooner rather than later. If they insist that they're not going to agree with this, that or the other thing, and they're not going to sit down and talk to us about it, well, that makes it very difficult to take into account their decisions."

On January 12, Wells released a four-page statement the government gave to the unions at a December 16, 1991, meeting, which predicted a $114-million deficit without major cuts. The statement listed a series of several items with the cost beside each one, which "may be considered later to eliminate $55 million of the potential deficit." The list contained such things as: the cost of one hundred employees — $2.5 million; cost of each one per cent salary increase for public employees — $11.5 million; cost of overtime above straight time rates — $8.5 million; cost of standby and callback above straight time rates — $3.6 million. Wells said the government did not say which options it preferred, but asked the unions for their views on restraint. But CUPE's Bob Matthews said, "You don't give up something, especially to this government, you spent fifty years negotiating, because it will take you another fifty years to get it back."

Two days later, March said the unions were going to meet Wells to offer their suggestions for cutting government spending. "There are many options we're looking at." He said they rejected the government's list of options because "they all require legislative changes to collective agreements. To do anything different would be to relegate public administration in this province to a banana republic. The agenda Clyde Wells has set for himself is an anti-union, anti-worker, anti-economic stimulus course. Quite frankly, we think there is another course."

Matthews said he didn't agree with Wells's claim the government couldn't borrow any more money because it would lower Newfoundland's credit rating one notch. Matthews said the action would do "very little" damage, since most of the debt is already locked in at long-term debenture rates.

By agreeing to several meetings with the unions, and at least giving the impression he was interested in their views, Wells had managed to soften some of the hostility from his last budget. Unfortunately for him, all the good work he'd done over the previous few months disappeared in a few minutes when he unilaterally dismissed the union ideas as "not realistic . . . sort of wishful thinking." Wells said wage costs are sixty-one per cent of the total provincial budget, a dilemma facing most provincial governments, so it is "inevitable that we must deal with our budget problem, in part, by reducing our wage expenditure cost."

Seven public service unions already had contracts calling for six to seven per cent raises for the 1992-93 fiscal year, and Newfoundland Teachers Association president Morley Reid said the union coalition was "not willing to soften [its] stand" against wage freezes. "We have collective agreements signed."

The unions had proposed a program of more borrowing to take advantage of low interest rates and help refinance government debt, selling off government-owned properties, reducing the cabinet (which Wells had already cut to fifteen from Peckford's twenty-three), and raising corporate taxes, which were at the same level they were in 1974-75, to avoid wage freezes or further layoffs.

Despite Wells's claim the union ideas were far-fetched and unrealistic, many of them seemed quite sensible. The unions proposed, for example, selling the four provincially owned

Holiday Inns, along with several valuable St. John's apartment buildings, such as Elizabeth Towers and Prince Philip Place; eliminating tax breaks for people earning more than $75,000 a year; cutting MHAs' pensions, or at least making them contribute more to their pension plans; decreasing grants and subsidies to corporations, about $165 million in 1991-92; offering the option of early retirement to employees; and establishing joint union-management committees in the workplace to identify and eliminate wasteful practices.

"It is not possible to deal with the problem of the magnitude that we have in the manner in which the unions have proposed," Wells said.

One day later, however, the magnitude of the crisis didn't seem as severe. Wells said a total wage freeze for public employees wasn't necessary to avoid further layoffs. "I don't think you would have to go all the way down to zero to avoid any layoffs, but I'm just saying that off the top of my head at the moment. I would have to check the numbers. But I believe you don't have to go that far to avoid layoffs." Wells had made reference to Ontario, where the NDP government had negotiated wage increases of one and two percent with its employees in return for job security.

CUPE's Bob Matthews said Wells hasn't made such an offer to the unions. "He didn't raise it [at their meeting], but I was sort of thinking he would raise it. I'm convinced if they had come to us a year ago to open the collective agreement .. then I'm sure we could have worked something out."

NTA president Morley Reid said he wasn't optimistic that the seven unions that already had contracts calling for raises would be willing to negotiate concessions with contracts already signed with the government. NAPE's Fraser March said Wells was too preoccupied with other matters, the Constitution in particular, to give the union proposals the attention they deserved. "The premier should stop dickering with the Constitution and deal with the affairs of this province," said March,

expressing his disappointment that Wells dismissed their proposals so quickly and didn't respond in writing. "That told us
what he thought of our proposals. No matter how smart he is,
he couldn't read that document in five minutes with any degree
of integrity. . . . The premier is treating this as a public relations scam."

In late January 1992, Simms called on Wells to borrow
money rather than lay off public employees or impose a total
wage freeze. "We are in extraordinary times, and the reasons
for borrowing in the short term are good reasons," Simms told
a Board of Trade luncheon at the St. John's Holiday Inn. "Once
the economy is growing again, then that is the time to take
measures to address the debt."

In February Baker said that even though it might delay
presentation of the budget, the government planned to meet
with union officials again to soften the impact of trimming the
deficit through layoffs and wage restraints. He said the government had completed its analysis of the union proposals, adding, "I'm hopeful they'll have some suggestions other than what
they've already given us." The only suggestion he liked was the
notion of joint labor-management committees to reduce waste,
but that's a long-term thing, not likely to have any meaningful
short-term impact.

The March 12 budget once again focused on the provincial
deficit, and although Wells didn't repeat his large-scale job cuts
in the previous budget, the government introduced new legislation, Bill 17, which basically extended the wage freeze for
another full year and capped at three per cent the maximum
amount public sector unions could receive through collective
bargaining the third year of the restraint period. The move
reignited union charges that Wells had again broken his word
and was out to destroy the collective bargaining process.
Unlike Bill 16, the new bill contained a few exceptions to the
general freeze, including a few groups of hospital workers and
some provision for pay-equity agreements.

"It seems to me if we are going to have a free collective bargaining system in this province, then we have to break that three per cent," March said. "If a union accepts that three per cent, what they're accepting is that the minister of finance has the right to simply stand up in the House of Assembly and state your increase next year is two per cent."

That is something of course, no union leader could accept. Not if he wants to keep his job. According to Wells, however, some of the union leaders did accept that privately. "Once [the union leaders] knew that we would probably invoke total restraints again this year . . . then they said we're not going to agree with you. And they told us in private, frankly, well, we know you have to do something. We know you had to make the decisions. But we can't be seen to be agreeing with you. We think it's wrong. We can't be seen to be agreeing that you can break collective agreements, but we understand what you have to do. And we'll have to put on a bit of a show. . . . Now that's what Morley Reid and Fraser March and the other leaders of the union said to us."

Reid, who represents 8300 full-time and 1500 part-time teachers, says he told Wells the NTA understands the province's position the first year at zero, and perhaps even the second, "but not the third. . . . Yes, I said the NTA understands, but I also said it would be absolute punishment to accept any kind of restraint the third year." Reid flatly denies saying that the union couldn't be seen agreeing with the government. "That's not correct."

He says the government's action was "undemocratic. They negotiated an agreement that was binding on both sides. If the government can undo it with legislation for two years in a row, there's something wrong with the process. A contract is a civil right."

March, who has switched from being a Liberal to a card-carrying New Democrat, believes a common front by the unions would either force Wells to back down or force him out of office in the next election. March and others see the dramatic shift to the right under Wells as creating a political vacuum in Newfoundland that could, for the first time, elevate the NDP to something other than a minor nuisance in the elections.

Despite the heavily unionized character of Newfoundlanders, they have not been willing to vote for the NDP, likely because, historically, most of their governments, Liberal or Tory, have been left-of-centre in any event, so there never has been room for the party. The NDP's backing the end to the seal hunt, in response to mounting international pressure, did little to endear the party to most Newfoundlanders.

One man who believes there is room now is MHA Jack Harris, the sole New Democrat in the House of Assembly. Harris says the government's actions in breaking the collective agreements have really hurt its reputation, even among non-union Newfoundlanders.

"A pragmatist would have found an excuse not to sign the contract a few days before the [1991] budget. He would have put off the signing ceremony. But they didn't. To me, that's a sign of someone who feels he is above respect for the collective bargaining system. He doesn't have to honor anything. To me, that was a great shock. And now he's doing the same thing again in Bill 17."

Harris said the NDP never got a foothold in Newfoundland because "Joey declared himself to be a socialist, and he was a New York street-corner socialist . . . the 'man of the toiling masses' he used to like to say. . . . Confederation was revolutionary for Newfoundlanders. . . . They were brought in holus-bolus to all those social programs . . . so you didn't have the pressure for social change you found elsewhere." Actually, there has always been pressure for social change in Newfoundland as there is elsewhere. It's just that Newfoundlanders have never looked to the NDP to supply it.

A February 1992 poll, asking which of the three leaders Newfoundlanders preferred as premier, showed forty-eight percent for Wells, compared to eleven per cent for Tory leader Simms, and eight per cent for NDP leader Cle Newhook. But thirty-three per cent of those polled didn't know or wouldn't say. What's more, the Wells figure was way below his mid-80s ratings just after Meech Lake, and it came after Simms had only been leader for a few months and hadn't had much of a chance to establish his presence in the house or in the province at large.

March said the NDP has "the potential of crawling through this window of opportunity and inheriting the centre-left protest vote. If they do, they could do well. I'm not saying they're going to win the government. But there's the start of something here."

Not everyone agrees. Dave Alcock, a provincial arbitrator who has helped settle disputes with NAPE and other provincial unions, says the unions have done well in Newfoundland because "they know how to play the political angle. Now the Wells government seems to be taking them on and so far with little fallout. Some employers are glad to see Wells take the unions on. . . . The Wells government is not hurting from doing that. . . . The government is getting away with it, showing it's not afraid of unions or kowtowing to them.

"There's a lot of mistrust, though, between government and the unions. Wells may be putting the labor movement back ten years. His biggest problem, some say, is his inability to designate authority. And he's lost respect from some ministers. He's called some of them 'silly' in public . . . and a lot of old Liberals are not happy Wells hasn't appointed them to positions."

Wells's hard-nosed labor strategy has brought the traditionally hostile unions closer together than they have ever been. Several of the major unions are even discussing joint bargaining to give themselves more clout, and in May 1992, NAPE boss Fraser March and CUPE staff representative Bob Matthews publicly agreed that if they don't work together, "we are going to sink together."

Matthews said the fight is no longer just fiscal. "This is punishment. He [Wells] is out to gut our collective agreements. He thinks we are overpaid, we have too many benefits . . . and unless we stop him now we will not have collective agreements in this province in a few years."

CUPE's newly elected provincial president Wayne Lucas said at the same time that "Wells better prepare for a fight at the ballot box and a possible provincewide strike," sentiments echoed by March, Reid, and other major labor leaders in the province.

While the labor movement itself has been unable to attain political power in Newfoundland, it has consistently determined who does hold power. One thing seems certain — without some serious fence-mending most union members aren't going to vote for Wells next time.

14

If at First

A YEAR AFTER the demise of the Meech Lake accord, Official Ottawa was still boiling about Wells. On September 23, 1991, the day before Brian Mulroney unveiled his Renewed Canada campaign, Constitutional Affairs Minister Joe Clark, responding to a reporter's question, snapped that forging a constitutional deal was "not a question of satisfying Clyde Wells. It's a question of satisfying the fears and needs of Canadians." But Clark knew as well as anybody else that Wells represented much more than himself, or for that matter, his province. He knew that in English Canada, Wells was still considered a hero by many of the sceptics he and Mulroney were hoping to woo with their new constitutional proposals. He also knew that much of the popularity Wells continued to enjoy had less to do with Wells per se than it had to do with the widespread malaise in the country toward politicians in general, and a downright visceral hatred for Mulroney in particular.

Whatever his private thoughts on the Newfoundland premier, Clark understood that Wells had captured the imagination of so many Canadians as much for how he stood, Horatio-like, against the collective forces of Meechdom, as he had for what he actually stood for — his own steadfast, simplistic vision of what federalism really means.

Wells's arguments against the Meech Lake accord had been so persuasive that MPs from all parties reported running into what they called the Wells Syndrome in their home ridings. Windsor New Democrat Stephen Langdon gives an example: "People see 'distinct society' as making Quebec special, even if there are no privileges attached."

The truth is, however, that there were privileges attached, which is why so many applauded Wells's stand. Despite constant claims to the contrary by his critics, and a widespread misunderstanding even by many of his fans, Wells never once disputed the rather obvious fact that Quebec was, and is, a distinct society. His concern was the unique powers that distinct status might give the province. The week before Mulroney unveiled his new plan, Wells told the Law Society of Upper Canada, "I see nothing wrong with acknowledging that Quebec is indeed a distinct society, but that doesn't make it distinctly different in status and rights and jurisdiction as a province."

Another sure indicator of just how the Ottawa Establishment viewed Wells was that on the very day the new federal proposals were announced, a front-page feature by pro-Meech *Globe* columnist Jeffrey Simpson, based on interviews conducted many weeks earlier, examined what the headline writer described as "the hard-headed man from the Rock." In it, Simpson wrote that the premier's "determined opposition to the Meech Lake accord and his unshakable certainty about his own correctness still haunt the federal government." There it was. Right on the front page of our self-declared "national" newspaper, an unmistakable declaration by Official Ottawa that they had seen the enemy, and it was Clyde Wells.

The column naturally infuriated Wells; Simpson's comparing Wells's popularity in Quebec with that of hockey player Eric Lindros (who refused to play for the Nordiques) was especially galling, no doubt. Wells saw the piece's placement and timing deliberately orchestrated to draw the proverbial line in the constitutional sand: on one side — the proper side, of course — stood the federal government, most of the provinces, and many, shall we say, thoughtful Canadians; on the other, looking to Wells for direction, and perhaps salvation, were those who were so unwilling to bend to accommodate Quebec that they risked the destruction of Canada itself.

For several months after the death of Meech, Ottawa appeared too stunned by the setback to do anything about the constitutional impasse. By the end of October, Wells was publicly demanding that Ottawa fulfil its promise to set up a national committee or convention or a parliamentary committee, something to resolve the issue. He claimed the decision by Quebec to appoint a provincial commission to examine, among other things, whether it should even stay in Confederation, along with decisions by other provinces to set up similar commissions — with different aims, of course — was threatening national unity.

Three days later Mulroney announced he had named twelve non-politicians to the so-called Citizens Forum, under the colorful but often bizarre chairmanship of CRTC boss and former *Ottawa Citizen* editor Keith Spicer. Their task was to tour the country seeking the opinions of the elusive "ordinary Canadians," and report back by Canada Day, July 1, 1991. Wells applauded. Many did. But apart from squabbling about expense accounts and spending $24 million in record time — much of it on consultants and high-tech satellite hookups around the country — the Spicer Commission ultimately contributed little of substance to the constitutional debate.

It is not likely his intention, but there are times Wells seems to go out of his way to offend Quebec. Just before Christmas 1990, for example, a few days after saying he'd be happy to appear before Quebec's Bélanger-Campeau Commission on his own constitutional future, Wells ripped into the deal Ottawa and Quebec had completed on immigration, a bilateral agreement that gave Quebec, among other things, sole jurisdiction over immigrants coming into that province.

"It's not up to the federal government and one province to make an arrangement that alters anything in the Constitution," Wells said. "If Ottawa is prepared to make that kind of arrangement for one province it should, I presume, be prepared to make it for all the provinces that want it."

Ottawa might do that if other provinces wanted it, but the issue has historically been more important for Quebecers, who, for better or worse, have concerns about protecting their cultural and linguistic balances that other provinces simply don't have. In addition, Ottawa makes special arrangements all the time with various provinces. The multibillion Hibernia deal and various programs to bail out the troubled fishing industry are just two that are geared to Newfoundland and nobody else. Indeed, Wells has complained consistently about federal-regional development policies that, instead of concentrating solely on the regions worst off economically, have tended to spread the money everywhere, thus diluting the total pool and making it impossible for the have-not areas to gain ground on the others.

His comments might have been better expressed a few weeks later, once the euphoria of the deal for the federalist forces inside Quebec had waned somewhat. Montreal *Gazette* columnist Bernard St. Laurent was prompted to write that most Quebec federalists wished Wells "would keep quiet for a while." He cited a recent Centre de Recherches sur l'Opinion (CROP) survey conducted for the TVA television network and *L'Actualité* magazine showing that sixty-four per cent of Quebecers favored sovereignty and demanded a 1991 referendum.

In January 1991 Wells came out full-bore for the notion of a national constituent assembly that he said could, over a four- or five-year period, draft a made-in-Canada Constitution unsullied by the politicians. In addition to the Spicer Commission, at the

time, Ottawa had already set up a Commons-Senate committee, under the joint direction of Edmonton Tory MP Jim
Edwards and Quebec Conservative Senator Gérald Beaudoin,
to study the amending formula and report back. In addition,
six provinces had already set up provincial constitutional
commissions to do much the same thing, a move Wells flatly
refused to contemplate. Instead, he argued that the constituent
assembly could take the recommendations from all these
various commissions and distil them into draft principles that
would ultimately be placed before the people for a public vote.
The idea had been tried before, of course, specifically in what
became known as the National Convention in Newfoundland,
which recommended to the U.K. choices to be offered the
people in a referendum on their own constitutional future.

But the idea of a constituent assembly has obvious draw-
backs. The Meech Lake process showed that it is difficult to
get eleven people to agree to anything, let alone to expect a few
hundred delegates from across the country to reach consensus.
Like many of the cherished ideas Wells promotes, it is more
the sort of thing earnestly debated in second-year political
science courses, where historical and political realities can be
ignored.

Wells's fervor for the Triple-E Senate is a case in point. In a
June 5, 1991, speech to the special colloquium of Carleton
University's school of public administration in Ottawa, the
Newfoundland premier made a persuasive case against the
current unfairness in the distribution of federal largesse in this
country, offering the Triple-E Senate as the magical solution
to make all provinces equal. "The overwhelming influence of
the sixty per cent of the members of the House of Commons
who represent the two massive economic engines of Central
Canada is the primary cause of Ottawa's adopting a symptom
treatment rather than problem-solving approach to correcting
regional economic disparity," he said. "Only with the Triple-E
Senate will we have the political ability to ensure national

legislative jurisdiction is exercised and economic policy is developed and implemented in a manner that will provide for the equitable development of the economy across all parts of the nation. Real and sustained economic balance will only be achieved if and when we achieve political balance."

If only it were that simple. General Motors didn't build in Oshawa because Canada lacked a Triple-E Senate. Giving Newfoundland the same number of senators for its 580,000 people as Ontario's nine million people would not have convinced the Steel Company of Canada to build in Port-aux-Basques instead of near the major markets in Hamilton. What's more, the federal system hasn't been the one responsible for Newfoundland's squandering its enormous natural resources; it's been the provincial governments, and before that their own national and colonial governments, which have exchanged these vast resources for the quick fix of a few thousand temporary jobs.

Wells seems to think that even if all provinces had, say, ten senators each, those senators would rush off to Ottawa and be strong, true blue representatives of the national good. In fact, they'd be politicians, partisans, members of a caucus, just as the current senators and MPs are, subject to the usual constraints, which are a fact of life under a party system.

The other reality is that no Quebec premier could ever agree to a system where Quebec is reduced to "equal" representation — which isn't equal at all, given the population disparities — with Newfoundland.

Throughout 1991 Wells kept pushing hard for a new round of constitutional talks, even if Quebec chose not to participate. "I don't see what the alternative is," he told the *Calgary Herald* editorial board. "Quebec can't vote for sovereignty and association with Canada. It takes two parties to agree. Quebec can't dictate that this is the way it's going to be."

In the meantime, while Wells championed the cause of more open public discussions on the Constitution, he continued to deny Newfoundlanders that chance, rejecting Opposition demands for a provincial commission on the Constitution. "Each of the provincial commissions will tend to focus on the prime concerns of that province," he said, "and the national issues are not likely to be discussed, at least not in a national context."

Maybe. But those supporting provincial commissions saw them simply as one step in the overall process leading toward a national consensus, not as an end in themselves.

At a St. John's news conference in February 1991, not long after having said Ottawa should renew talks with or without Quebec's involvement, Wells said he remained hopeful Quebec would join any new round of talks. He also dumped on Quebec's recently released Allaire report, calling on Quebec to open negotiations with Ottawa, without the other provinces, on a host of demands that would give it significant new powers and dramatically reduce the federal role in Quebec. "The report," he said, "amounts to the dismemberment of Canada as a nation. It reduces Canada to an economic and defence association of ten otherwise insignificant states," and would give Quebec a "privileged position" most Canadians couldn't stand. He said the report's recommendations were "not compatible with the fundamental constitutional precepts shared by most Canadians outside Quebec."

Perhaps not. But it soon became official policy of the Quebec Liberals — the so-called "federalist" party of the province — and a stark indication of what Canadians inside Quebec thought about those fundamental constitutional precepts so important to Wells.

On February 12, 1991, in a highly touted constitutional speech to the combined Empire and Canadian Clubs in Toronto, Brian Mulroney issued a strong plea for Quebec and the rest of Canada not to give up on each other, saying he was prepared to accept major changes in the Constitution but was not ready to reduce the federal government to an empty shell.

Reacting to Mulroney's speech, Wells offered the first indication that, for him at least, those boundaries were beginning to shift slightly. He said he could accept the notion that some federal powers could be transferred to the provinces, but like Mulroney, he stressed it could only work if the provinces in turn gave up control of such areas as the environment, where provincial boundaries make little sense.

On the eve of the March Quebec Liberal Party convention, which adopted the Allaire report as official policy, Wells again called for a constitutional convention to produce a new Constitution ensuring Quebec a limited veto over changes touching language and culture and its civil law system. But Quebec Intergovernmental Affairs Minister Gil Rémillard said he didn't much care what Wells thought about Quebec's role in Confederation. "I have no interest in what Mr. Wells has to say. . . . [He] refused to honor his own signature [on the Meech Lake accord] and other than that, I don't think it merits comment."

Rémillard said Quebec would only negotiate constitutional issues with Ottawa. "We are going to discuss with the Canadian government, and Mr. Mulroney can consult who he likes." That prompted Wells to say, "Quebec has a perfect right to decide who will speak for Quebec, but Quebec does not have the right to decide who will speak on behalf of the other provinces. To suggest that they will talk only with the federal government is, in my judgment, to effectively say that no discussions will take place."

Former Newfoundland Liberal leader Bill Rowe does not believe Wells is personally anti-Quebec at all, though he's not surprised Quebec views him that way. But he says there is an aspect about Wells's acceptance of the public adulation over his anti-Meech position that is disturbing.

"On the one hand, when people started to write him letters across Canada saying, 'Stick it to the frogs. C'mon, Clyde, get those frogs,' a sort of bigoted, redneck reaction, Clyde was the first to decry this. He said he didn't want to be a lightning rod for all the bigotry and prejudice. He sent off letters to people saying, 'No, no, you misunderstood me. It's got nothing to do with that. I love the French.'

"And I'm sure that's his honestly held position," says Rowe. "I have no doubt whatsoever he despises bigotry and prejudice and the anti-French sentiment in anglophone Canada.

"On the other hand, when Clyde has been criticized . . . he has not hesitated in saying, 'While I may have been alone with the premiers and the prime minister, I wasn't alone in Canada. Seventy per cent of Canada at the time supported my position on Meech Lake. That's how the people of Canada felt.' At the same time, he knows, of that seventy per cent, a significant majority is the redneck vote he says he rejects."

In a March 1991 interview with the *Evening Telegram* editorial board, Wells said there definitely had to be a referendum before Newfoundland would agree to substantial constitutional changes. He said the province will "not be squeezed into a time that will not allow a referendum," saying that he prefers a national referendum; failing that, a provincial referendum would be held before his government would agree to a new package. Nor can it be just a straight majority. "It has to be a majority of the people in the country that is reasonably representative of the different parts of the country." He suggested the current amending formula requiring an overall majority representing at least seven provinces and fifty per cent of the total Canadian population would be a good yardstick to use for a referendum.

Later that month, Quebec's own Bélanger-Campeau Commission said a Quebec referendum on sovereignty should be held by October 1992 if there is no acceptable constitutional deal by then. Wells said the rest of Canada can't make Quebec an offer that quickly to hand over new powers to Quebec. "I don't think its possible. . . . [Anyway,] this commission has no right to establish a deadline for the other nine provinces and the two territories of Canada. It's not my deadline. I don't even know if it's the deadline of the government of Quebec. I don't think it is."

It soon would be.

On May 22, 1991, Constitutional Affairs Minister Joe Clark met privately with Wells for two hours in St. John's, emerging to say the bitterness over Meech is history. "We're treating the past as past. The country's at stake. There were serious differences last year. Nobody minimizes those. Nobody wants to repeat them.

"We will now get on together to try to see how much common ground there is in the future. I cannot predict how much there will be except I was encouraged by the tone and the content of this first conversation," said Clark. "Several will follow."

Wells said the exchange was "full and fair and frank and quite friendly and pleasant," but cautioned he wasn't going to be telling anything to Clark or anybody else "to endear myself to them and to make life easier in the future. We have to retain the ability to express sincere views and convictions."

A week before the first anniversary of the death of Meech, Clark announced a new parliamentary committee composed of fifteen MPs and ten senators, who would travel the country seeking a consensus on proposals being developed by Ottawa. Co-chaired by Winnipeg Tory MP Dorothy Dobbie and Quebec Tory Senator Claude Castonguay, and dubbed "the committee to end all committees," it would soon run into serious internal difficulties. Even before it was launched, however, Wells was dumping on it, saying he couldn't understand how a committee could take a proposal "developed in secrecy" and obtain a consensus among Canadians. "I'm very apprehensive about this particular process."

Meanwhile, on June 20, the seventeen-member Edwards-Beaudoin Commons-Senate committee recommended that any constitutional referendum should require a majority vote in each of four regions — the West, Ontario, Quebec, and the Atlantic provinces. The committee rejected the constituent assembly concept — although its NDP members split from it on that one — and called for an end to the closed-door process of Meech as well as mandatory public hearings early enough in the process so that proposals could be adapted to meet public concerns.

It also called for a native veto over constitutional amendments dealing with native land or aboriginal or treaty rights, and proposed a new amending formula designed to give Quebec an absolute veto, a formula that would require most amendments be approved by Parliament, any two Atlantic provinces, Quebec, Ontario, and any two western provinces representing half of that region's population.

Wells complained the report flew against the wishes of the people, most of whom told the committee they favored a constituent assembly. He said it "reflects the political agenda and explains why I think having this kind of a parliamentary committee deal with these major issues has a lesser chance of success than a constituent assembly." As for setting up his own provincial committee, Wells said once again he'd have to think about it, but if that's the method all the other provinces are using, "then I'd say it's probable Newfoundland will do it as well."

In August, responding to a leaked report to the draft of federal constitutional proposals prepared by Clark's eighteen-member cabinet unity committee, Wells told *Toronto Star* reporter Edison Stewart that "the recognition of Quebec as a distinct society is really nothing much more than acknowledging an undeniable sociological fact."

The next day in Rivière-du-Loup, believing that Wells had changed his position on the distinct society provision, Mulroney congratulated him for making a "very important statement" and showing greater maturity than in the past. All Wells had said, as he'd said before, is that he had no objections if Quebec was recognized as a distinct society in the preamble of the Constitution. He clearly told the *Star* his objection to the provision in Meech Lake was its recognition of the role of the Quebec government and its national assembly to preserve and promote the province's distinct identity. "That's what gives them the special legislative status that I have objected to in the past," he said.

A few days later, in Yellowknife, Wells said Canada's aboriginal people are the only group entitled to special constitutional status. "To the degree we have to vary the principle of equality . . . it can only be justified for the aboriginal people. This is the kind of accommodation we have to make. We must make a reasonable accord so that the aboriginal people can live the traditional way of life, if they so choose."

Finally, shortly before Mulroney unveiled his "Renewed Canada" in September, Wells acknowledged there was no chance of a constituent assembly, so he grudgingly announced appointment of a provincial constitutional committee chaired by then justice minister Paul Dicks with seven MHAs altogether — four Liberals, two Tories, and a New Democrat — plus an equal number of unelected representatives. Even so, he made no mention at the time of public hearings, giving the committee authority only to "receive . . . representations and presentations," and flatly refusing to clarify this vague directive when asked to by reporters.

Memorial University Professor Patrick O'Flaherty, an old schoolmate of Wells, wrote in the *Ottawa Citizen* that "Wells had fallen into the habit of thinking that only he can handle Newfoundland's brief in the Constitution. . . . When cornered, he always comes back to his imagined role as the spokesman for 'the people of Canada.'" What's more, with Newfoundland's economy in a free fall, "the public is unlikely to put up with much more constitutional grandstanding from a premier who has done so little to help them get jobs."

In October Wells finally agreed to hold public hearings on the Constitution in Newfoundland. Around the same time, Mulroney released his long-awaited, mammoth twenty-eight-point unity package, ranging from Charter amendments to guaranteed property rights, to aboriginal self-government, an elected Senate — but not Triple-E — a Canadian economic union free from interprovincial trade barriers, more provincial control in immigration, culture and job training, to the all-important distinct society provisions.

The distinct society clause was similar in form to the doomed Meech Lake clause, but instead of being contained in the body of the Constitution, where it would have more impact, Mulroney now suggested putting it in the preamble and the Charter of Rights. Like most politicians, Wells greeted the package cautiously, but said the proposals were so "broad and all-encompassing" that consensus would be difficult to achieve. "You have to give Clark credit for making a tremendous effort," he said. "I'm not sure they've achieved a proposal that . . . will get widespread public support. . . . I think a great deal of work and discussion and adjustment has to be done."

Wells went on to say Ottawa must persuade Canadians that its constitutional proposals are best for the country. "They don't have to persuade me. They have to persuade the two-thirds of Canadians who would not agree with the [Meech Lake] proposals."

In Quebec, Bourassa had given his initial approval to the federal proposals, but he later emerged from the opening session of a two-day meeting with his ninety-member caucus to say he and his cabinet had adopted a tougher line and now would accept no arrangement that does not give Quebec a veto over changes to federal institutions. "The right of veto is a fundamental demand," he said, adding that his five basic demands from Meech still stand.

In October, despite repeated denials from both Clark and Mulroney that they were planning a national referendum on the Constitution, Government House leader Harvie Andre confirmed that the government proposed to table legislation soon that would enable a referendum to be held.

Wells finally delivered his formal response to the federal proposals during a two-hour hearing before his own constitutional committee in the House of Assembly on October 22, 1991. He seemed to catch observers off guard by arguing that Quebec does have the right to be a distinct society and exempt from portions of the Charter to pursue that aim.

"Some limited subordination of individual rights to collective rights within Quebec, if that is what the people of Quebec want," he said, "may not be an unreasonable concession to accommodate the legitimate concerns of a province that is, by reason of its culture, language, and legal system, distinctly different from any other province in the country.

"While philosophically I, personally, and perhaps the vast majority of Canadians, would prefer to see the Charter apply to every part of the country and to each individual in exactly the same manner, if the majority of citizens of Quebec want their individual Charter rights to be somewhat subordinated to their collective rights, then it is difficult for the citizens of any other province to say, 'We don't want to see that happen in Quebec.'"

Wells also called for aboriginal self-government and promoted his idea for a U.S.-style senate, repeating his long-standing notion of protecting Quebec's interests by giving its senators a double majority in the new Senate. The speech was widely reported as Wells's having changed his position on the distinct society provisions. Within a day, Wells was on a Toronto open-line radio show denying this. A few days later he told Southam News reporter Joan Bryden that if Ottawa thought Wells was now on-side they'd better think again. "It's an irony that people were rushing about last year to go head over heels to tell the people . . . that I was absolutely refusing to recognize the fact that Quebec is a distinct society. It was totally wrong, totally contrary to everything I've ever said. This year, they're rushing head over heels and saying I'm accepting whatever's recommended, and that, too, is equally wrong."

Wells said he opposed the original distinct society clause because it was "conjured up to mask the fact that they were trying to put in place a special legislative status for Quebec." This time, Ottawa was proposing to insert the clause directly into the Charter, and he said he was prepared to consider that, but on condition the clause would apply only to Quebec laws, not to federal laws or those of other provinces as currently proposed. He called it "a big 'but,'" which has been largely overlooked. "You can't have federal laws applied differently in Quebec than they do in other provinces. That creates a special status and I don't think that's right."

Wells added that most reports also overlooked his concerns about inclusion of a second distinct society provision in the proposed Canada clause, listing the fundamental characteristics of the country, including Quebec's special responsibility to preserve and promote its distinctiveness. He said it's difficult to determine precisely what impact it would have in its current vague form, but if it meant Quebec could gain special legislative powers, then his position "is no different than it was last year on that point."

He outlined what he called the "three equalities" that, in his view, must be in a renewed Constitution: equality of individuals, equality of the provinces, and equality between French- and English-speaking Canadians.

Even Gil Rémillard, never inclined to say anything positive about Wells in the past, called the premier's apparent softer line on the distinct society clause "interesting." He said Wells's comments "seem to reflect a more open spirit on the distinct society and other points. . . . But before commenting further, we have to see how he follows up. I think probably Mr. Wells has a better understanding now and I think that now it's obvious we can have a more constructive discussion with Mr. Wells and other premiers." That, of course, was before Wells began to hotly deny he had softened his view, as if the very notion of compromise was an attack on his manhood. Nova

Scotia Senator John Buchanan, the only premier who sat through the 1981-82 constitutional deal, the 1987 Meech Lake agreement, and the 1990 death of Meech, says, "There's a serious contradiction here, because among his objections to the Meech Lake accord, the most important was the distinct society, where he believed this was giving something to Quebec more than the other provinces had. Not a special status, but he believed the distinct society clause would override the Charter of Rights. He sincerely believed that.

"I didn't. I still don't. But the contradiction is that he now publicly says if the people of Quebec want those words 'distinct society' in a constitution, so be it. I don't understand how he could change his mind so dramatically in a period of less than two years. But he has. What he says now is that he really has no objection to the distinct society clause if it means language, culture, and the system of Quebec laws. Well, that's all it meant in the first place. It didn't mean anything else.

"Now his bottom line is the Triple-E Senate. . . . I'm a great supporter of that as well . . . but you can't have it all. I mean you can't bring down a constitutional amendment as he did in 1990 primarily because he believed the distinct society clause is wrong, and now turn around and agree with it and say my problem now is the Triple-E Senate."

During fall and early winter 1991 the Dobbie-Castonguay committee began rapidly self-destructing, turning into a farce, a force for national embarrassment rather than national unity. Early on, NDP Leader Audrey McLaughlin said she was considering withdrawing her party's support of the committee to protest what she called Tory patronage. The committee was planning to more than double its $3 million budget to $6.5 million, including $2.7 million for an advertising campaign and consulting contracts. In a letter, four NDP committee members — Lorne Nystrom, Lynn Hunter, Phil Edmonston, and Ian Waddell — complained specifically about a $190,000 contract for Roger Tasse, Mulroney's former constitutional adviser, and an

$85,000 contract for John Perrin, a former Dobbie campaign worker hired as the committee's executive director. Both contracts expired when the committee was to report in March 1992.

For all the charges of patronage by the NDP, however, it turned out that Nystrom, who sat on the steering committee that hired the two men, had agreed to the hirings before the contracts were let. When the Tories pointed that out, Nystrom replied weakly that, yes, it was true, but "there was never any discussion of salary."

But before the shouting died down from that incident, Edmonston and other New Democrats threatened to boycott a private meeting with Bourassa, who had told the committee that, as a "basic courtesy," he would meet with them, but in private in December. Dobbie said the committee, which was supposed to conduct its affairs publicly, "wants to meet in the open whenever it possibly can . . . but we have no control over the agendas that are being set by other premiers, and we've agreed to be flexible."

On top of that Ontario Premier Bob Rae postponed his planned session with the group because of his dismay at the committee's internal feuding.

At one public meeting, Sheldon Godfrey, a lawyer and board member of the Ontario region of the Canadian Council of Christians and Jews, said he supports enshrinement of Quebec as a distinct society, but believes the wording of the proposal would give special rights to Quebec's French-speaking majority and turn other Quebecers into second-class citizens. That's not the sort of thing the committee wants to hear. Two Quebec Tory MPs — Monique Tardiff and Gabriel Desjardin — rudely walked out on the man, and Quebec Liberal MP André Ouellet complained it is "regrettable that the gentleman who is supposed to speak on behalf of a national organization that promotes goodwill and understanding would come and present the views he did." Godfrey said later, "I didn't expect to make friends, [but] I did expect they would listen."

Obviously he expected too much. For all the constant talk coming out of Ottawa about tolerance and understanding of Quebec, there is little said about its being reciprocal. Many MPs, usually Tories from the West or rural Ontario, have discovered to their chagrin the depth of bullying and rudeness that seems to come with even the slightest hint that the Holy Grail of Quebec's distinct society is not sacred.

In early November, still hampered by internal chaos and partisan backbiting, the committee went to Winnipeg where, once again, it became embroiled in a dispute, facing charges of stacking the public hearings with expert witnesses who favored the federal proposals. University of Manitoba constitutional law professor Bryan Schwartz, author of a widely recognized study on the Meech Lake accord, was not invited to appear, while Winnipeg lawyer Patrick Riley, one of the few Manitobans who fought to save Meech, was heard by the committee even though he was not on the official witness list. He was pencilled in by Castonguay, whom Riley had brought to the province to twist arms during the Meech crisis. Manitoba Liberal Leader Sharon Carstairs, a key player in the process, was denied a chance to testify, as was Manitoba law professor Jack London, who was legal counsel for the Assembly of Manitoba Chiefs, main organizers of Elijah Harper's successful procedural battle in the Manitoba legislature.

The committee's negative publicity swelled to the point that both Mulroney and Clark publicly warned the committee to clean up its act. Liberal Leader Jean Chrétien said it had become "the laughingstock of Canada," and Mulroney, who didn't disagree, said "we'll watch closely" to make sure they perform more effectively. Clark said he would meet with Castonguay and Dobbie "as quickly as possible" to sort out the problems.

He didn't meet them quickly enough. Because of poor advance notice, in Steinbach, Manitoba, only one person arrived prepared to address the committee, while a few others came to listen to the event; in Gimli, there was only a small crowd to applaud when witness Ron Cassels said, "We're rebelling because we're getting French shoved down our throats with our own money"; in St. Pierre-Jolys, just three community members showed up, including a woman who came to help with the refreshments; in Thompson, many of the thirty or so who turned up complained they had only heard about the meeting at the last minute and had no information to help them prepare briefs; a mere two presenters showed up at the Portage La Prairie city hall for an afternoon public hearing, including Roy Lyall, president of the Reform Party of Manitoba, who complained, "They have ripped every business out of this province and relocated it in Montreal"; and in Churchill, where they drew about forty people, the meeting was dominated by native issues.

Castonguay, a well-respected Quebec businessman and for-mer senior provincial cabinet minister, complained publicly that he was "definitely not very happy" with the committee's role so far, and the inexperienced Dobbie got into hot water over a Manitoba high-school newspaper article that quoted her as saying Quebec's French-only sign legislation was "the most stupid, dumb, and bigoted thing Bourassa did."

The planned public hearings in northern Ontario were cancelled altogether, and the committee slinked back into Ottawa to regroup and plan a damage-control operation.

To complicate things further, Rémillard advised Ottawa to go back to the drawing board and rewrite their "unacceptable" proposals. A couple of days later, Bourassa softened the re-marks slightly, agreeing that some of the proposals weren't acceptable, but others couldn't be "categorically rejected, that is to say, without discussion." Turning up the political heat, Chrétien announced that Dobbie "is no good," demanding she either resign, or the Liberals would quit the committee. The NDP demanded major organizational changes or it, too, would walk.

In the meantime, disagreements in cabinet stalled the referendum legislation. Clark, who was not supporting a referendum, had said earlier, "On issues of this kind, referendums are either divisive or redundant. If there's a consensus, we don't need it. If there isn't, it's divisive."

On November 13 Clark, saying the time for "silly party games" was over, unveiled his alternative plan, saying Canadians would be asked to talk about the Constitution through five major conferences rather than the travelling committee hearings. Clark said he had not given up on the committee and would not ask Dobbie to resign, although both she and Castonguay offered to quit. In Quebec City, Rémillard quickly announced that his province would not participate in the regional constitutional conference.

After a week of fumbling around, the unity committee hobbled back to work. Chrétien had backed off on his demands for Dobbie's head, claiming in return for that he was given assurances of a new push for referendum legislation, an opposition veto over management of the committee, and an immediate start on the drafting of legal texts for the federal unity proposals. Once again, Rémillard said Quebec's plans for a sovereignty referendum were "untouchable."

To help get the committee on track, Clark brought in senior bureaucrat David Broadbent, a no-nonsense former military man, to relaunch the process. Broadbent, as deputy minister of veteran affairs, had been credited with saving the Spicer Commission from its own organizational chaos when he was named its executive director. All this was too much for Castonguay, and on November 25 he resigned as co-chair, blaming ill health, and was replaced by Senator Gérald Beaudoin, a constitutional scholar with more than a hundred essays and articles on Canada's constitutional law to his credit. Beaudoin had co-chaired the earlier Commons-Senate committee with Jim Edwards, and in the 1970s was a member of the Pépin-Robarts Task Force on Canadian Unity.

Once again, pressure from Quebec changed the federal government's constitutional agenda, as Clark bowed to pressure in a meeting with Quebec Tory MPs and said he would not bring in legislation for a national referendum before Christmas. Mulroney's Quebec lieutenant, Health Minister Benoît Bouchard, said the word "referendum" is "scary, the word is provocative, the word shocks in certain cases. There are bogeymen in Quebec, and one of these bogeymen is the word 'referendum.'"

Perhaps. But five months later, Clark, Mulroney, Bouchard, and the other Tories were saying a national referendum was the only way to solve the unity crisis, promising to call one in the fall if they couldn't reach a political consensus on a deal with the premiers before that. As for Bourassa, all his tough talk about a Quebec referendum on sovereignty also disappeared in April when he told a magazine interviewer in France that the referendum would not be on sovereignty after all, but would be based on the final federal proposals, even though at that point he didn't know what they were.

In a remarkable display of poor timing in late November, Bouchard announced a $300-million federal-provincial business-aid package for Quebec, which quickly escalated into a symbol of the country's deep divisions and sparked an ugly mood in Ottawa and elsewhere, prompting premiers in British Columbia and Newfoundland and most provinces in between to complain that what's good for Quebec must also be good for their recession-ravaged turf.

As the new year began, the Beaudoin-Dobbie committee had finally begun to function, but Alberta Premier Don Getty threw a spanner into the works by demanding an end to official bilingualism and multiculturalism laws, and listing tough new demands for his support for the constitutional package: a Triple-E Senate; no veto for Quebec unless Alberta has one, too; a distinct society designation for Quebec only if the province receives no new powers; and ratification of any new deal by the people, possibly through a referendum.

Wells, still trying to learn French himself, with little success, said of Getty's call for an end to official bilingualism, "I don't share his view. Canada is a bilingual nation." He did, however, side with Getty on the Triple-E Senate when he appeared before the joint Commons-Senate committee in St. John's on January 14, 1992. It was just one day after Bob Rae had testified before the committee in Ottawa that the idea, "stated baldly, is not acceptable to Ontario." Wells asked, "Why are we so afraid of doing what is principled? Why do we want to create a preferential position for any part of the country? What's right is a proper Triple-E Senate."

Wells also said that anything less than a Triple-E "is a denial of the fundamental principles of federalism, and there can be no justification for such a denial," adding that constitutional change "cannot result in special status or legislative power for one province or territory that others do not enjoy, and cannot result in a privileged position or superior benefits for one group of citizens over others."

The next day in Montreal, Bourassa said that other provinces should shelve their constitutional demands and settle "the Quebec question" first to save the country, saying premiers should be careful "not to destroy the country" by insisting now on such issues as bilingualism, property rights, and Senate reform. He'd told Getty a day earlier by telephone that the Alberta premier "runs the risk of making Canada's situation even more fragile" by attacking bilingualism, and he dismissed Wells's call for an American-style senate as "inappropriate," and again attacked Wells for bringing down the Meech Lake accord.

Bourassa, speaking to reporters after a Liberal meeting, also criticized Rae for saying that Ottawa courts disaster if Ontario and the other provinces are left out of constitutional deal-making. Bourassa said the problem with the current round is that "everyone is arriving with their own agenda . . . property rights, a social charter, Senate reform, bilingualism." For

Bourassa, of course, there was only one agenda. And the next day, Rémillard not only rejected the Triple-E Senate but insisted Quebec has a constitutional veto over Senate reform.

Four days later in Halifax, Ottawa sponsored the first of its five regional constitutional conferences, supposedly designed to allow "ordinary Canadians" to have their say, but in fact loaded by the usual array of politicians, academics, lobbyists, and special-interest groups, which always dominate these issues. Of the two hundred delegates in Halifax, for example, about forty were so-called ordinary Canadians who had answered newspaper ads inviting them to apply to attend.

The buzz word among the hand-picked delegates was Clark's "asymmetrical federalism," simply a sneaky way of conferring special status on Quebec without actually saying so. Under that system, Quebec would take control over many federal powers while a strong federal government would remain in control in the rest of the country.

Things were pretty much the same during the subsequent series of carefully stage-managed conferences: in Calgary, where delegates said they wanted Senate reform but not Triple-E; in Montreal, where delegates trashed federal proposals for an economic union but embraced Bob Rae's social-charter idea; in Toronto, where the delegates dismissed the federal property-rights proposal, agreed to keep the controversial "notwithstanding clause," and where the distinct society issue took another turn when Assembly of First Nations Chief Ovide Mercredi demanded a distinct society for natives; and finally, in Vancouver, where delegates called for a high-falutin "Canada clause" to be "brief and inspirational" and capture both the "essential unity of Canada and recognize and celebrate its diversity."

All this activity was well covered by the media and no doubt warmed the hearts of the participants and the various advocacy groups, which were pushing their own agendas. But in the end, it didn't amount to much. None of the major players —

the politicians, who will actually make the decisions — showed any sign of shifting their positions as a result of this orgy of constitutional theorizing.

If anything, the mood was getting nastier. House leader Harvie Andre, the political equivalent of an angry pit bull terrier, speaking in Truro, Nova Scotia, attacked both Getty and Wells for their "insane" demands, claiming their position is "either do it my way or to hell with the country. That is insane. And somebody should take Wells and Getty, and any-body else who's behaving that way, and find a deep lake and they can explore the bottom of it. These guys drive me crazy." Calling for "tolerance," and demonstrating none himself, Andre said, "It was Clyde Wells's decision that killed it [Meech Lake] and I'll never forgive him. . . . He, at the end, backed out of his agreement and stood back."

Later, Andre claimed his comments were taken out of con-text, although he didn't explain how such quotes could be meant in any other context. But he did write to Wells and Getty to say, "I sincerely regret any misunderstanding my comments may have caused."

An internal Bloc Québécois paper obtained by *L'Actualité* magazine outlined a strategy to paralyse Parliament if the federal government refused to recognize a pro-sovereignty result in a Quebec referendum; as well, public opinion polls were depicting Bloc leader Lucien Bouchard as the most popular politician in Quebec. In February Bourassa told re-porters in Brussels there would definitely be a Quebec refer-endum in the fall, either on federal offers, if they're good enough, or on his version of "shared sovereignty," a proposi-tion wherein Quebec and Canada become two sovereign states with a joint "economic confederation."

By the end of April Clark was saying Canada's new consti-tutional deal would likely be a two-part package — the first needing approval of at least seven provinces, the second re-quiring approval of all ten.

Clark also managed to offend Quebec anglophones by saying the federal government would not have any special responsibility to Quebec's English-speaking minority if the province seceded, sparking dozens of angry calls to Montreal radio open-line shows. He said Quebec's aboriginals would be exceptions because of their special history.

On February 25, 1992, the day before the Beaudoin-Dobbie committee's report was scheduled for release, Mulroney wrote each premier to invite the provinces to send a delegation to Ottawa to meet federal officials on March 6 and discuss the next step in the constitutional amending process. As expected, however, the committee did not give birth to its proposals easily, the whole thing almost coming unglued over some last-minute wrangling, delaying the report another day, after a meeting well into the night resulted in an uneasy truce among the warring political parties.

The 130-page package failed to find a constitutional amending formula, offering instead five options, all of them giving Quebec a veto for any substantial change to national institutions. Indeed the proposals decentralized power far beyond anything else ever suggested by the federal government, and recognized "the inherent right" of natives to self-government, plus an elected Senate.

Clark said the committee report "has moved Canada forward towards unity." Others disagreed. Alberta deputy premier Jim Horsman complained about the attempt to give Quebec a veto but not the other provinces. "We will be very happy to be an equal partner. But we will not be a second-class partner, and that is what the report would have us be." B.C. Premier Mike Harcourt said a constitutional veto for Quebec was unacceptable. Reform Party Leader Preston Manning said a referendum on the package would probably fail.

Not all federal Tory backbenchers were thrilled either. Mississauga West MP Bob Horner said, "A Quebec veto over the House of Commons and Senate? Give me a break." Ontario

Tory caucus chairman Bill Attewell was concerned about the devolution of federal powers and Quebec's status as a distinct society. "Someone is going to have to persuade me to see the logic on the question of the Quebec veto."

The day after the report was released, in Corner Brook Wells said the talks about economic co-operation among the four Atlantic provinces were too important to be hijacked by talk of constitutional change. "I find it difficult to get excited about this report. . . . I have grave doubts that this course is any more likely to provide a resolution than the Meech Lake accord, because it's too similar to it." He declined comment on specific aspects of the report, however, until he had read it.

Wells flew to Ottawa early the next day to meet Mulroney on the fishing crisis — the meeting where Mulroney pooh-poohed his suggestion to send in the navy to get rid of the foreign fishing trawlers — and after returning he told reporters at the House of Assembly he did some skimming of the report, but still hadn't read it thoroughly. He'd read enough, however, to say the committee's suggestion for a Senate with "equitable" representation from each province according to population is "totally inconsistent with what the western provinces have asked for. It's inconsistent with what we've asked for. So I find it difficult to believe they [cabinet] will find it acceptable."

On March 12, meeting in Ottawa with Mulroney, Clark, the provinces, and native leaders, Wells and everybody else agreed to attempt to reach a national-unity deal by the end of May, about ten weeks away. The idea was to conduct a series of alternating meetings of officials and first ministers, held in private, with "regular public reporting of progress," on various issues culminating in a first ministers' meeting if it is felt the talks could succeed.

Four days later, Bourassa announced he had no intention of returning to the constitutional bargaining table. He said it is "our Canadian partners' turn to make proposals," not

Quebec's. The same day, speaking in Vancouver, Wells said the ten-week deadline was an unacceptable approach and a "virtually impossible" condition. "In the end you're down to this deadline concept again where you've got until the end of May to do something to save the country, otherwise you will wreck the country. That's no way to deal with a Constitution."

He said an agreement "should not be based on threats that if you don't do a certain thing by a certain time, you will have caused the failure of the country. We cannot be rushed into accepting something that would not be acceptable if we had the time to stop and think about it and judge what needs to be done properly. . . . They've outlined a time frame, but if it isn't done by then, and it takes us into June and July and August and September, then so be it. We must take whatever time is necessary to do it right."

In Ottawa, Health Minister Benoît Bouchard angrily lashed out at Wells. Bouchard, who had voted against federalism in the Quebec referendum, was now Mulroney's chief Quebec lieutenant supposedly trying to sell federalism in Quebec. Nevertheless, whenever Mulroney made federalist speeches in Quebec, his Quebec ministers, Bouchard among them, remained virtually mum on the issue in their home province. Bouchard was strangely quiet, for example, when Bourassa blasted the process and refused to become a participant. But in response to Wells, Bouchard snapped, "We might not be in the same country if we continue to listen to Mr. Wells, and that's why I intend to get a deal by the deadline [May 31]." He said Wells said the same thing during Meech "and it was a disaster. If he wants to avoid another disaster, it's up to him. As far as I'm concerned, I don't intend to define Canada in accordance with Clyde Wells."

Nor, it seems, does Clyde Wells intend to define the country according to Benoît Bouchard.

And so, after more than two years of intense constitutional bickering, the penultimate countdown to this process may have finally begun. But the major players, while agreeing on some things, still have profound and, in some cases, seemingly unsurmountable differences.

With the Quebec-induced fall deadline for a resolution looming ever closer, the protagonists in this long-running, made-in-Canada war seemed as far apart as ever.

Wells said he'd learned during an open-line radio program in Vancouver just how strongly people in the West felt about recognizing Quebec as a distinct society. On the other hand, he said, Quebecers favor it as strongly as British Columbians oppose it.

He said he wished Bourassa would end his constitutional boycott and get on with the business of finding solutions, but even if he doesn't, "the country has to go on. Just because one province decides not to participate doesn't mean the country must stop."

Which is pretty much where everybody was when Meech Lake died in June 1990.

The tension eased briefly in late May when Wells and Bourassa met in Montreal, their first meeting since the death of Meech. Bourassa said the chances for a deal were now "more encouraging," while Wells said the meeting left him feeling "optimistic," although he cautioned that any new deal must please everybody, not just Quebec.

At the same time, the federal government was moving ahead with its referendum legislation, and Wells agreed to join Alberta, Manitoba, Saskatchewan, and Nova Scotia in the push for a Triple-E Senate.

On May 21, Clark announced a tentative agreement in which Ottawa agreed to shift power to the provinces in eight areas, ranging from housing to tourism to forestry.

Even Bouchard called it "an excellent day." But his optimism didn't last. A few days later the ongoing negotiations again fell apart, and Clark, who had got into the silly habit of setting absolute deadlines, again extended the May 31 deadline to

June 10, repeating his view that Canada would collapse if no deal were forged by that time.

Wells attacked a proposed constitutional agreement on native self-government as a "recipe for chaos." Still, the Commons approved its referendum bill, and the five-province push angered Bouchard so much that on June 10 he walked out on the federal-provincial talks claiming he had reached his "level of tolerance. . . . I don't believe we can reach agreement."

Two days later, Wells turned up the heat substantially by dismissing Saskatchewan's Senate proposal, which would have given all provinces an equal number of senators but a different number of votes on various issues, as a dishonest insult. What's more, Wells said that without a true Triple-E Senate, he would never agree to Quebec's demand for a veto over future institutional changes, a demand requiring unanimous consent because it meant changing the Constitution's amending formula. Wells said he wouldn't even present such a proposal to his legislature without first holding a provincial referendum in which he would "express in no uncertain terms" his opposition to it.

Many Wells critics immediately claimed this contradicted the premier's earlier promise that, as Bourassa told reporters, "if [Wells] is alone to block an agreement which will save the country, he will not block that agreement." Many journalists also picked up on the theme, and this alleged promise by Wells quickly became a regular part of the constitutional milieu.

The problem is, Wells never said it. He has directly denied saying it many times, but it didn't seem to matter to those pursuing the strategy of once again trying to isolate him as the bad boy of Confederation.

What Wells did say, and has often repeated, is that if he was the only premier standing in the way of an agreement he'd hold a provincial referendum. If Newfoundlanders voted in favor of the deal he would not then stand in the way, but would resign as premier.

By this time, however, the federal strategy of circling the wagons around Wells, clearly the most implacable of the premiers, had become clear. Once again, news stories began to appear singling out Wells as the lone ranger, despite the fact that Alberta and Manitoba in particular still opposed the Senate proposals, and in fact most provinces had expressed serious reservations about several of the latest suggestions.

In mid-June, two days after Pierre Trudeau had dinner at Wells's house — thereby rekindling the old notion that Wells was Trudeau's puppet, when all Trudeau was doing in town was working on a five-hour CBC documentary about his life — Joe Clark also came by for dinner. Later, Clark announced the two men had agreed to disagree. In a subsequent speech to the St. John's Rotary Club, Clark claimed Newfoundland would have the most to lose if Quebec separated — as if that's what Wells wanted — and even claimed the stalled Hibernia project would have a better chance of success under a renewed Constitution.

During a Newfoundland PC Youth meeting June 24, the federal Tories sent six cabinet ministers to the island to speak at the event and tour the province pushing the Constitution and criticizing Wells. Crosbie accused Wells of "academic fanaticism" in pursuing the Triple-E Senate, prompting Wells to respond that the smear campaign by Ottawa only showed they're worried they won't reach a consensus and will be forced to hold a federal referendum. He said Crosbie and the other ministers had come to Newfoundland simply to "try to pressure the Newfoundland people with threats."

On June 29, during a luncheon meeting between Mulroney and the nine premiers at 24 Sussex Drive — Bourassa continued his boycott of such meetings — the premiers agreed they would meet again in Toronto four days later in a last-ditch effort to salvage an agreement.

At one point, Mulroney was explaining that Bourassa's problem isn't so much PQ leader Jacques Parizeau as it is placating the youth wing of the Quebec Liberal party. Without their support, Mulroney said, Bourassa could lose twelve members of his caucus.

This prompted Wells to interject, "So what you're telling us, Prime Minister, is we're not here to save the country, we're here to save the Quebec Liberal party."

Wells left this July 3 meeting early to fly back to St. John's for an emergency cabinet meeting on Crosbie's imposition of a two-year moratorium on cod fishing. While the premiers heralded a tentative breakthrough on Senate reform at the meeting, Wells said the Senate "is not the only issue unresolved, believe me."

The proposal called for eight senators from each province, and two from each territory, with a series of special majorities needed to reject bills approved by the Commons. On natural resources legislation, for example, the Senate could kill a Commons bill by a simple majority vote; in areas with shared federal-provincial responsibility, such as agriculture, it would take a sixty per cent Senate vote; while on all other legislation, seventy-five per cent of the senators would be needed to kill Commons legislation.

It would also give Quebec a double majority for matters affecting the French language, which means not only an overall Senate majority but a majority of the eight Quebec senators. And to balance equality of the provinces in the Senate, the Commons would get seventeen more seats, ten of them in Ontario.

Meeting again in Ottawa July 7, the premiers agreed substantially to that package, with minor changes, which was a major breakthrough for the Triple-E boosters and an apparent setback for Ontario Premier Bob Rae, who had consistently dismissed the notion as "unacceptable."

The front-page headline in the July 8 *Ottawa Citizen* claimed, "A Deal at Last," after Joe Clark and the nine premiers formally agreed to the tentative breakthrough.

While there was certainly cause for some optimism, a deal

was still a long way from being done. Wells, for example, left the meeting saying, "I haven't agreed to a package. . . . I only agreed to Senate reform."

In addition to a modified Triple-E Senate, however, the package contained an expanded House of Commons, a veto for all provinces over future institutional changes, entrenchment of native self-government, a new distinct society clause in the main body of the Constitution, an economic union section aimed at reducing interprovincial trade barriers, and a new division of powers turning over jurisdiction to the provinces in seven areas, including job training.

Wells, objecting strongly to the native self-government provisions and distinct society clauses, hinted he would have his own provincial referendum. "I will not ask the legislature to approve those things with which we disagree."

Two days later, in a nationally televised news conference, Bourassa neither rejected nor accepted the package, saying it showed a remarkable amount of goodwill on the part of English Canada but expressing serious reservations about the "significant losses" to Quebec in the proposed Senate plan and concerns about the possible territorial implications for the province if the principle of native self-government came to fruition.

Still, Bourassa's response was positive enough to convince Mulroney to cancel his planned July 15 recall of the Commons, during which he'd intended to introduce a federal constitutional proposal in time for Quebec's October referendum.

At a July 10 news conference, Mulroney, echoing Bourassa's sentiments that the proposed deal is "provisional," said it is not "set in concrete," but does contain "the fundamental elements of an agreement."

Mulroney said he would not call an immediate first ministers' conference, but instead await the results of the negotiations by federal and provincial officials to fine-tune the offers. Then, if a full-fledged constitutional conference is called, Bourassa could end his two-year boycott and the country's seemingly endless constitutional saga could finally be put to rest.

Naturally, it could never be that easy. Even though Bourassa would soon officially re-enter the fray, constitutional bickering, like carping about the weather, is so central to the Canadian psyche that even if this round ends with a deal, the best we could hope for is a temporary lull in the haggling.,

Mulroney had not expected the July 7 agreement. He had hoped it would end in the usual deadlock, thereby justifying his plan to unilaterally make his own proposals.

And when Bourassa failed to dismiss the deal out of hand, sparking severe criticism in Quebec, he quickly demanded drastic changes, prompting Manitoba's Gary Filmon to say that Bourassa wasn't seeking compromise, he was "looking for a sign of surrender."

On August 9 the *Ottawa Citizen* published minutes from various June meetings between Bourassa and other premiers showing that Bourassa had privately accepted the principle of an equal senate. Yet, when Bourassa formally ended his constitutional boycott at a seven-hour informal First Ministers luncheon, August 4, in Ottawa, he denied it, saying he'd told Clark at a later meeting that he rejected an equal senate.

But Wells said, "Most of us at the (July 7) meeting had the clear understanding that what was being done was acceptable to Quebec." Mulroney subsequently called a full-fledged First Ministers conference for August 18, including native and territorial leaders, resorting to his standard tactic of threatening to go it alone if the premiers couldn't strike a quick deal.

It all sounded like a replay of Meech Lake, only by summertime Alberta's Don Getty, not Wells, had emerged as the high profile opposition to Mulroney and Bourassa. Wells, when asked, would clearly state his views, but he deliberately kept a lower profile, even leaving hurriedly after the July 7 meeting without stopping for the TV cameras.

Not that he had softened his position. To the contrary. Having helped win tentative acceptance of a modified Triple-E Senate, he, like Getty, wasn't about to easily retreat. By this time, however, Wells was again enjoying another rush of nationwide fan mail. But, with a keen eye to his own potential national political future, he quietly let Getty take the heat, avoiding a rekindling of the old hatreds, but all the while keeping his cherished first principles intact.

Epilogue

IN LATE SEPTEMBER 1990, Clyde Wells drew a lengthy standing ovation even before he'd said a word to a sell-out crowd of three hundred enthusiasts at a Liberal-sponsored luncheon in Victoria, B.C. During the speech, he was interrupted several times by prolonged applause and shouts of "Clyde Wells for prime minister." At the end, dozens of people lined up to shake his hand. One woman, tears in her eyes, gushed afterwards, "I'll never wash my hand again."

This was not an isolated event. Everywhere he went, particularly in the West, Wells was greeted more like a conquering hero than just another politician from the East. Even now, almost two years after gaining instant recognition during the epic battle over the Meech Lake accord, and despite a widespread public malaise about politicians and politics in general, Wells is constantly in demand as a speaker and frequently mentioned as a future prime minister. For his part, Wells does nothing to discourage this notion.

In an April 3, 1991, interview on CBC's "Fifth Estate," Wells told journalist Hana Gartner that he had not ruled out seeking the prime minister's job. "I say to you honestly I'm not carrying on an ambition to be prime minister of this country. I don't know what will happen in the future. [However] I can't sit here and honestly say, 'No, no, I would never, ever participate in seeking the office if the appropriate circumstances arose.'"

If Wells wasn't interested he would say so.

He continues to take French lessons from a private tutor and travels the country giving speeches at party functions, service clubs, academic organizations — essentially to anybody who has an ear and a platform for him. He has also brought former Newfoundland Liberal Leader Ed Roberts out of political retirement, appointed him attorney general, thereby creating an obvious heir-apparent to keep the party intact should he leave.

While Wells didn't enjoy the hostility the other leaders displayed toward him during Meech, he clearly revelled in the widespread public adulation and is building on it for a possible future run at the top job. In a June 1992 article in the *Gazette* Montreal journalist Benoît Aubin wrote that because of Wells's opposition to Meech, when he speaks "Quebec cringes, Ottawa listens, Toronto hears, and Calgary applauds."

Ironically, his grassroots popularity likely makes it more difficult for him to win the party nomination than it would be for him to win an election if he was the leader. Many in the current federal Liberal hierarchy, including several senior elected politicians, are envious of Wells's popularity with the public, hesitant even to discuss him, and not likely to offer him much support in his quest.

While his vast popularity naturally waned somewhat after the dizzying heights achieved during the Meech Lake dispute, it began regenerating itself in late spring 1992, as Wells again came to be singled out by Ottawa and many of the provinces as the unbending villain in the piece, rather than, as he sees himself, the Lone Ranger fighting to keep the world safe for federalism.

Could he be prime minister? Yes, it's possible, despite some heavy baggage, particularly the antipathy he generated in Quebec. Over time that, too, could fade, if the constitutional impasse is ultimately resolved.

Not only is Wells a different brand of politician from the slick, poll-driven types we've become accustomed to lately, the entire Canadian political landscape has dramatically changed.

If the old rules still applied, Wells wouldn't have a hope. Why not? Because as things stand, he wouldn't get many votes in Quebec, and as the federal Tories discovered time and again in the pre-Mulroney era, you can't win the country if you lose badly in Quebec. But the old rules are disappearing. We can no longer assume voters will behave in the traditional way, handing the bulk of the seats to the Liberals and/or Tories, and leaving a few healthy scraps for the NDP.

Not only are all three federal leaders unpopular, the Bloc Québécois and the Reform party are also likely to siphon off votes from the major parties. If the Bloc remains strong in Quebec, then the weakness there of a Wells-led Liberal party wouldn't be fatal. By the same token, the almost certain loss of substantial numbers of Tory seats, and some NDP seats, to the Reform party in the West would help the Liberals regardless of who is leading them.

If Quebec stops threatening and actually files for divorce, would English Canada suddenly turn on Wells as the guy who destroyed the country, or embrace him for standing firm and creating a country more at peace with itself? Nobody knows, but the odds for leading a Quebec-less Canada are with Wells. Face it, if Canadians are so pleased with the current configuration, why does Ottawa spend millions of tax dollars hiring people for television commercials to tell us how wonderful the country is? And why do they flatly refuse to release the results of public opinion polls on this very question?

Even if Liberal leader Jean Chrétien wins the most seats in the next election, chances are he won't have a majority and won't be around much longer, giving Wells the opportunity to run for leader.

Wells may not take it. As much as he might like to be prime minister, he is not incapable of walking away from politics altogether if he believed he'd accomplished everything he could. He did it once before; he might do it again.

Either way, when the time comes, Clyde Wells will make his position absolutely clear. He always does.

Bibliography

Byers, R. B., editor
   Canadian Annual Review of Politics and Public Affairs. Toronto: University of Toronto Press.

Canadian Bar Foundation
   1978 *Towards a New Canada: Committee on the Constitution.* Ottawa: the Canadian Bar Association.

Cochrane, Candace
   1981 *Outport: Reflections from the Newfoundland Coast.* Don Mills: Addison-Wesley Publishers.

Cohen, Andrew
   1991 *A Deal Undone: The Making and Breaking of the Meech Lake Accord.* Vancouver/Toronto: Douglas & McIntyre.

Coyne, Deborah
   1992 *Roll of the Dice: Working with Clyde Wells during the Meech Lake Negotiations.* Toronto: James Lorimer.

Gagnon, Georgette and Dan Rath
   1991 *Not without Cause: David Peterson's Fall from Grace.* Toronto: HarperCollins Canada.

Goulding, Jay
  1982 *The Last Outport: Newfoundland in Crisis.* Ottawa: Sisyphus Press.

Gutsell, B. V.
  1949 *An Introduction to the Geography of Newfoundland.* Ottawa: Department of Mines and Resources, Geographical Bureau.

Gwyn, Richard
  1972 *Smallwood: The Unlikely Revolutionary.* Toronto: McClelland and Stewart.

Hiller, James and Peter Neary, editors
  1980 *Newfoundland in the Nineteenth and Twentieth Centuries: Essays in Interpretation.* Toronto: University of Toronto Press.

Harwood, Harold
  1989 *Joey.* Toronto: Stoddart Publishing.
  1969 *Newfoundland: The Traveller's Canada.* Toronto: Macmillan Canada.

Hurtig, Mel
  1991 *The Betrayal of Canada.* Toronto: Stoddart Publishing.

Jeffrey, Brooke
  1992 *Breaking Faith: The Mulroney Legacy of Deceit, Destruction and Disunity.* Toronto: Key Porter Books.

Milne, David
  1991 *The Canadian Constitution.* Toronto: James Lorimer.

Mulroney, Brian
  1983 *Where I Stand.* Toronto: McClelland and Stewart.

Neary, Peter, editor
  1973 *The Political Economy of Newfoundland, 1929–1972.* Toronto/Vancouver: Copp Clark.

Newfoundland and Labrador, Department of Development, Tourism Branch
  1991 Travel Guide. St. John's.

Noel, S. J. R.
  1971 *Politics in Newfoundland.* Toronto: University of Toronto Press.

Peckford, A. Brian
  1983 *The Past in the Present: A Personal Perspective on Newfoundland's Future.* St. John's: Harry Cuff Publications.

Rowe, Frederick W.
  1985 *The Smallwood Era.* Toronto/Montreal: McGraw-Hill Ryerson.

Sawatsky, John
  1991 *Mulroney: The Politics of Ambition.* Toronto: Mcfarlane Walter & Ross.

Smallwood, Joseph R.
      Encyclopaedia of Newfoundland and Labrador. St. John's: Newfoundland Book Publishers (1967).

  1979 *The Time Has Come to Tell.* St. John's: Newfoundland Book Publishers (1967).

Thoms, James R., editor
  1990 *Call Me Joey.* St. John's: Harry Cuff Publications.

Vastel, Michel
  1991 *Bourassa.* Toronto: Macmillan Canada.

Wheare, K. C.
  1964 *Federal Government: Fourth Edition.* New York: Oxford University Press.

INDEX